"For me it quickly became clear that those clutching to the boat could not make it to shore under their own power."

ESCAPE UNDER FASCIST EYES

"Hold on to the boat and the floats!" I said quickly, and gathering all my strength, I hurried to catch up to those who knew how to swim. . . .

I caught up with the group. Domingo, Marquez, and the others stopped, treaded water. . . .

Meanwhile, the boat with the poor swimmers was almost motionless. "Put the floats under the canvas!" I advised. I had experience in rescue work on the waters of the Mezen.

Domingo did not understand at first, but when I showed him, slipping his bag under the canvas floor of the boat, he understood, then quickly pulled toward the shore. . . .

Soon, one after another, the other good swimmers came, dragging the inflated bags after them. They slid them under the boat's frame. Just as it seemed we were already out of danger, the enemy launch near the dam turned around and its running lights caught our attention.

"Hurry up! Faster!" Domingo said hoarsely. . . .

BEHIND FASCIST LINES

A Firsthand Account of Guerrilla Warfare During the Spanish Revolution

A. K. Starinov

BALLANTINE BOOKS • NEW YORK

A Ballantine Book
Published by The Ballantine Publishing Group
Copyright © 2001 by Col. Ilya Grigorevich Starinov
Translation copyright © 2001 by Jerman Rose

All rights reserved under International and Pan-American Copyright Conventions. Published in the United States by The Ballantine Publishing Group, a division of Random House, Inc., New York, and simultaneously in Canada by Random House of Canada Limited, Toronto.

Ballantine is a registered trademark and the Ballantine colophon is a trademark of Random House, Inc.

Map drawn by Michael Bechthold

www.ballantinebooks.com

Library of Congress Catalog Card Number: 2001116597

ISBN 0-345-48224-7

146062312

Contents

BEHIND
FASCIST
LINES

uernica

FRANCE

PYRENEES ANDORRA

Pamplona

I N

Teruel

Barcelona

Balearic Sea

Minorca

Castellón
de la Plana

Majorca

Valencia

Balearic Islands

Mediterranean

Cartagena

Sea

Algiers

ltar

Oran

ALGERIA

Spain Ahead

Moscow, November 16, 1936

The Moscow–Stolbtsy train had been ready for a long time. The steam engine puffed impatiently as if to remind the crowd there to see us all off that it was time to say good-bye.

The final exclamations, the fond farewells were heard, and right on schedule, the train gently started out.

There are so many people seeing someone off, I thought while looking out the window. But my eight-year-old daughter was not among them.

The last minutes reminded me of my parting with her.

I was standing near my open suitcase, which had been packed since morning, checking whether everything was ready for the trip, and Olya was fussing around me, trying to help, diligently adding completely unnecessary things while bombarding me with questions.

Occupied with my own thoughts, uneasy and anxious because of the impending separation, I forgot to answer her, or I answered so inappropriately that Olya felt that there was something wrong.

My little girl suddenly became very serious, then unexpectedly, she mournfully and softly began to cry. "Mama! Take me with you to the station, take me, please take me, take me . . . and . . . and," she sobbed.

I could not bear it. I snapped the lock on the suitcase, and tenderly hugged and kissed Olya. Then I quickly left the room, leaving her with my sister.

I was standing by the window, looking at the lights of Moscow, thinking about my daughter. Sometime in the future, we would meet again. Then I calmed myself and sat down.

My chief, Alexander Porokhnyak, an involuntary witness of my distress, wanted to get started learning Spanish that night, but I could not get interested in it.

After bidding me good-night, he climbed into the top berth and seemed to fall asleep.

The train traveled swiftly, the car rocked smoothly, it was long after midnight, and everything was perfect for rest, but I could not sleep; my dream was coming true. I was going to Spain, a country upon which the eyes of all the world were riveted.

Twenty years had passed since my graduation from the parish school in the village of Dorogorskoe, which was lost on the Mezen River, famous only because political prisoners were exiled there before the revolution. My father's words, spoken to me in 1915, were strongly impressed upon my memory.

"Well, Aniutka, praise God, you have learned to read, and you even know how to write. Little girls don't become soldiers, they bear children and don't need to read and write. Your mother and I can't read or write, and we have brought you five children into the world. It's time for you to get to work!"

"Help your parents, little daughter!" my mother added. "There is not enough bread to fill seven mouths until Christmas." They placed me as a nanny with the family of a local merchant, first for board, and then for a little money each month.

But I worked for the merchant only a short time. In the

spring, the two-year-old daughter of the merchant was climbing up onto the window sill, and I was so absorbed in a book that I did not notice, and the little girl fell out into the street! Thank goodness everything turned out all right; we both escaped with only a scare. But the finale was sad, the master and mistress learned what had happened, and they scolded me and dismissed me. That made my parents very unhappy.

After that, I worked as a day laborer. But I did not give up my books. Often forsaking sleep, I managed to read.

In order to earn a meager living and to help my parents as much as possible, for ten years, I worked as a laborer for wealthy landlords.

Once I worked for a wealthy reindeer breeder who had many hundreds of reindeer. It turned out to be a very difficult job, but I was young and not afraid of work. When he had had too much to drink, he would repeatedly say to me, "Anna! Let's marry you off to a rich reindeer breeder, you'll have a herd of reindeer, and you'll wear a long *malitsa*[1] with a hood of young deer fur. You will have laborers of your own." Fortunately that did not happen. The Soviets came to our region, and my future was completely and fundamentally changed.

Reluctantly, my boss went to the first general meeting, and when he returned, he pointed at his workers and said angrily, "They will rule now, but not for long!"

For me, a new life began—meetings, gatherings, discussions, antireligion propaganda, cutting wood. On March 8, 1926, I was accepted as a candidate member of the Bolshevik party. From 1926, after finishing the provincial course for women's organizers in Archangelsk, I worked for three years as the district women's organizer. This was followed by study in the Communist College and Yenukidze Oriental Institute, which I finished in 1935. After that, I was

[1] A *malitsa* is a wide deerskin overcoat without buttons that is worn with the hem over the head.

an interpreter at the Lenin International School of the Communist International. And there I was in 1936 on an international railway car on the way to far-off, mysterious Spain.

I finally became so tired that I drifted off to sleep. At the frontier station, Negoreloye, I woke up and went out into the corridor. Near our compartment, at a window, stood a nice looking, well-built young man in a good suit. When Porokhnyak came out, the stranger looked him over from head to foot. My chief guardedly touched me on the hand, and we went into the compartment.

"By his clothes, he's one of ours, but the devil only knows who," I said.

"Be careful," Porokhnyak said.

At Negoreloye, the frontier guards and customs officials carefully examined everything in the car and thoroughly checked our papers.

The train set out again.

We crossed the border into Poland without a stop. Our own Soviet border guards in their green service caps were left behind on the eastern bank of the small river. On the western bank stood the Poles. After a few minutes, the train stopped at Stolbtsy. The Polish signs were incomprehensible to me. All about us bustled tall gendarmes, clamoring porters, and vendors. I heard the offensive words *Pan* and *Pani*.[2]

Porokhnyak changed noticeably; he was somehow stooped and, as I later learned, not without reason. He had worked for almost ten years in the forces of the Ukrainian military district, for three of them, he had worked on partisan warfare. He was afraid that they would recognize him and not allow him through Poland; the Polish *pans* had their own accounts to settle with him.

[2] Trans. note. *Pan* is the Polish equivalent of Mister, and also the term used for Polish landowners.

The gendarme looked through my passport, smiled pleasantly, and returned it to me. Then he took Porokhnyak's passport. He examined it carefully and at length. From time to time, he would dart a glance at its owner. *"Proshu, Pan Porokhnyak!* (Thank you Mr. Porokhnyak)," the gendarme said at last, returning the passport.

The customs guards studied our luggage as if it was filled with diamonds but they confiscated only Soviet newspapers and magazines.

Porokhnyak watched as the customs inspectors examined the baggage of the other passengers. He turned his whole attention on them when they began to check the handsome stranger's things.

"He's ours, one of us, and it's possible that we are traveling along the same route," the chief whispered to me.

We sat again in the same car with the stranger. He really was a volunteer just like us. On the way, we learned he was named Pavel, a member of a tank crew.

Porokhnyak bought some newspapers and began to read. "They are lying!" he said. "If we believe them, we are already too late. In Republican Spain, there is complete anarchy. The rebels are in the outskirts of Madrid, and their leader, General Franco, is preparing to march into the capital."

In a newspaper dated November 6, 1936, were many photographs from Spain, of Moroccan soldiers and Gen. Francisco Franco himself. There he was, The Squab, with his retinue observing the course of battle through binoculars. In another picture, children were presenting flowers to the rebel general.

"Only one thing reassures me," Porokhnyak said. "I have known for a long time how the newspapers of the Polish landlords lie." He began to read one from the sixteenth of

November. "And this one is mistaken, too, but it does not predict the fall of the Republic soon," he said. "We will still make it in time," Pavel noted.

Looking through the newspapers, I recalled how on the evening of July 18, 1936, the students of the Spanish section of the Lenin International School in Moscow, where I was working as an interpreter, returned from one of the factories. They were tired, and as usual, they turned on the radio. That time, rather than the music, we heard instead that a Fascist revolt had begun in Spain.

On the following day, there was nothing threatening in the newspapers. But the students of the Spanish section were as agitated as an upset beehive. From Madrid radio came no gay music, no reports of bullfights, but calls to battle against the rebels, calls for the defense of the Republic, and reports were already being broadcast of the liquidation of separate centers of the revolt. The Spanish people stood in defense of their achievements. They won numerous victories despite the contrary reports from the rebels and their foreign instigators.

The following days brought news of the rout of the rebels in Madrid, Barcelona, and many other cities. Then the Italian Fascists came to the aid of Franco's forces. They began to assist the rebel generals openly, violating all the commonly recognized norms of international law. The Fascist intervention began.

It is well known that on the morning of July 20, the airplane on which the leader of the rebels, General Sanjurjo, was flying to Spain crashed during takeoff from the Lisbon airport. But the rebels had many generals, and into his place stepped the protégé of the German Fascists—Francisco Franco.

He had gained fame by his savagery in the battle against the Moroccan insurgents of Abdul Kerim. For his bloody crimes, he had been promoted to the rank of general in 1926.

In 1934, Franco took part in the massacre of Asturian miners and was named chief of the general staff. After the victory of the Popular Front in the elections of February 16, 1936, and in spite of the demands of the Communists, this inveterate Fascist was not put in prison, but sent as military governor to the Canary Islands.

Meanwhile, events in Spain were developing quickly and not at all as we wanted. A difficult task fell to the working people, to crush the revolt and repel the invasion of the Italian and German hordes that were sent to help Franco. But Republican Spain had neither modern arms nor a faithful officer corps. At the same time, the rebels received, unhindered, airplanes, ammunition, arms, and entire military units from Italy and Germany. The Anglo-American oil barons also helped the rebels by supplying fuel.

In defense of Republican Spain, a mass antifascist movement arose in many countries of the world. Motivated by a feeling of proletarian internationalism, antifascist volunteers went to Spain. Many of them understood very well that a terrible danger hung over the world.

In the Soviet press, there was then no information about our military aid to those fighting men of Spain, but no one doubted that the USSR was helping more than Spanish children. There was talk about repelling the Fascist threat. The Soviet people could not stand on the sidelines.

August 1936 was a month of hope and anxiety, a difficult month for freedom-loving Spaniards. Savage reprisals were carried out against supporters of the Republic in the towns and villages captured by the rebels, and progressive people everywhere were outraged by the crimes of the Fascists on the population of Badajoz, the Balearic Islands, and the brutal violence against the great Spanish poet, Federico

Garcia Lorca, who was shot in a ravine near Granada on the night of August 19.

On the train, which was carrying us west, I also recalled how my journey to Spain began.

Soon after the beginning of the revolt in Spain, our students, Spaniards with whom I was working, began to leave. On departing, they invited us to come to Spain. The first to go was my classmate at the Institute, Nikolai Andreev. When I heard about that, the dream of going to Spain was born in me, so I volunteered to go to Spain as an interpreter of English and Spanish.

However, I had to work at achieving my dream. My immediate supervisors did not make any promises, but did not refuse my request either. Eventually, I met with the director of the Lenin International School, Klavdia Ivanovna Kirsanova.[3]

I remember the rector coming to meet me as if it were today. She wore a mysterious smile as we greeted each other. She inquired about my health, work, and family affairs. We talked about events in Spain and about Soviet aid to the Spanish people.

"You are asking to go to Spain, but what about your daughter?" she suddenly asked me.

"I've already asked my sister to take the care of my daughter, and in case I should not return, the State will see that she is properly brought up."

"Good, Comrade Obruchaeva, we will take this into account! But in the meantime, all of this is just between us," Klavdia Ivanovna said with a smile.

Days passed. The events in Spain were widely covered by the Soviet press. I read the correspondence of Mikhail Koltsov, and was struck by the courage of the Spaniards and the valor of the author.

---

[3] The wife of Yemel'yan Yaroslavskii.

And all of a sudden an unknown woman came to my apartment. She introduced herself, Urvantseva—and warned that I must not divulge anything about which we were going to speak. Soon she asked me to go to her office and requested that I complete a large questionnaire. When I had finished, Urvantseva carefully read through it and said nothing, but I had already guessed that this was connected with my possible mission to Spain.

After several days, she stopped by my place and said with satisfaction, "Well it's good that I caught you at home. Get your things, let's go to the comrades who want to talk to you."

A half hour later, I found myself in a large institution not far from my apartment.

A tall, stately, military man with a coarse face and a thick head of hair spoke with me. I learned later he was G. L. Tumanyan. My questionnaire lay in front of him. "So then, you are ready to go on a long mission?" He looked at me in a friendly way.

"Yes!"

"And your daughter?"

"I have already made arrangements for my daughter. Relatives and friends will look after her."

Our conversation did not last long.

Gai Lazarevich was a man of few words, but I sensed that he already knew a great deal about me. We parted company warmly, and I understood that this would not be our last meeting.

They cautioned me again to say nothing to anyone.

Some time passed, and exactly at the appointed time, I was again in Tumanyan's office where I was introduced to a stranger and learned that they had appointed me his interpreter.

"I hope you are satisfied, Comrade Porokhnyak?" Gai Lazarevich asked the stranger.

"Yes, yes of course," he answered standing erect in military fashion and avoiding my eyes.

Looking at my future chief, I still did not understand what he would be doing in Spain.

Porokhnyak wore a new civilian suit, but it was evident that he was a military man. Apparently Gai Lazarevich noticed it, too.

"You are no longer a military engineer of the third rank now," he said, "but a citizen . . . Alexander Porokhnyak."

Soon corps commander S. P. Uritskii[4] received us, together with others who were leaving for Spain.

Semyon Petrovich spoke to us with a kind of internal enthusiasm. He warned that difficulties and dangers lay ahead but without fail we must live up to the great trust placed in us. He recalled the great trials that our people bore during the war against the White Guard and the foreign interventionists in 1918–1920.

Finishing his remarks, Uritskii said, "I hope you will do everything you can to help the Spanish people defend freedom and democracy in the struggle against the Fascist rebels and interventionists!"

We spent the night in Warsaw, and passed through Czechoslovakia into Vienna. The next day, we arrived by express train in Paris, where we had a chance to get acquainted with the French capital. On the evening of November 22, we left Paris for Spain.

---

[4] Komkor Semyon Petrovich Uritskii was an active participant in the Russian Civil War, but at this time was chief of Soviet military intelligence.

On Spanish Soil

We had a very mistaken understanding of the situation in Spain, and had only vaguely imagined the circumstances in which we found ourselves upon our arrival.

Early in the morning, the train emerged from a tunnel, and we saw the boundless Mediterranean Sea lit by the first rays of the sun. It slowly rose up out of the horizon. On the slopes of the mountains, orchards of tangerine trees and bright red flowers near little houses were already visible.

"This is November!" Porokhnyak said, noting the blossoms. "What is it like here in the summer?"

Out the window stretched the country that I had studied at the Institute, with people whom I already knew from my work in the Lenin International School. In the car, Spanish speech could already be heard.

The train stopped. The small platform at Portbou was filled with people who were meeting us.

"Salud, Camaradas!"[1]

"Viva Russia! Viva el frente popular!"[2]

The many bouquets, joyful exclamations of greeting, and strong handshakes moved us to tears.

On Spanish soil, I felt as if I were at home. The stirring

---

[1] Hello comrades!

[2] Long live Russia! Long live the Popular Front!

encounter with people who were giving the first armed rebuff to fascism brought us together, but not everyone was happy about the arrival of the volunteers. On the platform, I noticed a man with a narrow moustache and a black-and-red bandanna around his neck. On a belt across his shoulder hung an enormous pistol, and his face expressed a kind of dissatisfaction and rage. This was one of the many Catalonian anarchists. But I then still did not imagine what damage they were causing the Republican struggle.

The little town of Portbou was protected on the north, west, and east by mountains. On the slopes, industrious peasants cultivated citrus trees and grapevines.

While waiting for the next train, we walked around the little town and admired the boundless blue Mediterranean. On the horizon, unidentified ships appeared indistinctly, like toys. A warm breeze blew from far-off Africa.

If there had been no men with rifles, no slogans and appeals on the walls, no cries of young newsboys about the first victories over the Fascists, it would have been hard to believe that battles raged very near, that the Spanish Republic was in mortal danger, and the rebel generals were attempting with fire and sword to bring the Spanish people to their knees in order to establish dictatorship in the country.

Soon we left behind hospitable Portbou.

The sea disappeared. The train went into the mountains, passing vineyards, groves, flowers. In the stations were flags and banners. Slogans on the walls called to the struggle against fascism.

In the evening of November 23, we arrived in the Spanish Pearl of the Mediterranean—Barcelona, the capital of Catalonia.

Her green boulevards were sublime; her squares and prospects were beautiful. The large factories, long quays, and great port were impressive.

Everywhere flew the federal flags of Catalonia, the scarlet colors of the United Socialist party of Catalonia, the united party of Communists and socialists, the black-and-red banner of the anarchists, and in fewer places, the government flags of Spain.

In this inimitably beautiful great city with a population of a million, life was flourishing; the people seemed to bubble with life. On the streets, there was much greenery and many flowers. Music and songs were heard.

Automobiles filled the city. Furiously honking their horns, they scurried through the streets. The majority of cars bore the small flags of the anarchists with the inscription FAI-SNT. These inscriptions made a colorful show on many automobiles, painted on the back, on the front, and on both sides. There were fewer cars with the red flags of the Communists and still fewer with Republican flags.

In Barcelona, we parted with Pavel, our traveling companion from the tank unit. We had become good friends as if we had known each other for a long time.

"If we live, we will surely meet again!" Pavel said in parting.

"We will meet again," I said, although I was then not at all sure when this would be.

We did meet again, but that story is still ahead.

We spent the night in Barcelona.

"We have a very strict blackout," the administrator of our hotel warned us. "Be sure to observe it. Before you turn on the lights, close the blinds on the window. Be careful." Looking at us playfully, he added, "If they see a light, they may shoot you."

I didn't sleep at all because of the street sounds of automobiles, sirens, musical instruments, singing, occasional gunshots, and from time to time, exchanges of gunfire. The first time *that* happened, I left my room.

The elderly woman who was the attendant on our floor was cleaning.

"*Señora,* who is shooting?" I asked.

"Possibly the fifth column.[3] Their people sometimes, especially at night, come out of their hiding places and attack the people's militia, or perhaps it is the *milicianos anarchistas* shooting to show their bravery," she answered imperturbably.

I returned to my room and, without turning on the light, drew back the blinds and was surprised to see cars going back and forth with their lights on, violating the blackout.

The train for Valencia was leaving in the afternoon of November 24, and since we had time, we went into the city once more.

Barcelona spread out like an amphitheater around the shore of the bay. There was a war on, and there were few ships in the huge port, although before the rebellion, there had been up to five thousand a year here.

In old Barcelona, the houses varied from two to as many as five stories, many with numerous balconies. There were steep and narrow streets where it was difficult, sometimes simply impossible, for two cars to pass each other. In the new city, the streets were wide, the buildings beautiful, and there were avenues and parks, many cafes, flowers, and music.

What especially struck me about Barcelona were the

[3]At the beginning of October 1936, before the attack on Madrid, General Mola, one of Franco's competitors for the post of chief commander of the rebel forces, declared that there were five columns acting against Madrid: four from the front and the fifth—underground within the city itself. At that time, Madrid withstood the attack of all five columns thanks to the heroism of the troops that were defending the capital of Spain and to the assistance of the Soviet Union.

huge artistically rendered portraits of Bakunin and Kropotkin on the buildings occupied by committees of anarchists.

On several streets in the outskirts, there were still barricades of sandbags and of stones taken from the bridges. The downtown streets were crowded and noisy with newspaper vendors crying out information about the situation on the fronts.

In the cafes on the streets, numerous soldiers carrying weapons and wearing black-and-red neckties peacefully and happily drank coffee. From the jukeboxes issued the sounds of the Marseillaise.

The normal street activity gave the impression that the threat had passed, that the foe had already been beaten; in reality, a life and death struggle was going on.

"In these troubled times, soldiers at the front are suffering from bad weather, they are going hungry and dying, and here behind the lines wine and music flow. Many of these people have forgotten about those who are fighting," Porokhnyak observed.

The Republican government was located in Valencia. Both the military authorities and our advisers, to whom we had to report, were there.

After midday, we went on farther toward the goal of our trip. On the right were the mountains, occasionally hidden by green trees and orchards, and on the left the gray-green Mediterranean. In places, the railroad went right along the seacoast.

The train stopped often at stations, and only late in the evening, having covered 350 kilometers, did we arrive in Valencia.

In spite of the late hour, representatives of the Popular

Front organization met the volunteers with hugs, flowers, and greetings. In contrast with the meeting in Portbou, there were fewer black-and-red anarchist bandannas and neckties here. The city was in total darkness, but the muffled horns of automobiles could be heard.

On the way to the hotel, we finally saw consequences of the war: vehicles and carts of refugees, from regions occupied by the rebels, harnessed with mules or donkeys, with their meager household goods; and the refugees themselves with their children; the families of agricultural workers, laborers, peasants and intelligentsia, who had escaped the Fascists.

Suddenly the sirens began to howl, warning of the approach of hostile airplanes; automobile horns sounded. This was our first air raid, our first meeting with the enemy.

Most traffic came to a standstill, but individual cars with darkened headlights, desperately honking their horns, sped through the empty streets. We stopped in the doorway of a massive dark building as if to escape a downpour. The night was warm and starry. In the distance, explosions like rolling thunder could be heard. Finally, the long all-clear signal was sounded, and the street began to come alive again.

That night, Fascist airplanes bombed the outskirts of the city. But in the sunny morning, the news vendors cried out about the victory of Republican soldiers; on the square, flowers were sold, and on the crowded streets, there was music; yet another rebel attack on Madrid had been repulsed with large enemy losses. The Fascists again suffered failure. *"No passaran,"* "They shall not pass," sounded not only as a battle cry but as an expression of Republican confidence in the final victory.

The Spanish people rejoiced in their success, and we rejoiced with them. I was translating communiqués from the front, which were published in the Republican newspapers, for Porokhnyak, and he recalled how the Polish newspapers had leaned over backward to prove that the days of Republican Spain were numbered. But everything we had seen in Spain showed us that the Polish press was lying, and that the lying was done systematically.

Rejoicing in the recent defeat of the enemy, the people perhaps forgot that the government of Largo Caballero was not doing everything necessary to win victory, that international reaction was tearing down assistance to Republican Spain in every possible way and was aiding the rebels and Fascists, using as a cover false noninterference. But on that day, all the adversity could not cast a shadow on the victory of Madrid's heroic defenders.

The following day, a senior military adviser, who everyone fondly called "the Old Man" although he was only a little older than forty, received Porokhnyak and me.

On the way to his office, Porokhnyak talked about Yan Karlovich Berzin.[4] I was nervous, going to a meeting with him, and as it turned out, for nothing. Everything was simpler than I imagined.

Porokhnyak asked to go to Madrid.

"That won't work! The situation has changed. I am leaving you here . . . you have to begin with something small," said the Old Man. Then he spoke about the losses of the Fascists at Madrid, about the impregnable defense of the capital.

"For you, it is important that there is no continuous front line as in other sectors," noted Yan Karlovich smiling.

At this time, an assistant came in and reported that two other new advisers had arrived, and he gave their names.

[4]Yan Karlovich Berzin headed Soviet military intelligence from 1924 through spring, 1935. From April 1935 into the summer of 1936, he was stationed in the Soviet far east. In summer, 1937, he would once again, briefly, head Soviet military intelligence. He was purged in November 1937, executed in the summer of 1938.

"What luck!" Berzin said. "Get acquainted, Porokhnyak, Obruchaeva, and this is Sprogis and Citron. Comrade Porokhnyak, just now you help Sprogis with mines that can be made from common materials, the kind you taught partisans about in our schools."

On parting, Berzin said, "The Spanish people are a good people. We must help them defend their freedom and independence. Go to General Ivon, he will arrange everything."

On the way, Porokhnyak told me about how Pyotr Kyuzis (Ya. K. Berzin's real name) took part in a raid in the spring of 1906 to requisition materials for the Party. During this operation, Berzin was wounded and captured by the Latvian police. He was not yet seventeen, a fact that saved him from being shot; they did put him into prison.

After his imprisonment, Kyuzis worked actively in Riga, composing antigovernment flyers and distributing them. But his underground Party work was interrupted by a new arrest and exile to Irkutsk province. When the First World War began, Pyotr Kyuzis obtained forged documents, became Yan Karlovich Berzin, and fled to Riga, where he worked in the Bolshevik Party underground. Berzin participated in the Great October Revolution and in the armed defense of Soviet power.

Porokhnyak met with Berzin in the early thirties.

Berzin made a big impression on me. Something about him was sincere, charming, but he was so decisive that it was impossible to forget.

Contrary to our expectations, General Ivon turned out to be a Soviet officer, who made it possible for Porokhnyak to immediately begin work with a small group of would-be partisans. Ivon also turned Porokhnyak into "Rudolf Wolf," and me into "Louisa Kurting." Unfortunately, later on that subterfuge hindered us a bit; the Spanish knew that we were Russians, but they were surprised that we were not Ivan and Maria but Wolf and Louisa.

The next day, the newly coined Rudolf and I went down into the lobby of our hotel. The day promised to be a hot one, and I had put on a fancy hat.

Before entering the lobby, the guard stopped me and politely said, "*Senorita,* please listen. Allow me to give you some good advice. If you go out in that hat, the anarchists will take you for a Fascist, and then you'll find yourself in trouble."

I returned to my room and put on a black beret.

A Suitcase Full of Mines

After breakfast, we went out to the group's location in the outskirts of Valencia, where we spent the day working on partisan matters, which were unfamiliar to me. We made switches and detonating fuses, and later, we set them. Every day, we were occupied with such prosaic details, the many difficulties of partisan activity, teaching people sabotage behind enemy lines.

In the Institute and in the Lenin School, I had not needed to speak about partisan matters, especially about such things as mines, fuses, and explosives. But in Valencia, my translations were inexact since I didn't have the necessary technical vocabulary. When Rudolf saw that those he was teaching were not doing what he expected, he corrected them; when they still didn't do what was necessary, he got angry at *me*. So I became nervous, and that made the situation worse. I barely lasted until evening. I returned home, tired and disappointed, thinking, This is not going to work out; it's just not going to work out. Rudolf was also upset and not only because I did not know many military and special technical terms but because everyone was beginning from zero, from bare ground.

The next day, we gave explosives lessons again, traveling once more with explosives, fuses, and mines that Rudolf made at the hotel in the evenings.

At first, it was as if the small bag and small suitcase of detonators and explosives that I had to carry were burning my hands. I was afraid that they would be set off by the bump of a suddenly stopping train, or that the police checks would reveal the explosives and that our identity papers would not protect us from anything. But everything went well. The fuses and switches worked only where they were placed, and no one ever arrested us.

At headquarters, they gave us Spanish-language instructions for demolition work, but they did not use many of the words and concepts that Rudolf used. There was nothing about mines and switches, or about incendiaries and other methods of sabotage.

The directions were written very formally with a large number of words that were incomprehensible to me. Since there was no special military dictionary available, I wasted a lot of time trying to understand this new activity at the same time as the students, often confusing words and concepts.[1] It was especially difficult when we set a mine with live primers, small, thin, copper tubes but how powerfully they exploded, splitting rocks, breaking boards. Blasting caps about the size of a piece of children's soap broke rails.

"Set it and get away. A car or a train comes along, and it is blown up," Rudolf said.

Our students, who were almost fifty years of age, at first were very distrustful of Rudolf's mines, but when the fuse in a dummy mine blew up after an automobile drove over it, a stout, gray-headed, would-be guerrilla named Antonio enthusiastically exclaimed, *"Formidable!"* Suddenly understanding the significance and possibilities of the

---

[1] Many of the other interpreters also had trouble with military terms. On account of this, a military translation course was organized. The course was conducted by O. N. Filippova near Valencia, but I could not get to it.

mines, he began persuasively to convince the others what it was all about.

Gradually the students became fascinated with mines, and Rudolf showed them all the latest techniques.

Two students were especially interested in mines, an electrician, Salvador, and Antonio, who was an auto mechanic. Prior to the revolt, Antonio had been working in Toledo. Tall, lean, with a strong wrinkled face, in a leather jacket, with wide blue trousers, Salvador watched attentively, listened, and asked questions when he did not understand something. He was the first to prepare a mine with a button detonator, skillfully using a matchbox. There was no safety on the mine, and Rudolf advised him to install a reliable safety.

Antonio came to the class in his frayed overalls. He was the first who exclaimed *"formidable!"* when the mine worked in the exercise.

In general, there were good men in the group, but by age and by their physical condition, they were of little use for activity behind enemy lines as a member of a group of saboteurs, as Rudolf was proposing.

At first, the Spanish headquarters did not even acknowledge our existence; the regulations and manuals of the Spanish Army made no provision for partisan warfare so headquarters did not even put our people on an allowance. Our elderly students thought that the army would transfer them secretly behind rebel lines, with false identity papers, and that they would work there in strict secrecy, under deep cover. These dreams noticeably bothered Rudolf, however, at that time, he did not say anything definite about the methods of moving saboteurs behind rebel lines. He only taught them the construction of mines. Very soon the Spanish began to call him Rodolfo.

I was already interpreting more confidently. The students

set the mines, retreated from the dangerous place, and on the command "enemy!" they set off the blasting caps.

We had difficulty with material resources. The army allocated to the group only money for food. They gave Porokhnyak and me a salary, but we used it to buy supplies for making switches, fuses, and incendiary devices. The trainees brought a few things. But we had no vehicles for going out of the city to practice, so usually, we went to the end of the tram line, and then walked another three kilometers.

When I graduated from the Yenukidze Institute of Foreign Languages, I liked being an interpreter very much. I worked with people from Spain and Latin America who were in the Soviet Union, young Communists who were already hardened in the class struggle. They were people with whom it was interesting to work, and my knowledge of the language was completely sufficient to translate political and everyday topics. The work in Spain was completely different. Rudolf was training partisans all day long, and then at night, there were frequent practice exercises in the field. But Rudolf had no course summaries of any kind to work from, so there was no way to prepare for the lessons ahead of time, to look in the dictionary and note the new words. Rudolf only made an outline of the lesson ahead of time, usually on one page. He had no textbook. Everything was in his head, but he clearly had a great deal of teaching experience, and he knew what he had to teach by heart. I soon found out that he had already taught partisans and demolition specialists for more than fifteen years. He had been the chief of a demolition team, taught partisans at special schools, and had taught in a transportation engineers institute. So the work was easy for him but hard for me.

When I met the interpreters of the other advisers, I envied them. They worked in legitimate military units, and they did not have the difficulties we did. They did not travel on street-cars carrying suitcases stuffed with explosives, primers, and fuses.

Rudolf was also upset with our working conditions and went to General Ivon, but Ivon could not help us in a concrete way. It was not necessary to convince General Ivon of the possibilities for sabotage behind Franco's lines; he understood very well. But it was necessary to prove it to the Spanish Republican Army command, which was still being formed in the course of a difficult war.

But our students did not sit idly by. Understanding what was happening, they presented our needs to the secretary of the Valencia Provincial Committee of the Spanish Communist party, Antonio Uribes. Uribes invited us to discuss the matter.

When Rudolf and I entered Uribes's office, there were a few people there. One of them, a man named Martinez, jumped up from his chair and came up to me, hugged me, and slapping me on the back cried, "Anna! *Ola! Que tal?*"

Rudolf was at a loss to know what was going on until I explained that I had known Martinez since 1935 at the Lenin International School, where he was studying and I was working as an interpreter.

In spite of interruptions by phone calls and his noticeable fatigue, Comrade Uribes ascertained our possibilities and needs during the conversation.

"Courses, real courses, and a workshop are needed, we will be able to make and use new and cheap weapons for blowing up trains, vehicles, airplanes," Antonio said.

"There will be everything; without fail it will be; we will have a fine regular army, and there will be partisans," Uribes replied.

Uribes and Martinez reminded us about the complex situation in Republican Spain.

"The industry of Catalonia is capable of supplying the Republican Army with ammunition and, to a significant degree, with arms. But it is working at far less than full capacity," Uribes said. After a short pause, he added, "The bourgeois Republicans, who head the local Catalonian government, the so-called *Generalidad,* do not want to share, in a real way, in a military way, the riches of Catalonia with the rest of Spain. The anarchists cause especially great harm, making demands that cannot be fulfilled in wartime, like the observance of an eight-hour workday. They oppose the creation of a strong regular army. There are many demagogues among the anarchist leaders, even some of our avowed enemies. Some commanders of anarchist units even set up secret arms caches—they intercept transports with arms and military supplies that are headed for the front. Shouting about anarchy and insubordination, the anarchist leaders carry out terror in their own units against those who begin to understand and see the necessity of rallying all antifascist forces.

"There are also brave men among the anarchists, but they often are their own worst enemies," Martinez put in. "In the years of reaction, at the time of the trolley drivers' strike, an anarchist in Barcelona got into a trolley park on a hill and released the brakes of a few trams, set them on fire, and pushed them down the hill. A great panic arose, but nothing useful was accomplished, and the reactionaries got to shout about the banditry of the workers."

The Party Committee gave us a few more men and a place in Benimamin, a suburb of Valencia, where we organized a school for training partisan cadres. Later on, that school became our base and a rest house where the saboteurs could come after completion of missions behind rebel lines.

The next day, Rudolf and I were received at the Party Central Committee, which was guarded because of the activities of the remnants of the fifth column and the anarchists.

When we arrived, Jose Diaz stood up from behind the table and came out to meet us. He firmly shook my hand. I introduced myself and presented Rudolf. Diaz invited us to sit down. He appeared tired but vigorous.

Rudolf began to state his views and proposals, which arose from the training of the groups. Diaz listened attentively to my translation. He answered slowly, and it was easy for me to translate. Sometimes he nodded his head as a sign of agreement or said, *"Si, camarades!"*

During the discussion, a stately woman in a black dress came in unexpectedly. Before this meeting, we had often seen her photographs, so we immediately recognized *"La Pasionaria."* Rudolf immediately interrupted his report and Jose Diaz introduced us to Dolores Ibarruri. She took an active part in our discussion. She spoke quickly, and I did not have time to translate everything she said. From our conversation with the leaders of the Spanish Communist party we understood that its Central Committee would work hard for the development of the partisan struggle behind rebel lines.

The following day, the Central Committee provided the necessary equipment for the school. And most important of all, twelve men arrived under the command of a Capt. Domingo Ungria. They came in three light cars and a truck.

With the arrival of Domingo's group, our work increased. Again drill and practical exercises, but it was getting easier for me, and even Rudolf was not so nervous. Now he had helpers. Our "little old men," our *padres* (papas) as the newly arrived men called them, helped teach organization and sabotage techniques.

Now when we went out on exercises, we went in cars and

conducted exercises against roads, railroads, and other objectives.

December had arrived in "Little Spanish Africa," as the Spanish call the narrow band of lowland of the Levant (the provinces of Valencia and Alicante), which adjoins the Mediterranean and is separated by mountains from the rest of the country. It was warm, even at night, and sometimes downright hot. During the day, there was a clear blue sky, a hot sun, and occasionally, after midday, at great altitude, there were small tufts of clouds.

It was the time to harvest oranges. The crop was excellent, but it was difficult to export the fruit because of the interventionist blockade. The prices of oranges were low, and much fruit remained under the trees, covering the ground with a golden carpet. During breaks, we enjoyed fresh, aromatic, delicious fruit.

Near Valencia, we admired the remarkable irrigation system that had been built over the course of hundreds of years. Along canals fed by the mountain river Turia flowed the cool, life-giving moisture that watered the orchards and gardens. The canals could be seen along the road; they spread out through the fields and orchards. In some places, the road passed under the canals. In one spot, they were harvesting corn, and alongside they had sown wheat. Only 150 kilometers south of Valencia, near the city of Elche, we found ourselves in real subtropics.

"It's just like in Africa!" Domingo Ungria exclaimed as he admired the tall palms. "The Moors who conquered Spain built the first reservoirs and canals. After that, Spaniards began to develop a system of watering and irrigation. The climate in Spain is very varied. In the mountains, at an altitude of more than two thousand meters, there is snow, and down below in the valleys, there is heat, but because there is not enough moisture in the valleys, there is also drought. That is why if you bring water to the land, then in the valleys, which are protected on the north by high mountains, you can get two or even three harvests with irrigation."

Domingo stopped and waited while I translated what he had said for Rudolf. "Of course, it is one thing to build reservoirs and canals and another to distribute the collected water. Everyone tried to take a little more water from the canals. That is why a *tribunal de agua,* a water court, was created here. One for the whole country. It consisted of seven judges who sorted out all the disputes and distributed the water. The decisions of this tribunal were final, and they were not subject to appeal."

"Where did the tribunal sit?" I asked.

"It sat in Madrid, once each week in the cathedral, and continued in this way for five or six centuries."

In this way, admiring the canals, groves of tangerines and oranges, we arrived at the place where we had our lessons. But instead of a lesson, Domingo, glancing at his watch, said loudly, *"Es el tiempo para comida!"* Time for dinner.

No matter where we happened to be, and no matter what we were doing, at two o'clock in the afternoon, the Spaniards, without fail, reminded us about dinner.

"Let's continue after dinner!" they said. So as a rule, when we went to the field, we took everything necessary for dinner.

When there were no night exercises, we returned to Valencia toward evening. In spite of the war and the blockade, the third largest city of Spain[2] did not stand still in the evenings— movie and vaudeville theaters and bars were open, and the cafes were full. Even so, in the morning the city woke up early. Newspaper vendors cried out the news, the bazaar bustled, and on the streets fresh, bright, fragrant flowers were sold. Factories and workshops were open, and many of them had already switched over to the production of military supplies for Re-

---

[2] Before the revolt, its population was almost 350,000, and with those who had been evacuated from regions occupied by the enemy and from Madrid, it reached almost half a million.

publican soldiers. But in the port, second in size after Barcelona, few ships rode at the long moorings.

On Sundays, our students showed us the sights of Valencia. We saw the buildings of the university, which was founded in 1500, and the paintings of Goya, Velasquez, and other masters. Valencia was beautiful and unforgettable. But the charms of this blessed region were far from accessible to all. Once during lessons in the outskirts of the city, we noticed some pipes sticking out of the ground. Little children were playing among them.

"Who are these cave people?" I asked Domingo.

"Workers. They cannot get an apartment even in a half-cellar. Many have moved to well-built houses requisitioned from the Fascists, but not all have managed to do so. Many refugees have come here."

On one warm day, I dropped into a dugout "apartment." It was dark, damp, and stuffy. A thin ray of sun struggled through the single window in the ceiling. The furniture was wretched, just an old chair, a homemade table dug into the earth, two benches, and a cupboard with a small door that would not shut. The master of the apartment left home for the people's militia, to fight so that workers like him would no longer have to live in dugouts.

The young, thin housewife who lived there met me and said warmly, "Sit down please." As if justifying herself, she added, "There is just no way to get another place to live! We can't afford city apartments, and we could not get our own house. My husband is a worker, and they pay him little, and there are taxes on the land, and on each window and door. When we have beaten the Fascists, we will move to a good house," she said confidently.

It is impossible to forget our shooting range at Paterna. One day we arrived there early in the morning for lessons, and near an earthen bank, we saw targets and bodies of dead people. Among them were young and old, well-dressed men, women, and children, and poorly dressed peasants with calluses on their hands.

"What is this?" I asked Domingo in horror.

"Villains, miserable cowards and murderers! This is the work of the anarchists."

"Can't they be controlled?" Rudolf asked.

Domingo waved his hand in his distinctive way and answered, "No! The government is powerless to guarantee the observance of the laws, so the bandits from the anarchist column, and the fifth column, too, take advantage of this fact."

Later, in the evening and at night, when I listened to gunshots, I assumed that anarchist bandits were doing their dirty work again. Their murders had nothing in common with the execution of counterrevolutionaries, who deserved their death sentences because of their deeds. Later, at the insistence of the Communist party, the government put an end to the crimes of the black-and-red bandits.

Paterna was intended for instruction in shooting. Occasionally, we set off small charges, mines, and hand grenades there as a part of the training of the demolition specialists, and we also taught rifle and pistol marksmanship.

The military training that I had received at the Yenukidze Oriental Institute in Leningrad, where I was studying in the Latin American section of the Department of History and Economics, helped me a great deal. At that time, I never imagined that my passion for shooting would be so beneficial for me in the future.

"Again in the apple!" Domingo said as he examined my target. "Learn to shoot like Russian women shoot!" he added, addressing his own saboteurs.

We also shot at night, for which one had to put luminous points on the front and rear gunsights.

Especially enamored with night shooting were Rubio (which means fair haired) and Marquez, who had excellent night vision and could shoot quickly. We tried to use illumination from below, but we recognized that this ruined our camouflage. In addition, to avoid giving away our shooters' positions, we devised various ways of reducing the sound and flame during firing. Here our experienced auto drivers, Rubio and Pepe, came to our assistance, making pistol and rifle silencers. Unfortunately, they turned out larger than the pistols themselves, and the saboteurs rarely took them on missions. Eventually, they just threw the things away in favor of carrying more grenades.

However, the proponents of silent shooting figured that one could take out a sentry unnoticed with such equipment. I tried to shoot with a silencer, but it reduced my accuracy and instead of fetching the apple, the bullet often left "to get milk."

Along with partisan training, we taught all the men to administer first aid for wounds or poisoning. A doctor conducted the first lessons, and later a doctor's assistant, sent by the Valencia Committee of the Communist party. I assisted them, using the knowledge I had picked up in the Russian Society of the Red Cross ("ROKK"), courses for regional women's organizers in Archangelsk.

When the doctor and his assistant departed for the front, our lessons did not stop. Before leaving, the doctor entrusted to me a complete first-aid manual. We already had the necessary medical supplies, but it was difficult to conduct my first independent lesson. I had to prepare a great deal, and I often referred to the course outline.

After the arrival of Domingo's group, Rudolf began to spend more time on the tactics of action behind enemy lines. Our first students, the older ones, had mastered the techniques, and they longed for work behind rebel lines, but in tactical exercises, they gasped for breath during a quick march, not just when going up a mountain but even where the going was flat. Our "papas" were clearly not suited for a sortie behind enemy lines, and the Central Committee of the Spanish Communist party decided to use the veterans as instructors.

In the middle of December, Rudolf and Domingo were unexpectedly summoned to the general staff and ordered to prepare to take part in the operation for the liberation of Teruel.

Liquidation of the Teruel salient could prevent the rebels' breaking out to the Mediterranean Sea and splitting the Republican territory into two parts. The occupation of Teruel by the Republicans would shorten the front line and guarantee reliable communication between Valencia and Catalonia.

The rebels occupied only inhabited areas along the railroads and highways that connected Teruel with the rebel and interventionist rear. Republican troops to the north of Teruel held the other parallel highways. The only continuous front line was in the immediate area of Teruel.

Rudolf and Domingo spent a lot of time sitting with their maps, marking the positions of rebel forces mentioned in communiqués. Between small circles and strips marking rebel positions, there were forests and mountains that no one occupied.

"The anarchists can let us down," Domingo said. "These *bandidos* never fight seriously, and are only armed courtesy of the Republic, which they can attack from the rear," the captain said angrily and loudly with the approval of his closest assistants, Rubio and Buitrago.

Rubio was an experienced driver, strong and always in a good mood. In Republican uniform, with a large pistol on his belt, he took care of his Hispano-Suiza as if he was in

love with the car. As a rule, Rudolf sat next to him, and
Domingo and I sat in back. Around the city, Rubio drove
carefully, but at the slightest opportunity increased speed;
outside the city, he loved to pass.

Domingo often took his eight-year-old son Antonio with
him to the training sessions, which made the boy's mother
angry. But Antonio implored her without resorting to tears. I
never saw the boy cry.

In the detachment, they called Domingo's son Antonio Junior to distinguish him from Antonio senior, and yet another
Antonio. He became an integral part of the unit. As the son of
a cavalry officer, he knew how to ride, and his mother, a stout,
good-natured woman worried that he not fall off and fall under
the horse's hooves, but after his father began to study sabotage,
Antonio's mother once found fuses and dynamite charges in
the boy's pockets. "Dynamite!" she read on the charges. "Dynamite! My God, he will blow himself to pieces!"

"Leave the boy alone! It's only a dummy! We only have a
little dynamite and that's for actual sabotage," Captain Ungria tried to convince his wife.

At thirty-eight, Capt. Domingo Ungria was lean. Of aver-
age height, black haired, and swarthy, he was very quick
tempered, but exceptionally energetic and caring. And, as I
was later convinced, he was very brave. He quickly became
friends with Rudolf, but he mastered the techniques of demolition work slowly and asked questions basically about tactics. At first, he entrusted the technical matters to others, but
Porokhnyak knew how to make even the captain himself
mine roads and bridges. And the captain eventually mastered this science.

When he was angry, the commander of the detachment
sometimes wrongly chastised his men, but they quickly forgot the offenses. They loved him for his courage and his

care for them, and because he could get things that others could not, and because he always stood up for his men, and even because he was demanding and strict. They forgave him his hot temper and other shortcomings.

Domingo's assistant was Antonio Buitrago. He was twenty-one, with a powerful physique. He was strong, handsome, and brave, and he had already made more than one sortie behind enemy lines. He was recently married to a beautiful and jealous young woman. Antonio's younger brother Pedro fought at his side. Only eighteen, Pedro, nevertheless, carried a pistol just like his older brother.

All of the drivers attended the lessons. Among them was twenty-three-year-old Juan. He had thick hair and a small mustache, which neither spoiled nor beautified his handsome face. Juan was very attentive and conscientious. He had earlier joined the ranks of the People's Militia along with his own Peugeot. The other driver was Pepe. A very small man, he seemed frail but drove his Ford like a classical dance master. Strange in a Spaniard, Pepe did not drink wine and did not smoke, and all of Rudolf's attempts to break him of his bad habits during dinner were unsuccessful. At two o'clock in the afternoon, Pepe was already looking at his watch and, at the first opportunity, reminded us about eating.

I remember the black-haired Marquez. For a Spaniard, he was excessively phlegmatic. During lessons, he always paid close attention; he not only wanted to learn about everything, he wanted to do it himself. Marquez also listened attentively to Rudolf's stories about partisans. He admired the actions of Siberian partisans behind Kolchak's lines.

In the evenings of early December, I had to translate a lot. Fortunately, by then, Rudolf was trying to speak less and show more, to have the men practice more on the road, in the orchard, and in the workshop. He also paid special attention to safety. He took dynamite from the engineering depot, shot it, and it exploded. Rudolf began to dilute it with machine oil and potassium nitrate. The treated dynamite did not explode when shot, but it was weaker and did not always explode when the detonator went off.

First Sortie Behind Rebel Lines

At last all preparations were completed, and on December 13, 1936, after breakfast, when the sun already warmed the earth in the south, Domingo's group left Valencia for the Teruel front in three cars and a truck. In our trunk were two boxes of dynamite and as much TNT was put in the truck with the provisions.

After we passed through the checkpoint, Domingo held up the column and once again gave instructions to the drivers. Crossing the railroad, Rudolf suggested another training exercise. Domingo agreed, and I had to open my suitcase with the training mines. They were quickly placed and the engineer of an approaching train did not notice them. No one onboard saw the faint flash of the fuses in the ballast. Having finished the training exercise, we went still higher up the twisting road into the mountains. The sun was shining brightly all the way, but in the shadows, it was already chilly.

The farther we went into the mountains and away from the Mediterranean coast, the cooler it became and the fewer the orchards. When we crossed the Sierra de Gudar, we literally seemed to be in another country. Nothing remained of the subtropics. We found only sparse vegetation on which flocks of sheep grazed.

We passed two mules, walking one after the other, pulling

a high wagon loaded with firewood. Seeing our cars, the old driver stopped the animals, leaned back, and after setting the wooden brakes, greeted the passing soldiers. His wrinkled face broke into a joyous smile.

We arrived near Teruel toward evening and, in accordance with our orders, stopped in the village of Alfambra, which, like Teruel, was almost a kilometer above sea level. The houses in the village were thick walled and made of stone, but they had no stoves, and fireplaces did not provide the necessary warmth; they were chilly, even cold, inside.

In the village, there were many soldiers from other units who were to take part in the assault on Teruel. The poorly dressed peasants and their wives cordially welcomed the troops who had come. The children examined the vehicles with curiosity. The people were happy, hoping that the Republicans would soon liberate Teruel.

After sunset, it quickly became cold, and everyone dispersed. Our group was billeted in the house of a poor peasant. The floor was stone, the roof low, the windows small and in the middle near an interior wall was a soot-covered fireplace. The shutters were closed, and it was cold and dark in the room. Our host brought a little firewood, but we did not use the fireplace. We washed up and, after we had put out sentries, lay down to sleep.

During the night, I woke up, having heard the howling wind; covering myself a little more warmly, I was happy that it was still dark and I could lie under my overcoat and rough blanket.

In the morning, the air-raid siren began to howl, and the vehicles, which had gathered in the village, began to leave. Pepe and Emilio kept their heads—they quickly started their motors and transported our explosives into a field.

The Fascist vultures dropped their bombs from high altitude and missed the target. Domingo knew that with such a concentration of troops as that at Alfambra, the enemy planes would return frequently to bomb Alfambra, so after a little reconnaissance, we relocated our partisans to the village of Orrios, where we left the group and went to the commander of the Teruel sector.

The commander—the anarchist Benedito—received us in the presence of other officers. After listening to Domingo, he scowled then looked at me and Rudolf and greeted us casually. The conversation was short. The commander gave us our assignment, be ready to take "tongues," that is, prisoners for interrogation, and to wreck lines of communication. Domingo suggested conducting sabotage on the railroad and automobile roads by which the Teruel garrison could receive reinforcements. Benedito agreed, but on the condition that telegraph communications would also be destroyed.

On the Teruel front, I encountered Nora Pavlovna Chegodayeva, whom I had met through my work at the Lenin International School. She was working as interpreter for the adviser Walter, inspector of artillery of the Republican Army (in actuality he was future chief marshal of artillery, N. N. Voronov). Chegodayeva and her adviser spent a lot of time at the front.

Nora Chegodayeva was a highly qualified interpreter. She knew Spanish, French, and German very well, which was much to her benefit in Spain, since many officers in the international brigades did not know Spanish.

The Republican positions were in the mountains around Teruel. The cloudless sky, a real Spanish sky, reminded me of the sky at Kislovodsk. In winter, it is warm, even hot, in the sun, and at night it is cold. The men from Valencia did not like this.

In the mountains, where the wind was especially piercing, it was difficult to work, but at Teruel these difficulties were increased by the cold. When we arrived, I was dressed for summer, but here it was really winter, and there was snow on the mountains.

Domingo had to send a car to Valencia for warm things, oranges, and other provisions.

I shared the opinions of the men from Valencia and Andalusia about the weather at Teruel, but, as if to spite the weather, Rudolf was enthusiastic about the landscape.

"Conditions here are favorable for our first sortie," he told the Spanish comrades, who were sitting by the fireplace to escape the cold. "This is a plateau without steep mountains, there is no continuous front, the population is sparse, there is forest for concealment, and not all the leaves have fallen from the trees. And the fact that Teruel Province is one of the most backward and poorest in Spain, even that is good for us. The enemy has only one railroad and one highway, and there are few populated points along them."

"But other things are worse," Domingo said. "Around Teruel our militia detachments are usually under the command and influence of anarchists, and I have not yet managed to find the scouts we need, and none of our men knows the area."

It was difficult to find scouts. During discussions with candidates, we had to maintain security and could not speak about the aim of our mission. Scouts had to be reliable men who would not be afraid and would not refuse to do the work at the last minute, and who would not sell us out to the enemy. It took us twenty-four hours to find two anarchist scouts who were familiar with the area and who had frequently been behind enemy lines.

On the morning of December 16, a courier from the commander arrived at our position in a dusty Peugeot: a short, black-haired anarchist with a large pistol in a wooden holster. Without knocking, he entered the room where Domingo, Rudolf, and the scouts were discussing possible alternative routes behind enemy lines and summoned us to "comrade Benedito."

Domingo, Rudolf, Rubio, and I left for the headquarters of the commander of the Teruel sector. At the first opportunity, Rubio passed the Peugeot of the anarchist courier, who was soon hopelessly behind.

This time, Benedito was elated and met us in friendly fashion and even offered us seats.

Quietly, as if being careful the outsiders did not hear him, he asked Domingo, "Are you ready for a sally behind enemy lines?"

"Completely ready!" Domingo answered quietly.

The commander looked at the captain intently, leaned closer to him and, almost in a whisper, said, "Start out today. Tomorrow, around four in the morning, disable the communication line that parallels the automobile and railroads about twenty to twenty-five kilometers north of Teruel. Blow up the poles, cut the wires, close both roads."

Domingo tried to say something, but the commander looked at him so that he stopped on the word, "Min—"

"Above all cut off telegraph and telephone communications!" Benedito demanded. Then he wished us luck, leading us to understand that all instructions had been given and we must leave.

Half an hour later, we were back in Orrios. Rudolf and Domingo decided to take twelve men on the first sortie, the rest would remain in reserve. Those who were chosen for the trip began preparations. I saw that even Rudolf changed into *alpargatas,* (half boots, tops of cloth, soles of rope).

"You are planning to go, too?" I asked.

"Yes!" Rudolf answered as he adjusted the *alpargatas*. He acted as if we were talking about a regular departure for an exercise.

"Why didn't you warn me? Can you possibly think about going without me?" I said, offended that he would leave me. "You know that without me you are completely deaf and dumb; you hear but don't understand what the Spaniards say, and you can talk to them, but they will not understand. Without me, especially at night, you will be of no use to the group."

Rudolf had not expected my arguments and couldn't make much of a reply.

"I am your interpreter, and I will go with you," I declared and began to change my shoes for my *alpargatas*.

When I was ready to go, Domingo came up to me and said very sweetly, "Louisa, you aren't going with us. This is not women's business. My Rosalia would not think of going."

"Listen, Domingo, I didn't come to Spain to bathe on the beach, and you already know that I'm used to walking at night. I grew up in the north, and many times I had to walk along the forest roads and through the forest, sometimes alone and without a weapon. Here we at least have pistols."

"But here the rebels can see us."

"It is necessary to walk in a way so they don't. We have been training behind our own lines for two weeks, and now we will take an exam for real. I've also seen rebels and interventionists. In 1918, in our region along with the Whites, that is *our* rebels, we also had English interventionists. I was working as a day laborer then. The rich were happy, and they helped the Whites. But many of the poor were neither intimidated by the brutality of the Reds, nor went over to the Whites."

"They went into the Red Army or the partisans?" Domingo asked.

"In our village there were no partisans, nor were there battles. As soon as it began to get dark, the English sat in their houses and did not allow anyone to get close. The Whites, who were with them, protected them, and at night they didn't go anywhere outside the village."

"You mean they were afraid of the night. That's very good," the captain agreed.

My participation in the mission caused Domingo many problems—no one else wanted to remain at the base. "The woman is going, and what are we?"

On the way we stopped in at headquarters to get a situation report. The commander and his adviser Kolyev[1] noticed Rudolf and me in our marching gear. Kolyev called us aside. "Why are you going?"

"The first time, it's absolutely necessary."

"Well, what if the rebels capture you?"

"There is no continuous front line. We won't give them a trail to follow; we have delayed-action grenades for that, and we will return toward morning," Rudolf answered.

"You aren't planning to go with them, are you Louisa? Why are you dressed like that?" Kolyev asked me.

"As you can see, I am going! Rudolf is deaf and dumb without me!"

"Well, they gave you some boss," Kolyev said.

As we departed, he shook our hands and wished us luck.

More than once on the Teruel front, I met with Vladimir Yakovlyevich Kolpakchi and his interpreter, Lyala Konstantinovskaya. Once when I was complaining to her about the cold in the place where we were billeted, Konstantinovskaya

---

[1] Vladimir Yakovlyevich Kolpakchi

said, "Cold is bad but you can cover yourself up from the cold, but during the day I have to go to the brigades with my frantic adviser and at night sit with the Spanish officers over plans. Not long ago, I worked until I had to cut off my shoes because my feet were swollen from overwork."

We went by car to the sector from which we would depart on the operation. I was completely absorbed in thought and in a far from optimistic mood! Everything had happened so suddenly. All the while we had trained the men, there was never one conversation with Rudolf about our going with the Spaniards behind rebel lines. I knew that he had been behind Denikin's lines during the Civil War. Surrounded, he had worked his way back to his own area for five days and nearly got caught while crossing the front line disguised as a peasant. I knew that he had taught sabotage at the academy, but he was going behind enemy lines in a foreign country for the first time.

True, he had no family and would leave no orphans.

Rudolf said that although he was not born with a lucky spoon in his mouth, he was confident of success since "our ally is the night." I did not know then that he had sent intelligence agents across the border many times.

We arrived unnoticed at battalion headquarters. With the aid of the scouts, Domingo and Rudolf made arrangements with the battalion commander, and we made our way to the company positions from which we were going to walk behind rebel lines.

The front was completely different from what I imagined from my military training at the institute. There were no trenches of any kind. The soldiers were in a solitary, empty shepherd's hut. In the distance, in the direction of the rebels, was the forest and . . . the unknown. The company commander maintained that the Fascist covering force was located in another shepherd's hut about two kilometers to the west, and we could pass by unnoticed even in broad daylight.

"Let me have your scouts," Domingo asked the stately, clean-shaven company commander with the black-and-red tie.

"No orders!" the anarchist answered shortly, smoking a cigarette, and he did not give us the scouts. The captain ordered the men to take a smoke break.

Together with the company commander and the scouts we had brought, we examined the area for a few minutes through binoculars.

In front of us, we could see what seemed to be a dense dark forest. In front of the forest on the flat land, there were only sparse small bushes, which had at one time been grazed by sheep.

"Before nightfall, we can walk undetected along the dry streambed right up to the forest itself," one of the scouts said. I translated.

"We can go before dark," Rudolf agreed. "We just have to make arrangements with the company commander."

When we left the shepherd's hut where the small unit of anarchists was located, there was still more than an hour until dark.

We walked along the dry streambed, bending low. In front of us were our scouts and two intelligence agents, behind them Captain Ungria, Rudolf, and me; behind me Rubio with a submachine gun, and at the rear of the column the tall Antonio Buitrago.

On everyone's back were small white rags with pieces of rotten wood tied to them so that at night those who were going in front would be visible to those who came behind. Everyone was armed with pistols and knives. Most of us also had carbines.

In the middle of the meandering, dried-up stream there

was a real path that had been made by someone walking. From time to time, we went down so that we would not be seen, but the scouts, the agents, Domingo, and Rudolf checked the area.

"All clear," Rudolf said lowering the binoculars. "Now everything depends on the reliability of the scouts." These semiliterate peasants were proud of their membership in the FAI, the Federation of Anarchists of Spain. Moreover, they tried to persuade our men to go over to the anarchists.

"We need scouts who know the local area and conditions behind enemy lines well, so let's not try to convert these anarchists. If you annoy them, they'll leave us," Domingo said to Buitrago, who'd been zealously attempting to re-educate the scouts himself. "If necessary, intelligence agents dress in enemy uniform. The scouts stand for the black-and-red bandanna, so let some of our people wear them, let the anarchists think that their propaganda has been successful."

When we left for the rebel rear, Marquez put on a black-and-red necktie. He soon had the complete trust of the scouts.

A short twilight gave way to a dark, moonless night. Even the stars were not visible.

At nightfall, the forest toward which we were going dissolved into darkness. We moved more slowly to avoid giving ourselves away. Suddenly, the scouts stopped.

"Danger! We're near the forest! The enemy could be there! We've got to come out of the gulley. There could be a trap in front of the forest," one of the scouts whispered. The other one confirmed it. I translated.

"What do they suggest?" Rudolf asked.

"We need to get out of the streambed and walk carefully along the very edge of the bank. The moment an enemy flare is launched, fall down on the ground and stay still until it goes out." I translated the warning of the senior scout.

By this time, the stream proved more difficult. There was no longer a well-trodden trail. We ran into numerous gullies and other uneven spots. We walked slowly, stepping carefully. Every so often, someone would get into a hollow or get tangled in an exposed root and fall. Every noise could give us away to the enemy.

Soon we had to go into the mysterious forest. The tension intensified. It seemed to me, and apparently to the others, too, that a flare could go up at any moment, and then what could our small group do so far from our own troops?

"At last, we are in the forest," Rudolf whispered to me and, for the first time, firmly squeezed my hand. He understood that, not knowing the language, he would have been like a deaf mute without me.

"Tell the captain to stop for a minute," he said.

Everyone stood completely still at the edge of the forest. In the silence of the night, the rustle of the dry leaves that had not yet fallen could be heard. Possibly, enemy guard posts were somewhere nearby. Once again, we reminded everyone about maintenance of silence and camouflage, and about our signals. We set out. We walked almost without a sound. In front of us, the pieces of wood, which had been stuck on our backs, glowed like fireflies.

When someone broke silence, we would stop and listen before starting again.

It was even more difficult to walk in the forest. The roots of the trees stuck out of the ground; here and there, fallen limbs blocked the way. We could not see anything. As we walked, we had to lift our feet higher and put them down lightly in order not to trip over roots.

Rubio, who was accustomed to travel by car, stumbled and fell. We stopped. Everything quiet. Onward again . . .

The scouts stepped out briskly. They had already walked

this path more than once to visit relatives and close friends, and they assured us that they knew all the sentries and ambushes in the forest.

"The greatest danger is behind us at the edge of the forest," they said.

Rudolf and Domingo also walked confidently. I do not know what they were thinking about then, and even later, they did not talk about it, but at the beginning of the mission, I had the impression that we were going into the threatening unknown, and from the beginning, it was terrible. I had survived just such moments once when I was crossing over a deep swift river on a narrow board bridge. The board sagged so it seemed that you were just about to slide off into the water. But that time I went ahead . . . here there was nowhere to retreat.

The deeper we went behind enemy lines, the more confidently we walked. After about two hours, we stopped to rest and have something to eat. All around, a gloomy silence reigned. The night was dark and quiet.

The inveterate smokers begged to smoke. They were allowed to smoke, but only if they covered their heads with their jackets. The smell of tobacco was in the air, but the glow of cigarettes was not visible, and the flash of the matches and cigarette lighters was inconspicuous. We had taught this during our lessons. The chilly night air refreshed us quickly, and then we had to wrap up.

Suddenly, distant rifle shots broke the silence. In a few seconds, the sound of a burst of shots reached us from a distance, and everything faded away.

Rudolf sat alongside me, treating me to hot coffee, sandwiches, and chocolates. Again, we heard a distant, single shot, but everyone continued to rest peacefully.

"Our ally is the night!" Rudolf whispered. "The rebels do

not know that we are resting here peacefully." He continued to drink his coffee.

A breeze was blowing and, listening to it, I recalled my native north, when I was trying to find a couple of cows and a calf belonging to the man for whom I was working.

I had gotten lost, and night caught me in the forest. It was raining, and I had to cover myself with moss to stay warm. That was when I learned about fear! All around me were frightening rustling sounds, the calls of the night birds and animals, and I was alone with a walking stick. I wanted to climb a tree; it would have been safer there, but the rain squelched that idea, so I buried myself in the moss. I could not fall asleep. At dawn, I climbed a tree, looked around, and found the road. Now, behind enemy lines on a night halt, the forest was not so frightening.

Rudolf whispered, "Time to go." Domingo passed on the command.

The front line was far behind, but we did not feel the nearness of the enemy; we had complete faith in our scouts, so we felt more free.

The path was narrow; we were moving single file. I was between Domingo and Rudolf, and in order to translate, I had to turn around.

Alpargatas are indispensable footwear in the mountains. They do not slip, they are noiseless, and you can walk soft as a cat in them. It was bad luck that on the way we waded across a stream, not very wide but pretty deep. We could not find anything suitable for improvising a small bridge.

Our rag boots were instantly soaked. Our feet began to freeze. At the stops, Domingo gave those who were very cold a swallow of cognac directly from the bottle. And then we went on our way. At the next halt someone said, "Can we light a fire?"

"Are you crazy?" the others said. "No!"

Again we went on, staggering.

"Ah, it's a tough road," Pedro said with a sigh.

"Behind our own lines, you were a hero, and now you whine!" Antonio said to his brother. "We still have a lot of difficulties ahead of us. You may have to climb a mountain, and maybe you will be under fire."

"Aren't you ashamed?" Rubio said to Pedro. "A woman goes with us in silence, and you, you bastard, whine!"

We made yet another short stop. Around three o'clock in the morning, we came to the Teruel–Calamocha highway. We sat down about a hundred meters from the road and had a bite to eat.

To the north, a pair of lights soon appeared. They came closer, at first slowly, and then faster. A car passed, and we looked after its disappearing red taillights. We went to mine the road as a team, just like one of our night exercises.

Domingo's group had to destroy communications and blow up a small bridge. The width of the road was about ten meters, and the bridge was not high, just a single reinforced concrete span.

"Not enough explosives! What will we do?" Domingo asked, when we stopped under the bridge.

Rudolf did not answer right away. He measured the size of the beams. Then he brought the captain to the bridge pier and said, "Place the mines just like we did in our training on the reinforced concrete bridge on the Valencia–Albacete highway, only put a few more rocks to seal it."

"Okay," Domingo answered and added, "We can make a good seal here. There are many rocks."

"Car!" Rubio called.

Everyone held their breath. On the road above us, an automobile swept by. Domingo set to work with his people, and after waiting for another car to pass, Rudolf, part of the group, and I hurried toward the railroad along a dried-up stream.

We walked for about ten minutes, listening often, but everything was quiet. The bridge on the railroad turned out to be just as our guides had said it would be, made of metal and nearly eight meters long. We quickly set the charges, which had been prepared ahead of time, and set them on the telephone poles. We had very little time; we could not delay very long. The fuses on the bridge were expected to go at any minute.

We all gathered near the pier from which the mines spread out to both sides. Only Miguel was not there.

"What could have happened to him?" I thought. He was supposed to have mined the fourth pole, the last one from the right. And now . . . Just then from the direction of Teruel automobile lights appeared. As Rudolph asked "Should we go find Miguel?" Miguel suddenly turned up and whispered, "I barely found them!"

"Found what?"

"The fuses!"

"*Vamos,* that is let's go," said Rudolf, and we moved toward the highway.

At the first halt, Miguel told us how he dropped the fuses.

"The short ones fell in the grass, and I could hardly find them in the dark."

We had barely gotten to the highway when a bright flash lit up the area, followed by the sharp sound of an explosion. Other explosions followed. We crossed the highway and picked up the pace, hurrying to the previously agreed-upon meeting place. Suddenly a large fiery pillar lit up everything for a moment, then loud explosions were heard, and the earth shuddered beneath falling wreckage. The railroad bridge! The men were ecstatic, but car lights from Teruel interrupted our celebration even while the charges on the telephone poles continued to explode. We were so happy, we'd almost forgotten we were behind enemy lines. In just a few minutes the enemy could bring up trucks filled with troops, and then things could get unhealthy for us!

"Tell Domingo to order the team to get out of here quickly," Rudolf said, and before I had time to translate, he himself said to the captain, *"Vamos! Rapidamente!"*[2]

The return trip was a bit easier. Satisfied with their success, the men did not feel their fatigue. When we had gone about two kilometers from where the action had taken place, a flare lit up the sky. We quickened our pace.

The sun rose. Along the horizon stretched the snow-covered mountains, and the wind blew cold from them. The rumble of an artillery barrage signaled the beginning of the Republican attack on Teruel, but we were still behind rebel lines, and we did not hurry, hoping that the Republicans would capture the city. When we arrived back at our own positions, news of the liberation of the city had not yet come in.

Domingo sent his saboteurs off to rest, and we went to report to the commander.

"How strongly the charges exploded, how far the pieces flew!" the undersized, but hardy and quick, scout with the black-and-red necktie said with delight.

"It was no worse than an aerial bomb!" added the other, somewhat sullen scout.

"Of course, no worse!" agreed the first, "even better. Bombs from an airplane don't always fall on target, and

[2] Let's go. Quickly!

here, we hit without a miss. This will please Comrade Benedito!" he concluded.

The commander received us only after midday, and we were astonished when he strongly reprimanded us even though he had not heard Capt. Domingo Ungria's report.

"You're completely useless! You only make a lot of noise! The enemy is getting reinforcements! His communications work!"

"Listen to me, Comrade Commander!" Domingo began to explain. "Our plan was fulfilled and even overfulfilled. The poles and wires were blown up and the bridges destroyed."

But Benedito did not let Captain Ungria finish. Lucky for us, the commander was called out to a meeting.

"Is it possible that he expects fourteen men to determine the success of the operation?" grumbled Domingo.

"Don't give up hope," artillery adviser N. N. Voronov said to us, taking advantage of the moment. He had been present during the conversation. "Understand, the commander is nervous. The attack is not going according to plan, and our soldiers are taking greater losses."

"But what does that have to do with us? Our little group could hardly guarantee the success of the attack?" Ungria said.

"Of course not!"

Benedito came back and seeing that Domingo had not left began cursing him again.

We were all depressed by the behavior of the commander and his evaluation of our results. It was especially hard for the more animated scout to bear. He got red as a lobster and suddenly began to shout loudly, "We blew two bridges, we destroyed all communications. The pieces flew for a hundred meters. Fourteen men went out on the highway where a battalion was afraid to go," he shouted, waving his arms.

Domingo stood by the excited scout and cursed in a low voice.

Even Benedito was taken aback. Either the scout convinced him or he was too uncomfortable to continue the confrontation in front of Voronov. In any case he stopped shouting and said angrily, "All right. Rest! Get ready to go behind enemy lines again tomorrow!"

When we left, we were depressed. The scout and Rudolf were the most upset.

"Let him go himself, then he'll know what's going on," the infuriated scout said.

The older scout, no longer shy in my presence, used expressions which one should not translate.

Tired and sullen, we returned to Orrios.

We went into our room. The majority of the men who had been on the mission were sleeping. Some had bandaged their feet as if wounded. Those who had remained in reserve and five of those who had returned were waiting for us.

When they caught sight of us, they were happy, but then they noticed our expressions.

"What happened?" Antonio Buitrago asked.

"It's all right!" the captain answered briskly, but his men knew something was wrong both from the tone of his answer and our mood.

"Sleep! Sleep! And then today, we go again!" said Domingo. He sat on the floor and began to take off his shoes.

Rubio sat down next to him and quietly asked, "Why are you so upset?"

"They haven't liberated Teruel! That's why!"

They asked no more questions.

The next day, I had only just finished my morning exercises when they knocked on my door.

"Louisa! I have a serious question for you!" Pepe said after greeting me.

"Go ahead, ask."

"Louisa, while you were behind the lines, I was doing some reconnaissance. I learned from the local peasants that, not long before our arrival, some rebels in a car went on the Teruel–Perales highway and drove around Orrios. So why don't we drive on the Teruel–Calamocha highway?"

At first I did not understand what he was talking about and why he was asking me.

"Did you talk to Domingo about this?"

"No! Domingo is a cavalry officer. He would not understand. It's important that you agree with my suggestion and you tell Rudolf about it."

"Pepe, I don't understand, why drive on the highway? What for?"

Pepe anxiously smiled, thought for a moment, and began to explain.

"You walked on foot on this very same highway, you got tired and some of you got sore feet."

"Yes," I agreed.

"You got tired when you made about thirty kilometers in all, then what will it be like when you have to go even farther a second time?"

"Listen, Pepe, let's go to Rudolf and you tell him."

Just then a Peugeot stopped in front of the house, and the anarchist with the forelock who had been with us jumped out with an envelope in his hand.

"Where is Captain Ungria? This is a battle order."

Domingo and Rudolf also were no longer sleeping. The captain opened the packet, read the order, signed the receipt for it, and said, "Good! Everything is clear!"

The courier drove away.

The captain read the document again, gave it to me, and I translated it for Rudolf. The commander ordered us to conduct daily sorties on enemy communications north of Teruel.

"We need horses. Only cavalry can do this!" Domingo declared in a cheerless voice to the soldiers who had gathered around him.

That's when Pepe presented his proposal for carrying out sorties in automobiles.

Out of surprise, Domingo said nothing, and I had not yet had time to translate for Rudolf before passionate Rubio expressed his doubt, and Pepe martialed arguments to support his proposal. "If the enemy drove from his highway to ours in broad daylight, then why can't we do the same?" Pepe asked.

"We can! Of course we can!" Juan said.

Domingo and Rudolf decided to think over Pepe's suggestion.

The battalion commander, in whose sector the rebels had appeared in cars, not only agreed to help, but he also detached eight volunteers from the battalion.

When we arrived at a small grove that was located in no-man's-land, Pepe said, "Here is where the cars of the rebels came through." We drove along the dry valley, which had bushes growing on its slopes, toward the Teruel–Calamocha highway.

Four kilometers from our lines, we reached a field road and picked up speed.

The area was hilly, with small groves. The clay soil was cracked, and in some places, rocks with fantastic contours were visible. The midday sun shone brightly, and high in the sky there were occasional light clouds. The even rumble of the automobile engine was all we heard. The silence put us on guard.

"El cortico!"[3] Domingo said softly, pointing to a solitary shepherd's hut about a kilometer away.

After pulling into a small hollow, Rudolf suggested we stop and send out a scouting party. Domingo agreed. Rubio

---

[3] This is what they call a shepherd's hut in Andalusia.

and Buitrago went out, the rest prepared to support them with fire. The closer Rubio approached the *cortico,* the harder my heart beat. But everything came out all right, and we received the right signal.

We went up to the hut. Near it, a hungry overridden horse nibbled greedily on the grass. The horse shied away in fright from our soldiers.

We parked the cars under the canopy of the shade trees and went into the hut. No one was there. Household articles were scattered about. Where was the horseman, and what happened to him? Why did he abandon his horse? Or was he dead, and his steed returned home on his own?

Domingo, Rudolf, Antonio, Rubio, and the scouts carefully looked around. On the ground were the tracks of the enemy vehicles, but nothing indicated any danger. We went on another two kilometers without seeing anything suspicious. Then "Soldiers on the left! They've seen us and are taking cover!" Buitrago senior called.

"Stop!" Domingo said. The cars stopped. About eight hundred meters south of the road, armed men in uniform could be clearly seen. But who were they?

Rubio engaged the transmission, the car started with a jerk, but we did not have time to get to cover before they fired on us. Fortunately, the riflemen were poor shots, and we regained the hollow without any losses.

"Halt!" Domingo commanded. "Turn around," he said to the drivers. "The rest of you behind me."

The enemy directed fire at the cars, which could not be completely hidden in the hollow, but the vehicles and drivers were out of range. Our men returned fire, and the skirmish intensified. This was happening in no-man's-land in broad daylight.

"Look! They are retreating to the east, toward the Republicans!" Rudolf said. I translated, and the captain ordered a cease-fire. Domingo cursed.

"Break out the red flag," Rudolf said.

Pepe quickly took a small flag from his car and raised it on a carbine. In reply the group on the slope of the mountain unfurled a black-and-red bandanna on a rifle.

"Let me go for a parley!" Juan said. Rudolf and Domingo agreed. Our truce envoy walked unhurriedly toward the distant anarchists. The situation was very tense. Minutes of waiting seemed like an eternity. But Juan kept walking forward.

At last, to everyone's relief, an armed man stood up from where the unknown group was located. Holding a rifle in his right hand, he walked out to meet Juan. The envoys came together, they gesticulated, apparently they argued. After two or three minutes, Juan turned toward us and waved his hand, telling us to come.

"It is rare, but it happens," Rudolf observed. "We don't recognize our own troops." Our group had skirmished with an anarchist reconnaissance party.

"There are no Fascist detachments of any kind up to the highway itself," the reconnaissance party said.

In spite of the exchange of fire, which might have alerted Fascists to our presence, Domingo and Rudolf decided to move on. We drove along the dirt road without meeting anyone.

About five kilometers from the highway, Rubio suddenly stopped the car, jumped out, and began to examine the road. Only three meters in front of the car, across the road, two parallel cracks could be seen. Under close examination it was evident that the ground between the cracks was different from the rest of the road.

Rudolf carefully tapped the road up to the cracks and

between them with a small stick, and said, "It may be a wolf pit! With a mine!"

"It's easy to go around," Pepe said.

And so we did. We backed up about fifty meters and went through a field around the suspicious place. We went on more slowly, carefully examining the road. Soon we came out on a cart track where fresh automobile tracks could be seen. They led to the highway that connected the rebel garrison in Teruel with their main forces. From concealment behind the bushes, we observed the traffic along the Teruel–Calamocha highway from a distance of less than a kilometer.

We could also see the railroad bed, but no trains were in sight.

For the most part, only solitary vehicles passed along the highway and, very rarely, a column of ten or fifteen trucks. We did not see guards of any kind.

"We could go out on the road, join up with any of the columns and arrange some fireworks for the rebels," Domingo suggested.

Rudolf did not agree. "Another time, another place. We're too close to a large and already alerted enemy garrison," he said.

We followed the dry gulch closer to the highway, close enough to make out the faces of the soldiers. We turned the cars so that we would not be seen from the road and so it would be better to direct fire.

The cars drove off about twenty-five meters behind us, then Buitrago the elder staked in two mines and camouflaged them. Juan set a mine with an almost imperceptible string. Everyone worked calmly as if on a training exercise.

The enemy either did not see us or thought we were theirs. It probably never occurred to the Fascists the cars that had driven up to the road carried Republicans.

The group took up a firing position behind the rocks and patiently awaited the approach of a small column with freight. Initially, only solitary vehicles came, primarily cars. At last, a column appeared from the north. Everyone watched anxiously.

"Very good! Trucks, and it seems, without soldiers," Domingo whispered.

The column was already very close, the tarpaulin covers could be seen, there were twelve trucks in all. When the first one came up even with the group, Rudolf and the captain opened fire, and after them, the whole group fired.

The trucks that had come under our fire pulled off the road and one went up in flames. Some of the soldiers leapt from the cabs and bodies of the trucks into the ditches, others ran away. Then our group ceased firing and, bending low, made for the cars; from the north a large automobile column was getting closer. We assembled, the cars had been started, and we quickly set out on the return trip, leaving the mines that we had set earlier to cover us. From behind us on the highway came the sound of shots. We kept on the beaten track. The sun was in front and a little to the right. The rays of the sun, coming from the opposite direction, would hamper our pursuers.

To make pursuit more difficult, about two kilometers away from the highway we stopped and the demolition men planted mines. Once more, we went around the suspected Fascist mines and stopped. We set one small mine on the path that went around the cracks then drove on. Later, we learned that there really was a wolf pit on the road, at a depth of more than half a meter, and that the lead vehicle following us, possibly not knowing about the trap, hit it and was knocked over. The enemy set traps like that on roads that crossed the front line where there was no continuous defense line.

After a few moments, far behind us, we heard a dull explosion. No matter how much we looked back, no pursuers were visible. We assumed the Fascists backed off on their pursuit after hitting a mine.

After this mission, we were returning with lifted spirits. The volunteers from the anarchist element in that sector were the most happy. Little Pepe was especially happy with our success.

The next day, two groups of saboteurs went behind rebel lines and mined roads. That time, Rudolf and I did not go. By that time, the road was heavily guarded. And the enemy discovered one of our mines, and the other did not work. Rubio and his group captured and burned a fuel truck.

On the eve of the new year, 1937, anarchists unexpectedly held us up at a checkpoint.

A tall, lean soldier with a black-and-red bandanna around his neck shined the light of a pocket flashlight on our pass and said, "Get out! Come with me!" His right hand reached for his holster.

An angry Domingo climbed out of the vehicle. At the same time, Pepe jumped out. Rudolf and I stayed in the limousine. Behind us was the truck with our men.

"Take your hand off your holster and return our papers," Captain Ungria ordered. He whipped a small Browning from his breast pocket and stuck it almost to the chest of the anarchist who had taken our pass. Rubio held a Mauser; our other driver, Juan, held his Walther ready, and against the backdrop of a starry sky, two submachine guns could be seen, directed at the vehicle with the anarchists.

The tall anarchist took his hand from his holster and said to his assistant, "Jesus, let them by!" and he returned the pass.

The anarchists got quiet. Apparently, the submachine guns in the truck had a sobering effect.

Domingo could not stay calm for long, and snarled, "They don't fight, but they are masters at capturing vehicles in their own rear area. *Bandidos!*"

Valencia Workday Routine

The secretary of the Valencia Provincial Committee of the Spanish Communist party was satisfied with the activities of our group at Teruel.

"Things are looking up!" Rudolf said to me when we returned to Domingo's apartment from the Party Provincial Committee.

The captain's wife invited everyone to the table, but we were waiting for Juan. He had stayed behind to turn off the car. Suddenly we heard shots from the street. The men jumped up and ran downstairs. There was a lot of commotion. Rosalia and I went out.

In front of the doorway, near the Ford, lay Juan, head bent. On the asphalt, a dark thick stain was spreading. His right hand was as if to protect his heart.

Rosalia threw up her hands and shrieked with a high piercing voice.

Our men had already seized the murderers, two anarchists who defended their actions by saying, "We demanded his papers, but he went for his pistol."

A crowd gathered and buzzed threateningly. The anarchists, hands tied behind them, grew quiet.

"They needed the car!" someone in the crowd shouted. "They don't fight at the front, but they can steal behind their own lines."

"Shoot the dogs! Shoot them!" The shouts of the agitated crowd were heard.

But they also had defenders.

"What if the driver, instead of presenting his papers, pulled out a pistol?" I heard the strong tinkling voice. It seemed to me that I knew it. A car which had come up lit up the crowd with its headlights where the defender was, and I saw a tall figure with a black-and-red bandanna on his neck. It was the same anarchist who had detained us at the checkpoint near Teruel. A small group of anarchists with him began to defend the murderer, but the overwhelming majority of those who had gathered were against these unknown men, and the anarchists left in a hurry.

We buried Juan the next day. His coffin was taken to the Valencia cemetery, and there his friends and relatives carried it by hand. Except for me, the women remained in front of the gates in the carriage of the funeral procession. In Spain, the women were not allowed to go into the cemetery where they bury the dead, only the men went behind the fence.

Juan's tragic death shocked everyone. We had already gotten used to him and to the foolhardy Rubio and little Pepe. We said our last good-byes in front of the cemetery. Juan's father, a tall, round-shouldered, wrinkled old man, slowly came up to the open casket. He was standing firm, but when he touched Juan's high forehead, he began to tremble. The old man's dry hand convulsively tousled his silent son's forelock.

"Bandits! They murdered him!" The words exploded from him.

They placed the casket in a deep recess of the cemetery wall, covered the opening with bricks, and sealed it with cement.

The brother of the deceased came up to us. He was shorter than the one who had been murdered, with black hair and round face.

"Vicente," he gave his name. "Take me with you. I want to replace my brother."

Domingo took Vicente. And his car.

The next day, Rudolf was already practicing with Domingo's group on the Valencia–Cuenca–Madrid railroad, which no one was guarding. The men set practice mines under the rails, under the ties, and alongside the rails. Trains were passing, fuses were exploding, but the engineers did not notice. Everything was going well.

After lunch that day, they began to train in the use of *rapido* mines, high-speed mines. These had to be placed immediately before the passage of the train; the most skilled demolition men set mines with wheel-switch fuses of less than thirty seconds.

In the distance a train appeared. The saboteurs threw themselves on the railroad, mined it and quickly retreated. A passenger express approached. We could see the weak flashes of the fuses of the mines. Suddenly an engineer, who had noticed something was wrong, stopped the train. Soldiers with rifles and pistols in their hands began to run out of the cars, and the engineer also jumped out. They all went to the place where a practice explosion had gone off, and they found the remnants of our practice mines.

The engineer was gesticulating, pointing in our direction. He had probably noticed the demolition men running away from the railroad bed. We were behind a stone fence, in an orchard, 250 to 300 meters from the train. Our cars were two hundred meters from us. Before one of the passengers organized a search for saboteurs, we could be sitting in our car and getting away, but that might lead to an official investigation, and then they would get to us. It was necessary to head things off. Meanwhile, almost all of the passengers had left the cars, and a large group of soldiers gathered around the practice mine.

"Listen, Domingo, we have to head off a big commotion," Rudolf said through me. "Go to the train and tell them there weren't any and aren't any saboteurs, that this is the work of Republican demolition specialists."

Domingo had not expected such a suggestion and looking inquisitively at Rudolf, asked, "What if they pick us up and take us to Valencia and turn us over to the commandant's office?"

"Don't wait for them to take you. *Request* to go to Valencia, but first convince the senior officer on the train that this is not sabotage, that saboteurs don't set bricks."

"Let's go, Comrade Captain!" Marquez said.

"Okay, let's go!" Domingo said. Taking another four men with him, he headed toward the crowd.

From a distance, we could not hear what happened when Domingo arrived, but to our satisfaction, after about five minutes, the passengers began to return to the cars. Domingo and his men disappeared with them.

We got in our cars and drove back to the school. On the way, we found out that, against orders, the younger Buitrago had not covered the electrical fuse with ballast, so the blast of the practice mine had not been properly muffled. Young Buitrago's prank could have cost us dearly.

By the time we arrived at the school, Domingo had still not returned. We discussed the incident and waited impatiently for the captain. When he finally appeared, it was clear by his appearance that everything had come out all right.

"Everything is okay," Captain Ungria began. "True, walking up to the crowd was frightening. We heard them saying things like 'saboteurs,' 'fifth column,' 'Fascists.' "

The soldiers had discovered a practice mine, which, however, no one had decided to remove, so before they could come to their senses, Marquez bent down and pulled it out. "This is not an explosive, just some kind of brick!" he said loudly, and he smashed it on a rail.

"Back in the cars!" commanded the major who was there, and the crowd began to disperse.

"Wait a minute!" I said to Domingo. "Let me translate for Rudolf, he doesn't understand what's going on."

Domingo paused, and when I had finished translating, continued, "I decided to go on the train and tell the major what I had seen and how Republican demolition specialists had been working there and had left in a truck. The major proved not to be an alarmist." He already knew about the wrecking of trains behind enemy lines, and said, "It is not for nothing that demolition specialists practice near Valencia."

Later, Domingo told us he had once met that major at the front near Saragossa.

Then Domingo found young Buitrago and gave him a long dressing down for his carelessness. He warned everyone that no one should show such "boldness" in the future.

After returning from the Teruel front to Valencia, I lived in Captain Ungria's apartment. Rudolf spent evenings with him discussing the tactics of action behind enemy lines, telling stories about the struggle of Soviet partisans in the years of war against the White guard and foreign interventionists. They studied conditions at the front and in the rebel rear and spoke about the forthcoming campaign on the southern front, where it was planned to transfer our group, which had received its baptism by fire at Teruel.

I made friends with the group commander's wife, Rosalia. She had a little daughter, Theresa, and an eight-year-old son, Antonio. The little girl liked housework. At one moment, she would be doing the laundry, then the next she swept, then she rearranged her toys. A quiet and obedient child, although she was not yet six, she already helped her mother. Eight-year-old Antonio was bright, good, and brave beyond his years.

Rosalia often wept bitterly because she had left her

mother and two other daughters in rebel-occupied Seville. She knew nothing about them. It had happened like this.

In the middle of July 1936, she had come to Valencia with Antonio and Theresa, the rebellion had begun and the Fascists seized Seville.

A half year had already passed since the start of the rebellion, thousands of children had become orphans, many mothers and wives had lost their children and husbands, and thousands of children had perished. Rosalia always searched among the refugees for those who had news of Seville. For a long time, she had been unsuccessful in finding out about the fate of her family.

Our group was growing and was being trained continually, and we could have been sent to the front at any time, but we did not have enough explosives. One day, Rudolf learned that there were some old depth charges in Cartagena, and he got a note from Berzin addressed to Comrade Nicholas Kuznetsov, the Soviet naval attaché, with a request to help us out.

"At the front there is battle, but in Valencia there is the *corrida,*" Rudolf complained the Sunday I was seeing him off to Cartagena. Crowds of festively dressed people were flocking to meet at the *corrida.*

Refugees were walking along the street from the station, and next to them were volunteers, future members of the international brigades who stood out because of their ordinary clothes and because they were obviously amazed at the well-dressed crowds.

From fifty-four countries, the volunteers had rushed, full of resolve, to help the Spanish Republic.

"Yes, and among them are our Slavic brothers," Rudolf noted. "That's great! They can speak Spanish," he added.

At that time, I did not understand precisely what he

meant; if I had known what he had in mind, my fate would have been different.

Working with Rudolf was very difficult, and sometimes, he openly expressed his dissatisfaction with my translations. I had to interpret conversations with Captain Ungria and with members of his group, in addition to translating lessons, summaries of unit reports, and sketches of affairs at the front. It was like that from early morning until late at night. Sometimes I was so tired that I just could not continue.

But after our first sortie behind the lines at Teruel, Rudolf's attitude toward me changed sharply. He no longer asked me to translate reports and sketches from newspapers, and he no longer sent people to wake me. Instead, he bought me a small alarm clock so that I would not be late for breakfast.

In two months of hard work, I did not have a single day of free time. Only after Rudolf had left for Cartagena did I meet with my girlfriends from the Institute of Foreign Languages and the Lenin School.

The next day, Rudolf returned with the depth charges, which he had received from Nicholas. With the help of the Provincial Party Committee, Salvador obtained two large cauldrons, and Rudolf began *melting* the TNT from the depth charges!

This activity was not only dangerous, it was also exhausting. In the cauldron, filled with water, they put the large depth-charge cylinders, which weighed almost half a ton. They melted the TNT in the outskirts of Valencia, far from inhabited buildings. On the first day, with the fire blazing under the cauldron, the depth charge, and the water, the stout, happy laboratory assistant, Sancho Sastre, noted matter of factly, "It's dangerous to work with dynamite, but melting TNT is perhaps even more dangerous and difficult."

For two days, they melted TNT, pouring it out into forms. On the third day, headquarters summoned Rudolf and Domingo and ordered them to the southern front in Andalusia. Everyone was pleased, especially Domingo, who had long since requested to be assigned there with his group. The winter in Andalusia is warm, and the country was well known to Domingo because he was born there. And, of course, he wanted very badly to get his daughters and his mother-in-law out of rebel-occupied Seville.

Andalusia Ahead

The meetings were short. Part of the detachment was converted to a permanent school and remained behind. Almost half of the TNT was buried in the orchard near the school.

We left after breakfast, early, but life in Valencia was already in full swing. Although it was the middle of January, the season when in Russia they say "sun is for summer, winter for frost"; it was warm and fresh flowers were for sale on the street. The young newspaper vendors were already crying out the headlines, small trams squealed, and cars full of passengers scurried about honking their horns.

All of the men and the materials were put into three old trucks and five cars.

This time I was not the only woman. Rosalina went with us. Dressed in a military uniform, she was a beautiful, black-haired, young woman, suntanned as a mulatto, who would not part with her carbine. Not only had she mastered all the partisan mines, but even before our departure, she had demonstrated her ability to cook a delicious dinner.

The girl sat in Rubio's car. With her was our demolition man, Miguel, who had arrived with Domingo's original group. He was brown haired and strong and was almost always smiling. Unlike many of his friends, he was imperturbable. He clearly had fallen in love with Rosalina, and the feeling was mutual.

Domingo said good-bye to his Rosalia. She was not crying, but only cursed her husband.

"Well, where are you going with my baby? Leave him with me in Valencia!"

But Antonio was already sitting in the car. Domingo kissed his wife and said, "Everything will be all right. He will not die with the partisans."

"Mama, don't worry!" Antonio said, "I will remind papa to take care of our little sisters and grandma."

"Remind him, little son, remind him! But for him, everything is business, even war."

Half an hour later, we had left Valencia. Juicy, ripe oranges lay like golden globes under the citrus trees. The cars of Rubio, Vicente, and Pepe pulled out ahead, but we stopped near the trees; Rubio parked the Hispano-Suiza on the side of the road and ran up to a peasant who was gathering fruit. He offered money, but the peasant was offended, saying, "Take enough for the entire car. There is enough for everyone!"

"Take oranges for the road!" shouted Rubio.

The farther we went from Valencia, the poorer the vegetation became and the smaller the orchards. Only occasionally, small flocks of sheep could be seen. Toward dinnertime, we arrived in Albacete. Before the war, the city had been famous for its knives and other metal household items. Albacete is on an important highway, and it was connected by railroad with Madrid and the Mediterranean Sea. In early 1937, the city was the main base of the international brigades.

Until the rebellion, more than forty thousand people lived in Albacete. During the war, the population of the city grew significantly; natives, refugees from regions occupied by the rebels, and antifascist volunteers from fifty-four countries filled the streets.

Rudolf went to the aviators' headquarters, and there on the street, he met an acquaintance, a well-built pilot dressed as a Spaniard, who would not release Rudolf from his embrace for a long time.

"Why have you grown such a moustache!" he reproached my chief, still slapping him on the back.

"Douglas," he said, introducing himself to me.

"Probably the same sort of Douglas as I am Louisa?"

Douglas was really Ya. V. Smushkevich. He invited us to his place for dinner. And I began to envy the aviators' interpreters.

Rudolf had brought me to the end of the world; our unit was not properly recognized by anyone; our people did not belong to any state; we were living on a meager subsistence allowance allotted by the Party organs, barely enough to provide clothing no less arms. Yet our pilots were recognized as heroes and were participating in the war on all fronts. True, they had few airplanes, but on the other hand, they had a future.

Rudolf, as if he had understood my thoughts, sent me to the detachment's billet on a contrived errand, and stayed with Smushkevich. He returned late in the evening but brought surprising news. "Reinforcements have arrived for our company. Now we will have Slavs, Poles, Yugoslavs, Bulgarians, Czechs and Slovaks. There will be Germans and Austrians, Italians, Americans, Finns, and Frenchmen. Two Yugoslavs know Spanish very well and can speak Russian. Now it will be easier for you," Rudolf said to me in a satisfied voice.

"Perhaps!" I answered. His words had hurt me. I was thinking, "So he has that kind of reinforcements. Now he doesn't need me." I was beginning to think that I was wrong not to stay in Valencia.

"What's the matter, Louisa?" Rudolf asked pleasantly.

"Why didn't you tell me about your intentions in Valencia? What use am I to you now?" I asked and turned away.

"You and I are Soviets, they sent us together, and we will work together. You will be able to help me more now. We will be in action in the forward area of the southern front for longer periods, and I don't have the strength to manage alone. You have experience and with your knowledge of the language and the people, you will be able to stand in for me in many activities; you will have to send groups across the lines independently."

I awoke at dawn. It was cold outside. Passersby were dressed in overcoats, the soldiers were in wool uniforms, and some wore a hooded blanket that served them as an overcoat.

"This is the Meseta,[1] there are 'three months of cold and nine months of hell' on it," Domingo said, dressed as he had been at Teruel, in a wool service jacket, from under the collar of which peeked a knitted wool shirt.

From Albacete we went southwest, to Jaen.

The sun rose higher and higher; it was warm in the limousine, but those who were riding in the trucks wrapped themselves in their blanket overcoats while on the road, looking like the Napoleanic soldiers I'd read about in school. I was depressed, thinking about the unexpected changes that had taken place in connection with the presence of the international brigade interpreters. The semidesert region, its stunted grass

[1] The Meseta plateau, or Central Castillian plateau, is at an elevation of six hundred to eight hundred meters and occupies more than half of the Pyrenean Peninsula.

beaten down by sheep and goats, and even the appearance of the people, who were wrapped up in blankets and tarpaulins did not cheer me up.

When we had crossed to the southern slope of the Sierra Moreno (Dark Mountains) and began to descend steeply to the right tributary of the Guadalquivir River, a green valley covered with wild vegetation suddenly opened before us. About three kilometers away, near the river, a small village could be seen.

"We are in Andalusia!" Domingo cried happily. "Look how everything has changed! So much greenery—orchards, forests, and the famous Andalusian olives."

Sure enough, we could see orderly rows of olive trees arranged on large tracts of land. The trees were covered with small, ripening olives.

As the road wound down through the mountains, Rubio was quiet, steering the car skillfully while braking. "It's dangerous!" he said finally, pointing to the ravine with his head. "One moment's carelessness and you can crash."

After half an hour, we came down to the tributary of the Guadalquivir, the Guadalimar River, a wild mountain stream. We crossed it and halted. It was almost noon. In spite of the fact that winter was in full swing, the sun warmed us as if it were summer. Even high in the mountains, no snow was visible. At the foot of the mountains, at an elevation of eight hundred meters, it was warm, and everything was green.

"We are in Andalusia," Domingo reminded us again. "Andalusia is almost a fifth of Spain, the most well-endowed part of it is the southwest."

"Unfortunately, more than half of it is now occupied by the rebels," Rudolf said, when I translated Domingo's words for him.

"That is why," Domingo answered, "we will be based and

operate behind the lines in Andalusia—and we can have the good fortune to see the wonder of Spain—Seville."

"It would be good for us to see it before summer," Rubio said, "then we will be in the *Sarten de Andalusia*[2] and will be warmed by the *Horno de Andalusia*,[3] where the summer temperature often exceeds one hundred degrees."

"But winter in Andalusia is good, especially on the shores of the Mediterranean Sea and the Atlantic Ocean. We will liquidate the rebels, we will drive out—better yet, we will *destroy* the interventionists—and then we will get a tan," said the captain.

We eventually passed through the junction at Ubeda, and twenty minutes later, we arrived at the Guadalquivir River, where guards patrolled the bridge. The river was deep and fairly wide; the swift water icy.

Along the valley, among green olive groves, orchards, and fields we came to Jaen, the main city of the province of the same name, with a population of sixty thousand.

More than forty years have passed since I left Jaen, but even now I can see the small city in my mind's eye, surrounded by orchards and olive groves, sheltered near the slopes of the mountains. The Fascists often flew from behind the mountains to bomb the peaceful inhabitants.

Having left the column at the entrance to the city, Rudolf, Domingo, and I went into Jaen to the Provincial Committee of the Spanish Communist party.

As we entered the office of the secretary, I was astonished to see there the same Filippe who had studied at the Lenin International School while I was working there as an

---

[2] The frying pan of Andalusia. This is what they call the plain south of the Guadalquivir between Seville and Cordoba.

[3] The oven of Andalusia. This is what they call the city of Ecija eighteen kilometers east of Seville.

interpreter. In the Soviet Union, I had frequently traveled with him as a part of a study group familiarizing itself with the achievements of the Soviet people.

He threw himself at me with a hug, saying, "Anna, you came to Spain. Wonderful!" I was happy to see him and forgot about my duty as interpreter and my cover as Louisa.

Fillipe was with the first secretary of the Provincial Committee, Cristobal Valenzuela. With Fillipe's help, we quickly settled all questions connected with our arrival in Jaen. It turned out that the comrades in Jaen had already prepared everything for our arrival—billets, food, and even reinforcements. They housed us in two buildings almost in the center of the city. Domingo, Rudolf, Vincente, Rosalina and I, Pepe, and Sastre were settled on the second floor of a small house directly across from a convent. Here we also organized a workshop for making mines, and downstairs, we built a storage area for the explosives. Blasting caps and string fuses were kept under Rudolf's bed and dynamite under mine. Another large building, also close to the convent, was set aside for our school.

"Such a neighborhood doesn't bother you?" Valenzuela said to me.

"The Fascists won't bomb their own; we're safe near the convent."

"That's what we thought, too, but it didn't work out that way."

The next day, the Jaen Provincial Committee of the Spanish Communist party arranged a supper. Members of the Party Committee, local party workers, and Communists who worked in the administration and in the army were in attendance. The adviser to the commander of the southern front, Col. V. I. Kolman (a.k.a. Wilhelm Ivanovich

Kolman), a handsome Latvian, about thirty-five, with a shaved head, was there. *Two* interpreters, a radio man, and a cipher clerk came with him.

When Kolman spoke with a Spaniard, the person he spoke to had to wait, listening, while the first interpreter repeated what was said in French, and then the second repeated it in Spanish. Listening to the answer, Kolman waited, while the Spanish-to-French interpreter repeated what was said in French, then the French-to-Russian interpreter translated everything into Russian. Sometimes the interpreters each made small errors, which resulted in substantial distortions.

At the meeting, we learned that all the leading personnel of the provincial committee had gone to the front in the first days of the rebellion, leaving behind only one member, the invalid Pedro Martines. Then the local anarchists really let themselves go. Instead of mobilizing forces for battle against the Fascists, they busied themselves with the organization of a commune and unauthorized expropriations.

Martines could not do anything to stop the anarchists. Only when the rest of the Party committee returned to Jaen were the bends and twists introduced by the anarchists eliminated and, without prior arrangement, land reform was carried out in the interest of the rural poor. The peasants selflessly harvested the olives in the front-line area and in no-man's-land, the zone between the Republican and rebel soldiers.

"Our province," Valenzuela said, "along with the province of Cordoba produces the greatest quantity of olives and olive oil. Beautiful, rich Andalusia. But her people are not lucky. In the year 711 the invasion of the Arabs began through it, and in 1936 the rebels began the movement of their troops from Spanish Morocco through Andalusia. The Italians landed in her ports, and with their help, the insurgents occupied more than half the province. The Italians are breaking through to Almaden where there are rich deposits of mercury and other minerals."

"But one must not forget the contribution of Andalusia to the revolutionary struggle," the other secretary, Aroca, broke in. "In our century, almost every year there has been a peasant uprising in Andalusia. In March of 1932, at the Fourth Congress of the Spanish Communist party in Seville, the sectarians were crushed, and Jose Diaz, a worker of Seville, was chosen as the general secretary of the new Central Committee."

"One cannot help but be proud of the fact that the Andalusians of the 5th Regiment showed fantastic fortitude in Madrid," Valenzuela added. Then he proposed a toast, "For the courageous Andalusian soldiers, for the swift defeat of the rebels and interventionists."

After supper, there were a few toasts, and a great deal was said about Andalusia, its wealth, its people, and about peasants who escaped from the rebels and who returned as members of the near-legendary 5th Regiment, and about the workers of the mines and metal workers who produced weapons for the Republican Army. And, of course, conversation turned to the damage caused by the anarchists.

"When the central authority was weak, the anarchists were like fish in water," said Valenzuela. "Even though they fought bravely in the first days of the rebellion in Catalonia, their leaders had no use for discipline and order, declaring them an encroachment on individual freedom. They considered the war a secondary matter, that the main business was the establishment of 'free communism.' Not wanting to allow the creation of a regular army, they got to the point that in August 1936, they called for mobilized Catalonians to desert their barracks. At the same time, at their meeting in the Barcelona theater Olympia, they passed a resolution of agreement to join the ranks of the people's militia for immediate attack on Saragossa, but emphasized their refusal to go into the regular army. You were at Teruel," Valenzuela continued, turning to us, "and you saw how the anarchists conduct themselves. The Party's calls for the formation of a regular army with strict discipline, the anarchists declared to be proof of the fact that 'the Communists have sold out to the bourgeoisie.' They create secret stores of weapons, they arm their own inactive columns. Finally, their demagoguery, the fight against discipline in production, the violent reprisals against their political opponents, especially against the clergy—including the burning of churches—play right into the hands of Fascist propaganda. Anarchist unions in Catalonia, the National Confederation of Labor (SNT), unite four-fifths of the organized working class and possess more power than the government. The headquarters of the Federation of Anarchists of Iberia (FAI) is located in Barcelona. These are no longer workers—they are politicians."

Valenzuela paused while I translated. After taking a sip of water, he continued.

"SNT and FAI are seriously preparing for armed struggle against Communists and socialists. They are forcibly carrying out the collectivization of agriculture. They are seizing enterprises and hoisting the red-and-black flag over them. The enterprises they have seized do not work on defense. They are, in fact, lost to the Republic."

"The anarchists were trying to stir up trouble here, too," Aroca broke in, "but we have kept them quiet so far."

The meeting with Valenzuela automatically brought to me the memory of my work at the Comintern's Lenin International School, where the Cultural Committee of the

Bolshevik party sent me in 1935 after I graduated from the Leningrad Oriental Institute. I worked as an interpreter in sector L, where Spaniards, Portuguese, and Latin Americans were studying. The work was very difficult. In the Institute, the instructors spoke with us very slowly, but the Spanish, especially the Basques, spoke so fast, like bursts from a machine gun, and they swallowed the ends of their phrases. Fortunately, the Latin Americans spoke more slowly than the Spaniards.

At the Lenin International School we had no cars or buses of our own, so we traveled on public transportation. During the winter, it was especially difficult to take groups on excursions to the theater or the movies. The students were dressed in quilted, black winter coats and wore hats with ear flaps, so they were warm enough. But in their home countries, they were used to going out in light clothing; they became clumsy as bear cubs in their heavy winter clothes. They did not know Russian. While they were getting on the trolley, I would have to stand on the front platform and watch to be sure they all got on. As the last one entered, I would say to the driver, "You can go now."

Sometimes, we had no rest even at night. Quite often we had to stay up at night to give medical assistance to students who suddenly became ill. It was a good thing that the clinic was close to our dormitory.

All meetings and lectures on general topics were held at the Volkhonka. Each interpreter sat her or his wards in one place so it would be convenient to translate for them. The hall was large, there were many people, and each interpreter spoke loudly, but it worked out. From the outside, it must have sounded like being in a noisy oriental bazaar. Some translated into English or German, others into Spanish, and Nora Chegodayeva into other Romance languages.

G. Dmitrov, Kolarov, Wilhelm Pieck, Palmiro Togliatti,

Nadezhda Konstantinovna Krupskaya, and Mariya Ilinichna Ulyanova, and other Soviet and foreign comrades often delivered speeches before the students. One had to have a tin throat and strong lungs, to speak this way for a whole hour so that the others would not drown you out.

The Soviets treated our foreign guests with respect. Once when we were in Dnepropetrovsk, a few of us interpreters had walked through a barrier into a park and were sitting on a bench. A policeman noticed and angrily whistled and walked toward us. We were speaking in Spanish. The policeman, having heard our conversation, said that crossing the barrier was forbidden, then he demonstrated this with gestures and saluted, then threw away the tickets that would otherwise have meant a fine for us, and left, thinking that we were foreigners. This was not uncommon. During excursions outside the city, when we had to stop at hotels, there were occasions when the locals, thinking we were foreigners, were surprised that we spoke Russian so well.

Yet another former student of the Lenin International School was present at that supper—Martinez. He kidded me, "It was not without reason that they took you for a Spanish woman in Dnepropetrovsk. You really speak Spanish so well that you could pass yourself off as a woman from Valencia." After supper we talked a lot about the Soviet Union, and I noticed that the Spanish comrades treated the Soviet adviser for the Southern Front, Wilhelm Ivanovich Kolman, warmly and with consideration.

In Jaen, Rudolf began everything again from the beginning. From early morning until late at night, he worked training new reinforcements, supervising the production of mines and grenades. True, he now had assistants—those students from the first group who had passed a substantial course of study. Some of them had been behind enemy lines at Teruel. I worked on logistics and kept up communication with the Provincial Party Committee. Getting enough supplies was very difficult since we had more than a hundred men, but our allowance was nowhere near enough. We were living thanks to the support of the Jaen Party Committee.

Partisans in Action

After about ten days, Rudolf left with one group for action behind enemy lines near Granada, and Domingo Ungria went with another group to Villa Nueva de Cordoba.

Against my wishes, Rudolf left me in Jaen, where about forty men were in training. Ivan Grande went with Rudolf, but Ivan Kharish remained in Jaen.

One day, while Domingo and Rudolf's groups were studying the situation in the enemy rear and planning sabotage, I had reported the first information about conditions there that we had received from Domingo, and I was delayed at Colonel Kolman's place.

He had a really small staff, the two interpreters and a radio operator named Nikolai Ivanovich Mironov, a happy man who always had a camera and was ready to sing at any moment. Working with Nikolai Ivanovich as a team was the cipher clerk, Ivan Alekseevich Garbar, a tall, reserved man. Apparently, he was as they say about his specialty, "everything's always in secret."

After supper, we were sitting near the fountain in a little courtyard enclosed by a high wall. There were flowers and a pool with fish.

Nikolai found a portable gramophone, and we listened to music, Spanish and Soviet, and I was quickly carried away to Moscow, to my home.

I wanted to sit and rest with Kolman's staff, but Pepe hurried up and, after greeting me, said, "Louisa! Sastre and Kharish are getting ready for a night exercise. They need mines and some kind of explosives, but you have the key!"

I began to take my leave, but Kolman decided to accompany me. After we sorted out everything needed for the exercise, we returned to his quarters, where "the staff" had already dispersed. Just the two of us were left, and we continued our interrupted conversation.

We talked about work.

"It's very hard for me with my interpreters," Kolman said, "conversing through two 'transformers.' " Just the appearance of my "guard" irritates the front commander, and when I begin discussions, he is clearly nervous, tapping the table with his fingers, while they translate from Russian to French and from French to Spanish."

Kolman paused, then continued, "Louisa! I have to talk with the Spanish commanders, I need to speak persuasively and concisely. I need a real interpreter. Come to work for me! What are you doing with Rudolf? He has two interpreters who can replace you. Working for me will be far better. You will feel fine in our little collective and won't have to worry about anything. Everything will be taken care of."

"And what will Rudolf think?"

"It only needs your agreement, and I will take care of the rest. War is war. They will order him to do it, and that will be that."

I was ready to agree, but our conversation was interrupted by a telephone call. Rudolf had found me, even there.

He said hello and, after inquiring about my health, said, "Everything is arranged with the local directors. Our artists can perform with the amateurs. Prepare seven guitarists at once," meaning: Everything is arranged with the command of the military sector. Our sabotage group can take action behind enemy lines with volunteers from elements located at the front. Prepare a sabotage group made up of seven men.

I reported the mission order to Kolman.

"All this can be done without you. Come to me right away, and you won't be sorry."

"I'll think about it," I said, bidding him good-bye.

"Don't wait too long. You've got to work with dynamite, and that stuff is always dangerous. Hurry up or Rudolf will hijack you off into the country somewhere," Kolman said as we parted.

His proposition made me really think. In reality, I was no longer working as an interpreter but had turned into Rudolf's assistant. In his absence, everyone came to me to solve problems. Living up to the responsibility was very difficult, but I felt that I was doing something useful. I helped to train men for operations and learned a great deal myself. But Kolman's proposal enticed me, and not because "Rudolf would hijack me into the country." I had grown up and worked in the country. In the country, the air is better, and it is more peaceful, but Kolman badly needed to replace his two "transformers," with one interpreter.

In the morning, I met Ivan Kharish. He was in a good mood.

"I completed my assignment ahead of schedule. I made all three types of mines," he said.

"Good," I answered. But apparently I answered in such a way that Kharish understood that something was wrong. "Is something bothering you, Louisa?"

I looked at Kharish, admiring his tirelessness, his discretion, his great life experience, and I wanted to share my intentions with him.

"Listen, Kharish, they have offered me a new job—interpreter for Comrade Kolman, what do you think about this?"

Kharish gave me a perplexed look, and smiled. "What about Rudolf?"

"He no longer needs me as an interpreter!"

"But he needs not only interpreters. He also needs assistants."

"He has already found interpreters for himself, and he has assistants."

"No! Rudolf won't let you go. Remember how Ivan Krbovanets wanted to leave him. He followed Ivan to the station and didn't let him go. And he will not part with you."

"The higher-ups will order him to do it. He is a military man. You will get along without me."

"If the new appointment is up to you, then I do not advise you to leave. You'll go back home, but what will you tell stories about? What will you reminisce about? *We* are Republican saboteurs." Kharish paused briefly and looking straight at me continued, "I don't advise it, Louisa. We are used to each other."

As always, Esperanza came in unexpectedly. She worked with problems of supply and finances and performed the duties of secretary.

"Louisa! The Finns are asking for vodka again," she blurted out.

"No vodka! They came to fight, not to swill vodka."

Ivan Kharish said angrily, "If they need to drink, then they should go to the anarchists. They are still in port; they just arrived in Spain, and they want to drink their fill of cognac? Let them go over to the anarchists."

"No vodka of any kind!" I asserted and went to talk to the Finns. Seeing me, they immediately grew quiet. One of them understood English. We talked and agreed that we would drink only after a successful sabotage mission.

Just then I was occupied with preparations for Rudolf's

group of saboteurs. Having sent the "guitarists," I thought about whether I should agree to go over to Kolman or stay with the saboteurs.

Rudolf and the group were delayed in returning from Granada. Rosalina grew impatient as she waited for Miguel. She had even prepared a gift for him.

When Rudolf finally walked in, unexpectedly, I called out "Rosalina! Our boys have arrived!"

"Wait a minute, Louisa, wait!" Rudolf tried to warn me, but was too late.

Beaming, Rosalina ran into the room.

"Salud, camarades! Salud!" she called, but the ones who had arrived did not reply. Their faces betrayed confusion and grief. Miguel was not among them.

"Where is Miguel?" the girl cried.

Juan Grande took off his beret and said, "Miguel died in battle."

Everyone took off their hats. Rosalina threw herself into her room, sobbing.

Everyone tried to comfort her, but she did not calm down for a long time.

When Rosalina finally came to herself a little bit, I said to Rudolf, "Kolman requested that you go to him upon your arrival," and I remained with Rosalina.

Rudolf was out of sorts when he returned from Kolman. And in the morning, we left with the group for Villa Nueva de Cordoba.

Domingo had prepared everything for the establishment of a support base and the organization of still another branch of our school.

"I am forming a mounted sabotage platoon," he said to

Rudolf, not without pride, showing us the first eight horses, which he had obtained with the help of the Jaen Party Committee. The first cavalryman that I saw was Domingo's son, the sharp, eight-year-old Antonio. Very pleased with himself, he pranced about on a beautiful, even-tempered horse.

More than forty years have passed. Only brief notes have been preserved, and I have had to reconstruct much from memory, but there is little that is only in one's own memory. Fortunately, there are still people living who took part in these events, and they have helped me in many ways.

Yellowing newspapers of those times are preserved in libraries. The sketches of Soviet news correspondents, brief communiqués allow us to be more precise. February 8, 1937, the fall of Malaga. The offensive of the rebels and interventionists along the coast in the east was choked off west of Almeria; the barbarous shelling of this peaceful city by a German battleship; the government of the Spanish Republic declared the mobilization of men; February 25, the Fascists savagely bombed the small city of Andujar. The descriptions of the rout of Fascists and interventionists at Guadalajara and the communiqués about the repulse of the enemy attack at Pozoblanco are especially impressive. There are even reports about sabotage, about one of our units blowing up a train near Montoro.

Party political work had great importance in the difficult conditions of our activities. They often reminded us of it in the Central Committee of the Spanish Communist party, giving practical advice and rendering overall assistance. The political activity of the Communists, and of all the partisans of the unit under command of Captain Ungria, was directed toward strengthening the partisans' faith in the achievement of victory, faith in the power of their own weapons, especially mines, and the perfection of their military skills. Party political work was even conducted behind enemy lines.

Party political work was continuous and systematic. The chief methods of political agitation and propaganda were explanation and persuasion. During the course of study, and when resting, we conducted political lessons, discussions, and newspaper readings. Leaflets with colored drawings, which were supplied to us by the Central and Jaen Party Provincial Committees, were distributed among the population and enemy troops by partisan intelligence agents.

Clear drawings with expressive inscriptions were used to persuade the people of the necessity of the fight against fascism, to expose enemy propaganda, and to inform them about the successes of the Republican Army and about international solidarity with Republican Spain.

The leaflets were distributed with the assistance of intelligence agents, who acted deep behind enemy lines, and directly by partisans in the course of operations. When this was done, close attention had to be paid to make it safe for those who did it and so it did not enable the enemy to detect partisan bases.

Political security of military action also took into account the consequences to the local population of our military activities. Berzin warned us to carefully choose our objectives, and Rudolf and Domingo understood the value of not unduly bringing harm to the local inhabitants. They chose objectives the destruction of which would not touch the interests of the broad mass of the population and which would make the population happy for the success of the partisans, such as wrecking a troop train, or blowing up vehicles with rebels, interventionists, or military supplies.

In our free time, during lessons, and at our bases behind

enemy lines, the partisans begged Rudolf to tell them about the activities of Soviet partisans, so I had to translate his tales of the brave men who operated behind the lines of Denikin, Kolchak, and Wrangel. Rudolf could tell them a lot about such activities because he had worked with partisans at the end of the 1920s and in the first half of the 1930s.

Partisan Intelligence

While still preparing for departure to the southern front, Rudolf had endeavored to train intelligence agents along with the demolitions men. The experience of our group at Teruel demonstrated the necessity of having your own reconnaissance rather than counting on the reconnaissance of troops in action on the front. However, it proved to be more difficult to train intelligence agents than demolitions men. An illiterate peasant could easily master the subtleties of sabotage techniques and tactics, but he could not write what he knew about the enemy.

On the other hand, it was easier to translate the lessons for intelligence work than for demolitions. At the Lenin School I had already worked on problems of secret organization, cryptography, and the organization of communications for illegal activities, all of which proved useful. For intelligence work, the Valencia Committee of the Communist party specially selected a group of volunteers who best fit our requirements. The intelligence recruits were then trained with the demolitions men. The latter were trained in the manufacture and setting of mines, and the former carried out intelligence assignments.

Once, Domingo Ungria returned from the Central Committee of the Communist party with a young captain, who appeared to be only twenty years old; sometime later, we found out that he was already thirty. He was smart looking, clean shaven, and wore a new uniform. He was battalion commander Francisco Castillo.

In the course of the conversation it became clear that Castillo's battalion numbered almost twelve hundred men, and that he was establishing a large network of partisans and spies, that would work in rebel garrisons and other important objectives. Captain Castillo was a lawyer from an ancient aristocratic lineage. His full name was Francisco del Castillo Sain de Tejado. But he was a Communist because before the rebellion, reactionaries had killed his brother, lieutenant of the Assault Guard, Jose Castillo, just because of his antifascist convictions. So Francisco, then working in a notary's office, drew closer to the Communists, carried out assignments for them, and supported contacts with progressive circles of the intelligentsia. At that time he was considered a "sympathizer." When the rebellion broke out, Francisco Castillo did not hesitate; in the first days of the war, he took up arms and joined the Communist party at the front.

"I have many agents, but no experienced men for analyzing intelligence data, and communication is also bad. Sometimes information about the enemy is received so late that it only leads us astray. In general, we need help in training agents, organizing communication, and improving the quality of information."

With the arrival of Francisco Castillo, Rudolfo and Domingo Ungria devoted even more attention to the creation of our own intelligence service.

After arriving in Jaen and establishing contact with Francisco Castillo, Rudolfo and Captain Ungria began to organize an intelligence service.

There was an additional complication—Colonel Kolman, adviser for general military matters, did not have the interpreters, so I had to translate our intelligence reports into Russian for him.

The press of intelligence work so overwhelmed me that I had to go out to meetings, gather and process materials, and later organize assignments for the agents.

The deputy commander for intelligence and the chief of the intelligence service was Augustin Fabregas, a most experienced volunteer of the underground, an excellent organizer, and a wonderful comrade. He was almost sixty and often ill. I not only had to help him but also to fill in for him. "Louisa!" he would say sadly, when it was necessary to compose a report or dispatch. "You know what interests Rudolfo and Kolman, look into it and compose the dispatches."

The intelligence service covered a huge territory in the area of the southern front. You might say that the partisan intelligence network created by Francisco Castillo with the help of Rudolfo and Domingo Ungria, had an all-encompassing character; to a depth of one hundred kilometers into the enemy rear, there was nowhere our partisan agents did not penetrate, right up to the important military air fields. Besides obtaining valuable information, many of our agents also carried out sabotage with the help of homemade, delayed-action mines. Sabotage activity grew after we began to use small magnetic delayed-action mines. Placed directly on a train or automobile, the mines exploded after the vehicle had moved far away, or after the agent had retreated to a safe place.

My transfer to work with the intelligence service became possible because Rudolf succeeded in acquiring interpreters from among the members of the international brigades, and also because Rudolf worked so well with his driver that the driver began to understand him, so to speak, with just hints.

I tried to help Rudolfo learn the language, but he was just

not up to grammar. He expressed himself in a kind of Spanish with the drivers, but he just did not have the necessary vocabulary. Not knowing grammar, he used all verbs in the infinitive. He could not have conversations with the Republican command without me, especially during the organization of group movements in new sectors in the enemy rear.

The Czech, Jan Tikhii, and the Yugoslav, Juan Pequeño, as the Spaniards called Ivan Kharish, were the interpreters for demolition training and on independent sabotage operations behind enemy lines.

Ivan Kharish was especially attached to Rudolf, and I remember that when Rudolf gave a general lesson, Ivan always tried to learn more about the achievements of Soviet partisans during the civil war years. His curiosity was not without purpose; all of the information proved useful to him in Yugoslavia.

However Rudolf understood that trips to front headquarters and administration were burdensome for Ivan Kharish, so he enlisted Juan Pequeño only for translating on practical exercises and behind rebel lines.

The increasing scope of sabotage and intelligence activity required a corresponding increase in supplies. In spite of the assistance and cooperation of the Jaen Provincial Committee of the Communist party, our illegal and growing elements felt the lack of military supplies, explosives, gasoline, and other materials necessary for training and missions behind enemy lines.

More than once, I had to go with Domingo Ungria to the headquarters of the southern front, and there, together with our officers "knock out" all the necessary supplies. When Domingo asked me the first time I was surprised.

"You are a captain of the Spanish Republican Army," I said, "you don't need an interpreter."

The captain smiled slyly and answered, "I am a Spaniard, I have to speak with the top brass at headquarters. They can say to me 'You have no orders! You are not attached to us for supplies.' And that is that."

"But I don't have any kind of all-powerful documents," I answered.

"Louisa! For you they are not necessary. You are a Soviet woman, and that's all it takes."

So we went. The first time I went to headquarters I was worried, but they gave us such a warm reception that at first I even forgot why we had come. We were given orange juice and coffee and asked about the Soviet Union. The Spanish officers were surprised to learn that I had left my young daughter in Moscow and had voluntarily come to Spain.

While we were speaking, Domingo managed to get orders for supplies and a packet of coupons for gasoline.

"Spanish Republican officers just couldn't refuse a Soviet woman!" he said happily when we were back in our car.

After that, I often went with him and with other officers of the unit, and the staff always received us warmly. While I told stories about life in our far north, about bears and reindeer, the representative of the partisans invariably managed to get all the necessary orders.

News from Seville

No matter how much Domingo was occupied with the affairs of his unit, he never forgot about his stepdaughters or his mother-in-law who remained in rebel-occupied Seville.

One day, after a conversation about an upcoming mission behind rebel lines, Rubio said, "Comrade Captain! Can't we carry out a deep intelligence raid in Seville and, at the same time, find out about your family?"

Domingo stood up, paced around the room, then looked at Rubio. "No, at present it is impossible! We don't have enough experience to conduct a deep sortie in the enemy rear. And forget that I have relatives of any kind behind enemy lines. Don't remind me about this anymore."

"I know that no one must know, and I haven't spoken to anyone about it," Rubio said. Then, after saying good-bye, he left on assignment.

"Louisa," the captain said to me, "Seville is two hundred kilometers from the front line as the crow flies. I want very much to get the girls out, but I am afraid to bring harm to them. I am afraid that the rebels will intercept a messenger or, still worse, capture the girls on the way to the front. You know how badly I want to see them. But I have to be careful not to foul it up."

Domingo always questioned deserters from Seville about

what was happening there, but he never asked directly about his daughters and mother-in-law.

"How could we organize an intelligence network in Seville?" he asked Rudolf a little later.

"We need to find a deserter from Seville or one of the surrounding villages and check it out first, and then we might risk it," Rudolf answered.

Time passed. There were few deserters from the area of Seville, and we did not quite have the information we needed. But Domingo continued to accumulate data. The separation from his daughters bothered him very much; he was a good father to them. He guarded a family snapshot like a sacred object. "Look, Louisa," he said, showing it to me. "Here is our older daughter Eliza, she is already sixteen. And here the younger, Maria. And this is my mother-in-law with Antonio on her knee. And this is me and Rosalia. Such good daughters!"

The daughters really were beautiful.

"Thinking about how to get them out of Seville gives me no peace!" Domingo said while looking at the photograph.

Watching how Domingo got along with Antonio and how he cared for Rosalia's daughters, it was difficult to believe that none of them were his own children.

Before the election victory of the Popular Front in February 1936, Domingo had been in France as a political émigré. More than once, he had to emigrate to a foreign country to save himself from reactionaries. When he returned to his homeland, fate led him to the widow Rosalia.

She had known Domingo when he was still working illegally because he had hidden from the police with her family. Her children knew their affectionate uncle very well, and they were happy when he became their father.

One day, Captain Ungria arrived in Villa Nueva de Cordoba from Adamuz. Having noticed that the captain's car had arrived, Antonio ran out to meet him. Domingo grabbed the boy's hand, gave him a long kiss, squeezed him tightly, and caressed him more than usual.

Noticing me, the detachment commander kissed Antonio once more then let him go. When he was sure no one was near he said to me, "Today I learned that the Fascists are increasing their terror in Seville, they are taking hostages. This can't happen to my daughters.

"What is to be done? How can we save Eliza and Maria, if it's not already too late? Is it possible to risk sending someone there?" he asked me.

What could I advise in this difficult matter; it was not for me to decide such questions. "Ask the comrades for advice," I said.

"I'm afraid to ask anyone. I'm afraid that their help could ruin it for me. Any operational indiscretion could attract attention to the girls. In Seville, no one knows that the family of the widow Rosalia has become my family. Even in the detachment, only a few know—and only those who know how to keep their mouths shut."

"Then consult with Valenzuela. He is an experienced party worker. Maybe he will help with advice. And action," I suggested.

"Well, in the meantime, let's have supper. I'll sleep on it. Things'll be clearer in the morning."

At dinner, the captain drank more wine than usual and ate almost nothing.

"I have decided to send Ustaros's group to Seville," he finally said. "I will give them money. Perhaps they will be able to give it to the girls or even to get them out."

I knew the small-statured Luis Ustaros. He had participated in the operations at Teruel and was distinguished by his calmness, discipline, and courage. He had already made a couple of successful independent forays behind rebel lines on the southern front. In my opinion, he was more suited for this difficult operation than the very brave but excessively hot-tempered Rubio.

Domingo described the operation to Rudolf, and he did not raise any objections. No one in the detachment except me and Rudolf knew about the special assignment of Luis Ustaros's group, and only a few knew that they went to Seville.

Even Antonio, who on order of his mother, reminded his *papite* about his sisters, did not suspect about the mission.

Perez Salas

"That's enough delaying. Everything is ready. Let's go to Front Commander Perez Salas." I translated Rudolf's words for Domingo.

"Tomorrow we will go," Domingo answered with displeasure, not liking those meetings. "It's easier to go behind enemy lines than to go to him."

"Again you say tomorrow! No, we won't put it off. The groups are ready, but without the agreement of the front commander, we can't act," Rudolf argued.

And he succeeded in convincing the captain to go together to the front headquarters.

It turned out that the commander was not at his headquarters, but all of the problems were solved without him.

Domingo's negotiations with Col. Perez Salas were necessary for the deployment of his groups behind rebel lines in the area of the southern front. They took place after the first mission of our special group behind rebel lines near Granada and Cordoba.

Perez Salas's headquarters was in the small town of Andujar. We had passed by it several times. We had even been in it, but Domingo had always avoided the commander, so one day, Rudolf decided to meet the front commander without the captain. The duty officer announced our arrival, and we were quickly shown to a spacious office. From behind a large, old desk with fantastic carving, Perez Salas stood up. Wearing large thick-lensed, horn-rimmed glasses, the colonel was no longer young; he was tall, with graying hair and a sullen face.

He was not always well intentioned toward the advisers, but he was civil and polite. He asked us to sit down and offered coffee.

Rudolf laid out the plan of action of Capt. Domingo Ungria's detachment behind enemy lines: "A well-trained group, made up of five or six men, can go, set mines and escape without losses, after derailing a troop train, or destroying an infantry battalion, or a few dozen tanks."

I hardly had time to translate the words when the colonel interrupted and asked, "You mean the saboteurs set the mines and leave? Who will answer if a passenger train with civilians is blown up by these mines and not a troop train?"

"But in wartime, and especially on roads in the area of the front, civilians don't ride the trains," Rudolf replied.

Perez Salas frowned and was noticeably nervous. Before answering, the front commander let out a smoke ring and put down his cigarette. "We have a special kind of war. The population density of our small country is significant. Passenger trains do run on the railroads in the area of the front. They carry women and children whom we cannot kill."

"But we have the possibility of destroying only military trains . . ." Rudolf began. Just then the telephone rang, the commander excused himself and picked up the receiver. He listened, from time to time frowned, ordered something, took notes in a field notebook.

Before meeting Perez Salas, I had heard much about him.

They said he was stern, unsociable, and stubborn, but he knew his business, was decisive, and had great strength of will. They also talked about his unreliability and even his connections with the rebels. But there were also those who spoke positively about the strict but fair colonel, who had

not gone over to the Fascist rebels in spite of all entice-
ments.

So, remembering what I had heard about the commander,
I closely observed his discussion with one of his subordi-
nates on the telephone.

He impatiently listened to answers, spoke shortly, gave
orders clearly and, most important, took hard what they
were reporting to him.

No, I thought, even though the colonel may be sullen and
stern, he is caring and not at all indifferent to events. He is
probably an honest Republican officer!

It was evident that the commander was tired from the
great strain. Having finished the conversation, he slowly
hung up the telephone and apologized for the interruption.

All the same, it then seemed to me that Perez Salas was
not like a Spaniard; he was too sullen and strict. Spaniards
with whom I had occasion to meet were generally cordial,
happy; some were hot tempered. He was not like them.

The front commander called the duty officer and gave
him some kind of order.

As if he had forgotten about the trains, Perez Salas began
to talk about other things. "We have many advisers, volunteers come to us, but we have few tanks, airplanes, cannons,
and shells."

Rudolf tried to tell him about the difficulty of delivering
arms from the Soviet Union, but the colonel smoked silently
and occasionally an ironic smile floated across his face.
When I had finished the translation he said, "Yes, Russia is a
large and mysterious country. Russians have very great and
recent experience with civil war."

Then, having put down his unfinished cigarette, and
without giving me enough time to translate, the commander,
smiling kindly, asked, "Excuse me, *Señora,* are you also
Russian?"

"Yes, I'm Russian—not only Russian but Soviet," I answered with pride.

The commander was even more surprised to learn that I was a volunteer, that I had left an eight-year-old daughter in Moscow, and that I was not the wife but the interpreter of Rudolf Wolf.

"*Señora,* if I am not mistaken, you were born, grew up, and studied in Moscow or Leningrad?"

"In fact, I did study in Leningrad, and before my departure for Spain, I worked in Moscow, but I was born and raised in the village of Dorogorskoe, in the Mezenskii region, Archangelsk Province, a hundred kilometers from the Arctic Circle."

"That's very interesting! You mean you lived on the tundra, and in such a beautiful city as Leningrad, and in the Big Village, as some of you call Moscow?"

"No, *señor* Colonel, I didn't live on the tundra. The tundra is still farther north. In Mezenskii region, we are famous in all the province for our trees."

Rudolf silently drank his coffee, clearly bored; he did not understand our conversation.

Finally, noticing that the commander was very amiably and animatedly talking with me, Rudolf took advantage of a pause caused by a telephone call and he said to me, "Tell the colonel about our missions at Teruel."

I began my story with the first time we went into action against enemy communications. Contrary to my expectations, Perez Salas put aside his cigar, and listened to me attentively without interrupting.

"Yes, only Russian women are capable of this! The Russians have many partisan traditions. Your partisans operated on foreign soil even in an earlier time," Perez Salas said very amiably. And for the first time, a true, good-natured Spanish smile flickered on his face. But my reminiscences of the battle did not change the colonel's opinion about the destruction of trains, on which Rudolf had counted. The commander did not want to talk about that any more just then. "We will talk about trains again, *señorita.*" Perez Salas stood up, signaling that our lengthy interview had ended.

"I will be happy to see you, *señorita,* I am very interested in your country, and your people, but I hope that we will find something to talk about besides trains," Perez Salas said in parting.

Capt. Domingo Ungria, hearing my story about the discussion with the front commander first frowned angrily and then smiled maliciously. "Okay, we will see!" he said. "It is not in our interest to blow up passenger trains, but they won't condemn us for a troop train, and to make sure they don't get rid of us, we'll follow the commander's instructions."

Demolition Men Can Make More Than One Mistake

Along with blowing up and in other ways disabling automobiles and wrecking troop trains, the groups of our special detachment also tried to blow up tunnels.

Soon after our meeting with Perez Salas, Domingo came into Jaen very upset. He began to tell Rudolf about a big problem that had occurred.

"Perez Salas ordered me to destroy the tunnel in the Penarroya–Cordoba sector, he ordered the chief of staff to place sappers and half a ton of dynamite at my disposal. I sent Marquez with the sappers. The tunnel is large, but security there is weak, only two sentries on patrol, plus about five more in the guardhouse. They took out the guards and placed all five hundred kilograms of dynamite near the entrance to the tunnel. There was a strong explosion. In the morning, they retreated to the mountains then sat in the forest on the slope and observed what was happening on the railroad."

Domingo spoke hotly and quickly and Rudolf understood none of his Spanish.

"Wait a minute," I said to the captain and began to translate.

"You mean they rest after their good works," Rudolf noted, but I had not begun to translate this when Domingo continued.

"Before dinner there was not a single train, then just as the sun was going to set, a troop train approached from Cordoba. Well, they thought, it will smash some romantics, but the train just disappeared into the tunnel. After approximately an hour, another one was coming, but this time toward Cordoba, which means that it had to have passed through the tunnel. I was furious with Marquez. How could it be that half a ton of dynamite exploded without effect?"

Domingo continued to speak quickly and emotionally, and I hardly had time to translate. It turned out that the front commander had already summoned him, chewed him out for not getting the job done, given him another whole ton of dynamite, and ordered him to blow up another tunnel, and by doing this to stop traffic for a week.

"And you think that this can be achieved by exploding a ton of dynamite in a small tunnel?" asked Rudolf.

"Yes! The large tunnel is now heavily guarded, which they hadn't been doing before we showed up, but they are guarding the small one lightly. We will take out the guards, dig a hole from the top over the entrance, place the charge, explode it and block the tunnel. We will use up even less than a ton," Domingo declared confidently.

Rudolf disagreed with him, arguing that digging the hole would not be as easy as the captain imagined, and in addition to that he might not succeed in taking out the guards without noise. Rudolf made some calculations on paper and convinced Domingo that even under favorable conditions, it was impossible to delay train traffic even for three or four days, let alone a week, with a ton of dynamite blown over the entrance of the tunnel.

"But what if we arrange a train wreck and fire well *inside* the large tunnel?" Rudolf asked when Domingo had calmed down a bit.

"How can we do that," the captain asked, "when it is

guarded by almost an entire battalion? The intelligence agents saw the fortifications they are building in front of it. In all, they're about one and a half kilometers long. No, it is impossible!" After waving his hand, Domingo shook his head no, and then began to show on the map where the security agents said the guard was located.

"It's about half a kilometer from the entrance. We can blow up the train in the tunnel with the aid of a mine attached to the locomotive."

Rudolf explained how they were placed. At first Domingo was skeptical. Then they summoned Sanchez and told him about it.

"Let's give it a try," he said after he understood what was to be done.

We reported our idea to the first secretary of the Provincial Party Committee, Valenzuela. He helped find everything we needed, and by morning of the following day, two mines had been prepared and tested, again with the assistance of the Provincial Party Committee. A trial run was performed at the entrance to Jaen station. We had one of our partisans operate the locomotive so no one took notice of the unusual activity.

In the evening of the same day, a group of demolitions men, headed by Domingo, went out on the operation, taking with them the mines, a few dozen kilograms of dynamite and half a hundred home-made delayed-action incendiary devices.

After two days, Domingo returned satisfied and happy.

"Very good! Outstanding! We went up to the railroad more than a kilometer south of the tunnel. Trains were infrequent, and we decided to blow a troop train or a freight. We had good luck. A heavy train with double rods came. We set the mines and watched, being careful not to be seen by the patrol. We were prepared to take it out. We did not see the locomotive pick up the mines, but we managed to pelt the train with incendiaries. Many of them didn't stay on the flatcars but fell on the road. But they were not wasted because the ones that burned attracted the attention of the tunnel guards." The captain became quiet so that I could translate and then blurted out, "A muffled explosion could be heard from the tunnel."

"You need to report to the commander at once," Rudolf said.

"I already did. He listened attentively. He praised us. He said, 'Let's see how long traffic will be held up,' and he gave us an allotment of gasoline coupons!"

As it later turned out, the lead locomotive of an ammunition train had picked up the mine and went into the tunnel with it. Just as the demolitions men had calculated, the explosion occurred in the tunnel and wrecked the train. The cars and flatcars burned from the incendiaries. The rebels needed more than a week to put out the fire, to pull out the remains of the cars and flatcars and to repair the tunnel.

Before Spain, I had only admired the moon, especially on warm summer nights. In the winter in the north, the moon brightens the arctic night with its light. On a moonlit, frosty night one can see a great distance, and it is so bright you can read a newspaper. But in Spain on moonlit nights, I often heard the complaints of Domingo's men, "The moon let us down! It is impossible to cross open ground unnoticed."

Fewer operations behind enemy lines were conducted on moonlit nights, and then only where one could walk hidden in the shadows of the trees and bushes.

On moonlit nights, sorties across the front line over waterways stopped.

On one such night, Rudolf was sorting out a bag of mines belonging to a seriously wounded demolition man, and suddenly an electrical detonator exploded.

Fortunately, everything came out pretty well—one fingernail was completely stripped off Rudolf's right hand, half of two others were taken, and a few dozen splinters went into his hand and chest. They bandaged him up and sent him to Jaen along with a demolition man who had been wounded in the foot.

The experienced and careful surgeon, chief of the medical service of the Front, Frederico del Castillo, put a cast on the wounded demolition man and removed a large number of small splinters from Rudolf's hand and chest.

"It seems that demolition men *can* make more than one mistake!" the doctor noted.

Rudolf was not out of action. Even with a bandaged hand and suffering from pain in the injured fingers, he continued to work, sending the group into action against enemy communications.

"The inquisition really knew how to torture its victims when its interrogators put needles under the fingernails!" he said once as sweat broke out on his forehead. At that time, with his large ugly moustache, he seemed like a really old man, even though there was not one gray hair on his head.

Ivan Kharish—Juan Pequeño

The organization of movement behind enemy lines was very complex. It involved determination of the conditions at the front from the appropriate headquarters and the selection of a place on the map for crossing enemy defenses and of the route of the groups through territory occupied by the rebels, departure for the front sector, and specification and agreement on the spot of all questions for guaranteeing the success of the operation.

Such was the case one time. Ivan Kharish had given all the instructions for the preparation of the group for the proposed mission to his deputy, and sat in the car next to me. Rudolf was in front with Pepe, and we went to the sector where Kharish's group would have to cross the front line.

This was not the first mission for Ivan Kharish, and he was in a very good mood. He was talking and joking, but not wasting time. He carefully studied the locality and made notes in his field notebook.

The car drove along the white, dusty road, leaving behind a kind of smoke screen, which the weak wind slowly blew to one side. We were driving along a small valley, a swift mountain stream flowing toward us. Then we began to climb in a steep spiral up the mountain. Approaching the turns, Pepe invariably honked the horn and slowed down so as not to collide with approaching vehicles.

The slope of the mountain was overgrown with sparse pines and bushes. On one of the turns, the driver suddenly braked sharply and began to honk the horn at a donkey loaded down with baskets of olives that was slowly crossing the road. We then went through a grove of oaks where it was gloomy and quiet, then through a clearing strewn with small boulders. We passed olive trees on which there were more ripe black fruits than leaves.

Sitting next to Juan Pequeño, I automatically thought about how much the small man had endured in his life. I admired him, his courage and initiative, his persistence, endurance, and bravery in action in the enemy rear, which everyone already knew. During the debriefing following an operation, Domingo and Rudolf often recognized Ivan Kharish as the commanding officer of a group that in any difficult situation invariably completed its assignment successfully. The group destroyed important enemy military objectives.

Little Ivan was then thirty-three years old, and he had already managed to knock around the world. Unemployment in Yugoslavia forced Kharish, at twenty-three, to forsake his native land and to search for a living in America. They received him coldly in Canada, and after a two-year stay there, he decided to move on to Mexico where, although he was a good cabinetmaker, he was unsuccessful in finding suitable work. And so he began his travels around America, Guatemala, El Salvador, Nicaragua, Panama, Colombia, Ecuador, Peru, Chile, and finally Argentina. Ivan Kharish worked there not only as a cabinetmaker but also in the Party underground together with the Pole Fillip Vodopii.

News of the rebellion in Spain reached Argentina the day after it happened. The Party center in Buenos Aires brought the truth about events in Spain to the people and gathered the resources for rendering aid to the Republicans. Kharish and his friend Fillip Vodopii also requested that the Party organization send them to Spain. In September 1936, Kharish and his friends left Argentina for Europe in the coal bunker of a freighter.

"We traveled a long time," Kharish told me one day, "and when we reached Europe, I was so happy. It was wonderful that I had lived to return to my continent. You know several times I was close to death in the jungles and mountains of Latin America. Oh, Louisa, how I wanted to go to Yugoslavia, to my own Croatia, where I was born, where my people live! But all thirty passengers of our ship hurried to Spain, and events drove us. We were afraid we would be too late."

Ten years Ivan Kharish had worked in foreign lands, as he often said *"s trbuhom za kruhom,"* meaning, "for bread on an empty stomach." He had had a chance to experience every discomfort—cold, hunger, tropical heat, thirst, the humiliation of bosses, and the police.

"Was it really impossible to find work in Yugoslavia?" I asked Kharish.

"It was possible to work for free. I worked for free as an apprentice, when I was already a pretty good cabinetmaker. Louisa, you can't imagine our country. It has fertile valleys along the Danube and its tributaries, and its mountains are covered by lush forests. It has the seacoast of the Adriatic which is unmatched by anything else. It is protected on the north by high, barren mountains, and along the coast, there are a few dozen large and a few hundred small islands. The water on the Adriatic coast is always clean and calm, but only rich people can vacation on the wonderful Yadrany[1] coast. This is a country where the king lives very well with

---

[1] Yugoslavs call the Adriatic Sea the Yadrany.

his family and hangers-on, a country that foreigners plunder, and in which there are so many unemployed that they agree to work for a piece of bread, and even that is not always possible. Every year, tens of thousands of young people leave Yugoslavia to work in other countries, but even then, the majority of them, good specialists, eke out a miserable existence and die, foreigners, in poverty or even, let's speak directly, from hunger. Only a few manage to live through their difficulties abroad to return to their homeland for burial."

Kharish also told us what Yugoslavia had endured— "First the Turkish pashas plundered and enslaved us, then the Austrian magnates. And now (1937) it is the home-grown bourgeoisie and feudal lords together with foreigners. But the time will come, and I firmly believe this, that our people will be masters of their own country! Many of our comrades participated in Russia in the war against the Whites and now fight against Fascist bands. The time will also come to fight against the *chetniks* and the *ustasha* in order to cleanse our land of those on whose account I and many thousands of others had to forsake our motherland."

I admired his optimism, his love for his native land, his faith that there would one day be for him a true mother country, where men such as he would be masters of the country.

From the first day of his arrival in the detachment, Ivan Kharish, who became Juan Pequeño, because of his small size, attracted Rudolf's attention with his zeal and inquisitiveness. He learned partisan techniques faster and more completely than the others, seeing and making use of all their possibilities. He tried to learn as much as possible about the tactics of partisan warfare. Kharish questioned

Rudolf about the activities of partisans in Siberia, the Far East, Ukraine, and Belorussia, in the Urals, the Caucasus, and in the Crimea. He asked not only about partisans of the civil war but also about those of 1812–1813. A month after his arrival in Jaen, Juan Pequeño was not only going behind enemy lines but he was also teaching partisan techniques and tactics to the others.

He was upset by the suffering of the Spanish people, and he gave his salary to the needy as, by the way, many of our other partisans did. He helped those who had escaped from rebel occupied regions and at the expense of his own reward.

The car sped quickly along a pretty good road. Kharish was thinking about something, looking out the window, not knowing that I was recalling our conversations about what might become of Juan Pequeño in the struggle for Yugoslav freedom in light of his interesting and complex biography.

After crossing a small crest, the road leveled out, and we entered a forest of cork oak trees. In the heart of the forest, we saw a small flock of sheep bunched together near a spring. I requested that we stop the car. We took canteens and went toward the flock. Suddenly a dog burst in front of us, with its tail raised, and barked angrily, not allowing us to go closer.

An old shepherd, with a herder, a boy about twelve, began to shout at the dog, and after barking a few times in a conciliatory way, it retreated.

We drank cool, delicious water from the spring, filled our canteens, and said good-bye.

Having come out of the forest, we found ourselves on a rise. In the distance in front of us, as if we were not moving, were high mountains.

Eventually, Pepe pulled over, parked the car under a large tree with a spreading crown, and said, "Here we are! We can't drive any farther. We have to walk a bit."

We reached the command post safely, where a tan young officer with a pistol on a tightly cinched belt welcomed us warmly. The purpose of our arrival was already known to the battalion commander.

"Alfonso! Please, bring us coffee!" the battalion commander said to his orderly, without asking if we wanted any.

After drinking the small cups of coffee, Kharish, the battalion commander, Rudolf, and a few other soldiers went to the observation post. They were gone a long time, and I began to worry, especially when we heard rifle and machine-gun fire in the battalion sector.

"Everything is okay. This is an excellent place to move out from. Now we will go to Villa Nueva de Cordoba," Rudolf said to me. But we did not go; the air-raid signal sounded, and two enemy planes appeared in the sky. Apparently conducting reconnaissance, they flew low, wheeling around like real vultures. Suddenly, looking just like stubby cigars, bombs separated from the airplanes. At first, they flew almost parallel with the planes, and then steeper and steeper, they fell to earth.

We heard the muffled explosions beyond the olive groves, then the Fascists slowly turned and headed toward us.

"My God! They will see our car!" said Kharish.

"Possibly," the battalion commander said, as if it did not matter.

Meanwhile the enemy planes soared about three hundred meters over the road along which we had planned to return to Villa Nueva de Cordoba.

Ivan Kharish looked at his watch, and I glanced at it, too.

"Still more than an hour until dinner," he noted.

"By that time the Italians have to be gone. They are never late to eat. Let's have another coffee," the battalion commander suggested.

"No! Let me make my way up to the high spot, where your forward observation post is located," Kharish asked the battalion commander.

"But you won't see anything new from there, and the Italians will be able to see you," the captain answered.

"You're right. I won't see anything new, but I want to talk to the men who are up there. They will help clear up something." There was no stopping the group commander.

"Go ahead, I will send Antonio with you," the battalion commander said.

And so Kharish, Rudolf, and the youngest soldier, Antonio, headed toward the forward post, about six hundred meters from the command post. At first they walked along the trench bending low, then they crawled and scrambled, then with a short rush they reached the command fence and went along it until they were hidden from view.

I remained at the command post under the large olive trees. Ripe fruit littered the rocky ground.

"They will gather all of them!" said the battalion commander, having noticed that I had taken up a handful of fruit.

While I was at the command post, I automatically compared what was going on around me with what I had seen at Teruel. Here there was a calmness, a harmony in the work, a confidence in victory over the enemy, and military discipline. The Spanish Republican Army had come of age. Even so, I worried about Rudolf's going to the forward area in broad daylight. The Italians will catch sight of them and fire on them . . . and the planes are still flying . . .

But nothing happened. After half an hour, the Italians flew away, and the men returned. We drank more coffee, said good-bye to the hospitable captain, and went to the car. The dinner break had begun, the sky was clear, and there was complete silence on the front.

At one point on the way back, fresh craters from the bombs were visible from 50 to 120 meters off the road. We could still smell the explosives.

"There was a poorly camouflaged car here," a satisfied Pepe told us. "The Italians missed the first time, and then they flew by. Maybe they didn't have any bombs left. I thought they might have seen my Ford, but probably not, I broke off branches and covered it so well I couldn't see it myself."

We had not even left the crater yet when Kharish cried out, "Look! Another plane! He's lost or lagging behind."

"It doesn't matter whether he's lost or late or has already eaten dinner earlier than the others, we have to hide the car," Rudolf said.

The Italian was rapidly approaching at low altitude, but Pepe kept his composure, quickly pulled off the road, and stopped under a large tree with red pods. We took cover behind a stone fence, and everyone but me opened fire on the airplane.

In spite of the fact that it was dinner time, Republican units began firing on the descending airplane with rifles and machine guns. To me it seemed that it should not be hard to hit him, but he continued to fly, gaining altitude. So we got back into the car, and Pepe hurried for the base, once in a while glancing at his watch. Dinner time was coming to an end.

On the outskirts of Villa Nueva de Cordoba, women were

doing laundry in a stream, and freshly washed linen hung on bushes, drying.

In the evening, we moved Kharish's group behind enemy lines. The men arrived at the command post before nightfall. "Everything is ready," the captain reported, meeting us as old friends.

Kharish was in an especially good mood. He joked around, but he was on top of the situation; he had provided for every contingency, down to the smallest detail.

At one point, the battalion commander asked Kharish, "Why do you have so few cartridges?"

"Because we are carrying lots of explosives. We're not going for a skirmish. Ammunition is not much use to us. If we shoot, they can shoot back. The Fascists can bring up reinforcements in a hurry, but we can't expect help from anyone. The enemy can drive his wounded to the hospital, but we have to carry our own, and we have no medicine with us except iodine and bandages. But when can we set mines without attracting attention and a car is blown up or a train derailed, we can watch the results of our work from afar," Kharish said.

When the sun set, we said good-bye and parted without emotion. But I admired the men who went behind enemy lines, who had to be confident in their strength and in the success of the operation. Before the group left, Kharish again reminded us of the return time and requested, "My dear captain, be sure to alert the men, so that they don't fire on us when we return, and remind them of the password." This time Juan Pequeño bid me good-bye with special warmth and holding my hand said, "See you soon, Louisa!"

"Good luck. I will try to come to meet you," I answered.

Kharish's group silently disappeared into the approaching darkness. Rudolf and I remained at the command post.

Occasionally we heard shots, but eventually everything became quiet. After a little more than two hours the battalion's scouts returned, the senior scout reporting that the group had passed by the rebel forward posts safely.

Three days later, Kharish returned. The Soviet pilots had told Kolman about the troop train that was derailed.

A Base Behind Rebel Lines

As a rule, until the middle of February 1937, every time Domingo's groups conducted attacks on enemy lines of communication they crossed the front line twice. The longer they stayed behind enemy lines, the more the front changed, which they could not know about because of the lack of communications. That meant that during their return, they could run into enemy patrols. True, in some cases, we set up signal beacons to orient them. The beacons made it possible to signal changes in conditions or that it was impossible to use the primary route. We could even let the groups know the backup sector. Unfortunately, beacons were not suitable everywhere because of the local topography.

If there were no beacons, the groups had to cross the forward area very slowly. Sometimes, without realizing it, they wandered into positions held by our own troops.

Occasionally, after spotting an unknown group sneaking up, the Republicans would order the group to stop, tell the men to throw down their weapons and raise their hands—all without explaining who they were themselves. At least once that led to losses when the group opened fire on those they believed to be Fascists; within the detachment, the greatest attention was paid to the reception of our groups so that the Republican units would not take our saboteurs for enemy spies.

Experience showed that it was good to have secret bases behind enemy lines for delivery of supplies of food and demolition materials. The presence of bases behind rebel lines could make the activities of small sabotage groups easier and increase the number of opportunities for attacks on lines of communications and other objectives. The route to the target would be shorter, and it would not be necessary to recross the front line each time. On the other hand, it raised other dangers.

A stay at such a base was possible only as long as the enemy did not know of its existence. If the enemy managed to detect a base and attacked it suddenly in the first half of the day, it would be difficult for the sabotage group to escape before nightfall.

During the establishment of a base, both backups and decoys were provided, but the main concern was the maintenance of secrecy and careful camouflage of the main and backup bases, and the elimination of the possibility of an enemy surprise attack.

The first such base we established was an abandoned olive-oil-processing factory twelve kilometers northwest of Adamuz. The base was organized at the initiative and with the participation of a battalion commander of the Spanish Republican Army, Capt. Francisco del Castillo.[1] He quickly got involved in the sabotage operations of Domingo's detachment and took direct part in them. He was already a frontline soldier, and he understood the dangers of frequent crossing of the front line, especially during the return to our side.

The base was intended to facilitate strikes on the lines of communication and other Fascist targets on the approaches to Cordoba. It was already organized by the middle of February,

---

[1]Francisco del Castillo participated in World War II, often going behind enemy lines, and while I was writing these lines he was a recipient of a merit pension, living in Dnepropetrovsk.

but I went there later on when Rudolf did not have an interpreter.

We left Jaen for Adamuz on a warm, sunny day. We had not gotten as far as Linares when we stopped in the small village where the peasants had feasted us with fresh oranges in January. Although I had an English name and surname, and Rudolf Wolf, a German one, the Spanish with whom we worked still knew very well that we were Russians, that we were Soviets.

All of our secrecy was a sham because the "headquarters" of our advisers in Valencia had become quite well known, and we could not hide our citizenship from the leaders of the Party Provincial Committees and the command of the Spanish Republican units.

Many of our Spanish friends were surprised to "learn" that in Russia there were no Ivans, Pyotrs, Yegors, and Annas, just Fritzes, Malinos, Wolfs, Louisas, and so on. Even our Domingo Ungria was sure that my real name was Louisa and Rudolf's Rodolfo Wolf.

The peasant men and women from the village (I have forgotten its name), in which we had once stopped again treated us to wine and oranges. Many fine words were spoken about the Soviet people, especially the three fliers who one day, near Linares, had fought nine Italian planes within view of many hundreds of the local populace. Two of the enemy were immediately hit, and the rest turned and fled. Before long, three more were hit, one of which fell not far away. The pilot parachuted out of the plane.

By evening, we were in Adamuz, where Marquez's group met us. Ammunition, explosives, and provisions were loaded on mules, and by the end of the day, all of the equipment intended for the base was concentrated in the forward area.

At that time, stubborn fighting was taking place at Pozoblanco, but it was quiet in the area of our crossing. We observed the movements of hostile patrols through binoculars, studying the disposition of enemy posts, and with the coming of dark, we left the forward area of our troops and moved forward.

The hooves of the animals were wrapped in pieces of flannel blankets, and the men walked silently in *alpargatas*. The mules walked cautiously, as if they understood the danger. We would stop and listen—silence—and then continue forward.

In the darkness, we crossed ditches and streams, now and then going up the mountains and then going down again. It was tough going, and after climbing, we rested a bit. It seemed as if our march would never end. The darkness was terrifying. It was as if we had fallen into a barrel of tar.

It was almost midnight when Domingo stopped the column. He went up to a large tree, searched for something and swore. "I called for the guard, but he's missing," he whispered to me.

At last, a small light began to stir near the tree, and after two or three minutes, two partisans, whom I knew, came up to us and led us to the base.

The low buildings were dark and gloomy. There was no sign of people.

The guard led us into a sooty room. Crooked, short logs burned weakly in the fireplace, twelve partisans were sleeping on the floor wherever they could, and someone was snoring with a whistle. Near the fireplace were two guards who stood up and came to meet us. They turned out to be volunteers from Jaen, whom we knew.

The captain added wood to the fire and put on some cutlets. After half an hour, we had supper and spread out to rest. They took me away to a small gloomy room, not unlike a cell. It was dimly lit by a homemade lamp with olive oil.

I could not sleep. The squeaks and rustle of the rats kept me awake. I don't know how many times I reread letters from my daughter and sister that I had received from home. There were drawings on them of the Kremlin and Red Square, which had been drawn by my little Olya. They were more valuable to me than famous paintings. I went outside. It was very quiet. I could hear only the sound of the water falling over the dam of the hydroelectric station.

The sentries stood near the wall, on which hung pieces of rotten wood that glowed as if in a fairy tale. I looked at the sky, at a bank of drifting clouds, which slowly changed their whimsical outlines as they moved.

The chief of the guard was on duty. He recognized me and began to tell me about the base. *"No pasaran,"*[2] he said to me with pride. "All of these wires are connected with wires and alarms on the approaches to the base. Our men know where and how to walk and how to alert the guard. By breaking or even only pulling on a wire, they will give themselves away. Rudolf, Tikhii, the Finns have done a lot of work here," he said.

From below, on the northwest, the incessant rumble of falling water could be heard.

"The electric power station is two and a half kilometers away as the crow flies, but we have no orders to destroy it. The station itself serves as a screen for us," the captain told me in a whisper. "The Fascists wouldn't believe that saboteurs could be so close to the station and not touch it."

Below, two pair of headlights got closer to the power station.

"Fascists. They come to check the station, maybe bringing men or provisions. We don't touch them, we work on distant highways along which soldiers and reinforcements are sent to the front," my guide explained.

---

[2] They shall not pass.

The headlights disappeared at the power station. It was again dark all around, and as before, only the roar of the falling water could be heard from below.

Toward morning, I napped a little. In spite of my fatigue, I did not fall asleep quickly. I had a dream. I was in a small forest cabin, with one small window and a large iron stove surrounded by bricks. It was very hot. Almost the full length of the cabin was filled by a table thrown together from planks and over it, reaching to just under the ceiling, were two poles on which were drying foot cloths, felt boots, and clothes. The tired wood cutters were eating supper. The cabin was filled with the smell of drying foot cloths, felt boots, and clothes and also with tobacco smoke. The air was so thick you could cut it and stack it, and the glow of the kerosene lamp seemed to be drowned in the cloud of tobacco smoke.

The woodcutters, whom I knew lay on the plank bed, were not sleeping. I told them that the quota for timber cutting was overfulfilled on other pieces of woodland, and about the present situation, about events in our country and abroad. Everyone listened attentively. Some asked questions, and I answered. The howl of a hungry wolf was heard from outside, and everything disappeared into a haze. I found myself in a forest. The snow was up to my belt, and I could hardly move. I watched as two young woodcutters with a two-handed saw felled a large tree. The youths worked very well, cutting off the boughs, loading a sledge, and taking it to the river, where they made rafts. The call of the hungry wolf was heard again, and the horses whinnied with fear. I woke up. There was complete silence all around, but it was already light. The most dangerous time for partisans had begun. It was daylight when the safety of the partisans depended on careful camouflage and the skill of groups returning from missions who, if they had covered their tracks properly, had not led a punitive force to our base.

I dreamt about the cabin eight years after the last time I had been involved with timber cutting. Forestry had enormous significance in the first five-year plan. Resources were needed for obtaining new machines for the restoration of the national economy of the young Soviet Republic, and the export of forest products provided a significant part of the necessary foreign currency. Because of that, the Communist party paid a great deal of attention to timber cutting, in which I participated as women's organizer for the Mezenskii region.

It is necessary for a person to dream. During the night it had rained. From the olive grove came a fresh smell and a cool breeze. The sun had not yet appeared, but its rays already shone on the mountains, over which could be seen thin, fleecy white clouds. It was quiet all around, and only the guard reminded one of the war, and the fact that the base was behind enemy lines.

In the morning, Rubio and Alex's groups arrived from their mission. Alex was our only American, a brave commander of a sabotage group. They reported on the completed mission, ate, and went to sleep.

At the base, we had to walk so that not the slightest sign of life could be observed from a distance.

During the day, we warmed our food in the building over charcoal.

The little factory was hidden in an olive grove. East of it was a steep slope on which grew small olive trees and large leguminous trees. On the west and southwest was a slope into a valley where a small river flowed, and on the river was a high dam and hydroelectric station, and behind the dam a reservoir. Through the binoculars, you could see armed men walking on the dam.

The man on duty invited us for a light breakfast, coffee

with condensed milk, cheese sandwiches, salted olives, and oranges. Rudolf and some of the interbrigadists chewed on the long brown pods that were in abundance on the trees. The mules also ate these pods with special pleasure.

During the day, Marquez's group prepared for an operation. There were more than fifty men at the base. We had a radio receiver, and the men knew about all the news.

"The most dangerous time is before dinner," Rudolf explained. "The sooner after sunrise the Fascists discover us, the harder it would be for us to hold out until dark. If they attack after dinner, then we have to turn the enemy back at the far approaches, set delayed action grenades, and retreat to a backup base. We cross the front line to our own area at night."

Rudolf and Domingo began to prepare for a simultaneous operation to wreck a train and blow up two small high bridges on the railroad leading to Cordoba. The group under the command of the short, young, but already graying sailor, Ruiz, had to force a crossing of the Guadalquivir River in order to approach the Montoro–Cordoba railroad from the north, coming from a direction in which the enemy did not expect saboteurs. For the crossing, Ruiz and his men would bring a canvas boat.

I had a great deal of work translating the intelligence materials we received.

Dinner was at two o'clock sharp, and we ate under a huge tree, warming the food over wood coals that had burned down during the night. We had beans with canned meat. The portions were large, but some of the men asked for more. They gave out wine only by the glass. We also had cold coffee, left over from breakfast.

After dinner, most of us rested. The silence was complete. The guard and a few of those not going on the mission stayed awake. The sun was still high, and it was warm. The broad valley of the small river, which flows into the Guadalquivir, could be seen in the distance, even with the naked eye. Through the binoculars, it was easy to see what was happening on the plain—peasants were working in the fields.

Before sunset, three groups went on the mission. Rudolf, Domingo, and Jan Tikhii, who had managed to sleep, went with Ruiz's group. Another six men went with them to secure the crossing of the swift river and, in the case of success, to communicate the results quickly through Adamuz to the Republican command.

Night fell. I remained at the base where there were no more than twenty men. In the darkness over Cordoba,[3] the sky was lit up with a reddish-white light.

"It is the light of the electric signs," one of the partisans said.

What struck me about the base was the confidence in its security. Outside, a pair of sentries was standing. Inside, in the main room, the windows tightly battened down, the coals in the fireplace burned brightly, and the radio played gay music, alternating with news broadcasts. We were listening to music, and within three kilometers, at the power station, was the enemy. The front line was within a dozen kilometers. It was not continuous, and each of the sides was ready to repel an attack.

Juan Grande also remained at the base that night. He would go out the next day, but just then his group had guard duty, so he stayed awake. In the evening, he had checked the alarms and instructed the men in security procedures. He did not lis-

[3] The main city of the province of the same name with a population of more than 100,000 people. It is located on the high bank of the Guadalquivir River.

ten to music, but was outside almost all the time and only occasionally came into the room to smoke a cigarette.

That night I did not go to sleep for a long time, and Juan
Grande and I talked a great deal. The Montenegrin came to
Spain after escaping from an Italian ship. He was not married, but he had left an elderly mother and a married sister in
Montenegro. Juan Grande was brave and hot tempered; he
was poorly educated, but he had passed through a great
school of life. One of the first members of the international
brigades to begin to go behind enemy lines, he was like a
hunter tracking enemy troop trains and vehicles. He got a
great deal of pleasure out of blowing up the enemy's troop
trains and derailing them—ammunition, soldiers, officers,
and all! But Juan Grande was not a cruel man. He understood that not everyone in the enemy camp was fighting voluntarily, but that there was forcible conscription on the
Nationalist side. He was disturbed by the suffering of the
people who had been plunged into war by the rebels. He
could not calmly walk by those who were in need and whom
he could help.

When he returned after completing a military mission,
Juan Grande never took advantage of the allotted time for
rest, and he distributed his salary to those who suffered most
from the rebels.

After a brief rest, Juan usually went to Rudolf or
Domingo and asked them to send him on a mission again.

He often told me of Montenegro's stormy past. He listened enthusiastically when I spoke about the Soviet Union.
That night we were talking quietly when we heard the rumble of a far-off explosion. Juan Grande looked at the luminous dial of his watch. It was 12:48 A.M.

"Is it possible that it only seemed like an explosion because we are expecting one?" I asked.

"No. It is an explosion, a large explosion. It's not under a train, but on a bridge."

Ruiz returned with his group in the morning. His men were tired, their eyes red from lack of sleep, but happy and satisfied. It was as if they had forgotten that they were behind enemy lines and Juan Grande had to remind them of this.

"Where are Domingo and Rudolf?" I asked Ruiz.

"They went straight to Adamuz to report about the destruction of the train and to call in an air strike."

Before dinner, we heard explosions near Montoro. In the evening, Juan Grande left on a mission, and late at night, Domingo, Rudolf, and Tikhii returned to the base with provisions and happy news—pilots under the command of K. M. Gusev had attacked enemy vehicles that were carrying ammunition from the troop train the partisans had destroyed near Montoro. They had watched the ground attack from the Republican positions. Valenzuela, the secretary of the Party Provincial Committee, who had arrived at the front from Jaen, also watched.

The next night, Rudolf, Domingo, an escort of six men, and I left the base. We rode on mules, strong, gentle, and intelligent animals. We reached what we supposed was the front line. But exactly where the line was and where the enemy units were was unknown, and the uncertainty put us on our guard.

We dismounted, leading the stubborn animals by the reins. Suddenly, somewhere to our left, an exchange of shots started up. That meant the enemy was near, alongside our own line. Before Franco's revolt, our guide, the old peasant Jose, had worked in the oil factory and knew the area very well. "There is no one," he whispered. We crossed a stream. "Ours were farther to the east yesterday. Who is there now? We have a password, but who can guarantee that instead of a reply, we won't suddenly hear a machine-gun burst . . ."

After going a half a kilometer, we stopped, and the guide went off to one side. After twenty agonizing minutes, he returned with two Republicans. We were behind our own lines.

The partisans had diverted the enemy soldiers, delivering appreciable blows against them, forcing them to guard communications and important objectives day and night; they obliged the Fascists to keep an unwieldy punitive machine in the rear.

Battalion *Especial*

Domingo's detachment intensified its strikes behind rebel lines, and all the groups carried out the operations more successfully—they derailed trains, blew up automobiles with mines, blew up bridges, and destroyed tunnels.

In February 1937, near Cordoba, the detachment destroyed a train that was going out of Seville, and wiped out a few hundred Italian Fascist pilots and officers. Rudolf, Juan Grande, and Juan Pequeño accompanied the groups on that mission.

Domingo, Rudolf, and I then went to report to the commander of the southern front, Col. Perez Salas.

This time, he not only welcomed me warmly but also Rudolf and Domingo. He listened attentively to the report, occasionally adjusting his large glasses, then he asked a few questions about setting mines.

"Tomorrow, toward the end of the day, present your report and plans for deployment of the detachment behind rebel lines," he said to Captain Domingo. On that note the meeting was ended.

In the next twenty-four hours, many events took place. The most important was that we managed to get Fascist newspapers with obituaries and funeral announcements about those who had perished ("the valiant ones felled by death").

That afternoon, we again went to the commander.

Perez Salas received us even more hospitably. The colonel was delighted, looking through the newspapers with the announcements of the destruction of the Fascist airmen.

"Let's have your report and proposals!" he addressed Domingo. Domingo handed it over.

The commander quickly familiarized himself with the report and grinned.

"This is beyond my authority. Go to General Rojo; I will ask him to receive you."

Having written a cover letter by hand, the colonel warmly bid us good-bye.

After two days, Domingo returned from Madrid. "Everything was decided quickly and positively," he began to tell us.

"Our proposals have been approved. Enough begging! They named me commander of Battalion *Especial*! Look! Here's the stamp, here's the seal, and here is the order of the general staff."

In the large hall, which had been turned into a lecture hall, they gathered the saboteurs. They all listened with great attention to Domingo's story about his trip to Madrid.

"The creation of the Battalion *Especial*," Domingo said, "is recognition of the importance of hitting the enemy behind his own lines. It is recognition of our successes. It means a drastic improvement of the material conditions under which we live, but it is only the beginning."

The personnel of the battalion were given a higher salary. During raids behind enemy lines, there would now be sufficient dry rations, and uniform allowances would be allotted on the basis of wear and tear.

Thus, the successful destruction of a trainload of Italian pilots and officers fundamentally changed for the better the material and legal situation of our unit.

The destruction of the Italian airmen on the train near Cordoba became widely known.

At the base at Villa Nueva de Cordoba, where the sabotage units were located, there was a real invasion of correspondents from many Spanish and foreign newspapers. We were astonished at how quickly they found our location. That turned out to be because of the headquarters of the southern front.

In order to maintain security, Rudolf and Domingo tried not to be seen by journalists. The captain worked hard on this with those who took part in the operation and the staff. He impressed upon them the need for everyone to hold their tongues.

We received the journalists hospitably. We spoke with them, but as to the question of who and how the sabotage was conducted we politely answered, "The war is not over. Because of this it is too early to describe our means, methods, and people."

In contrast to the Spanish and foreign correspondents, Soviet journalists were in no hurry to penetrate our secrets.

Toward evening on the second day after the group came back from behind enemy lines, Mikhail Koltsov arrived at our base. By dress and appearance he was very much like a Spaniard, and he spoke Spanish like a true Castillian.

News of Koltsov's arrival at the base roused the entire staff. Not only Soviet people knew M. Ye. Koltsov well at that time. His articles were helping the Republicans in their struggle against the rebels and their Fascist allies. Everyone wanted to see the fighting *novinar*[1] as Ivan Bolshoi (a.k.a. Juan Grande, "Big Juan") called him.

"Please, introduce me, please, to the men who wrecked the train at Cordoba," Mikhail Koltsov asked me, after learning that Rudolf was not at the base.

---

[1]Croatian for reporter.

I did, and they began friendly conversations, but everyone remembered Domingo's order and held their tongues. They spoke freely about the weather, about how they got wet and tired, but no one said where they warmed up and rested. They explained that they had set large mines in order to destroy the train.

"This wreck is still too little for the Fascists!" Domingo proudly declared. "You know, we have seen the results of their barbaric air raids on Madrid, Andujar, Pozoblanco, and the other cities!"

"Did all the foreign comrades know Spanish?" Koltsov asked Domingo.

"No!" the captain waved a hand. "Two Yugoslavs, the Italians, and the French understand and can speak, but when they joined the detachment, the others knew only a few dozen words, but now they all can express themselves."

"How about the local population? Can they tell these are foreigners?"

"Our groups carry everything they need behind enemy lines and don't bother the local population. For work among the populace and communication with them, we use only Spaniards," Domingo answered.

"But what if someone falls behind at night?" Koltsov asked.

"So far, no one has fallen behind. He has a compass; he will get out!"

"Why did you join the partisans?" Koltsov asked Juan Grande.

"Because I came to Spain to fight Fascists."

"But you can fight at the front, where there are also many Fascists. It's simpler for foreigners there, and you don't have to know the language!"

"No! It is easier to strike behind Fascist lines; mainly you hit him where he doesn't expect it, when he's on his own side. At first I didn't understand this myself, but when I saw, then I understood that the rebels in cars and trains are like snakes in cages. You beat them until they crawl," Juan reported.

Koltsov was making notes quickly, but he did not ask any more questions on this theme. I did not hear what he and Rubio were talking about, but noted that he was satisfied with the discussion.

"After the destruction of the pilots' train, couldn't the rebels follow the fresh trail and find and destroy your base?" Koltsov asked Domingo.

"We will no longer return to the base behind enemy lines, but to a base behind our lines; the Falangists have short arms. Besides, we promote vigilance, relying on the people. With their help, we have already fished out a few enemy spies. The cowardly scum," Domingo answered.

"You are right about that. But not everything is in order with your security. For example no one asked me for any kind of papers."

"It's not necessary!" Domingo answered calmly, "They know you, but a stranger wouldn't get far. Our guards have already arrested more than one suspicious person and sent them to the commandant, and even detained them in the houses of the clergy, and they are like small fortresses."

Mikhail Koltsov did not stay to spend the night. He was in a hurry.

The next day, Ilya Ehrenburg arrived with a secretary and a portable typewriter. This guest was not in a hurry and agreed to stay overnight with us.

Domingo began to show Ilya Grigorevich his operation, and first of all he took him to the mounted saboteurs.

"What kind of a horseman is this?" the writer asked in surprise when he saw eight-year-old Antonio sitting on his father's thoroughbred trotter.

"This is my son!" Domingo answered with pride.

In honor of our guest, a dinner was arranged, which was attended by almost everyone who was at the base. Ilya Ehrenburg showed everyone who was there photographs and obituaries which had been published in Fascist and profascist newspapers. "They grieve over the destruction and complain about the partisans," the writer noted.

"When the enemy cries and complains, we are happy," Domingo answered.

"Enemies write and friends write," Ehrenburg said. "But our friends understand that the more rebels the partisans destroy behind the lines, the fewer enemy soldiers there will be at the front and the sooner there will be victory."

Finally, tired but satisfied, the writer went to rest.

In the morning, he said good-bye to the partisans and left, after saying, "I'll write, but I'll maintain complete confidentiality."

"Very good," the captain answered.

"Just so it doesn't turn out badly for us," Rudolf requested.

Ilya Ehrenburg really did write about the train wreck, and he fulfilled the promise he had given us.

"Yes! A big conspiracy! But now we have been recognized, and they can't dump the blame on the local partisans," Domingo said, when I translated for him Ilya Ehrenburg's sketch, which was published in *Izvestiya,* March 23, 1937.

Rubio and the Others

The destruction of the train with the Italian pilots near Cordoba eliminated all our concern about material support, except for communication. Rudolf arranged with Kolman to use aviation for communication, and the groups were given signals that they had to give our pilots, but that system was not reliable, mainly because the Republican Air Force was loaded down with other assignments.

We alerted the battalion commanders in the sectors to which the groups were supposed to return across their lines, and the battalion commanders reminded the company commanders, but sometimes the groups were not there at the appointed time. This was the case once with Rubio's group. It went out on a mission to capture tongues on the Espiel–Cordoba road, along which enemy soldiers who had advanced on Pozoblanco were being supplied.

The group should have returned on the third night, but we waited for it in vain, even beyond that time. It was as if they had disappeared. This was of special interest to V. I. Kolman because he needed the intelligence information.

"Rubio's not lost," Pepe assured us. "It is his anarchist habits. He just captured an important car and decided to drive around behind rebel lines. He left a love in Merida. He showed me a photograph. Beautiful!"

"Yes, I know that he left his lover in Merida," Domingo

recalled, "but he can't risk going there. From Espiel to Merida is more than 150 kilometers."

"He can do it!" Pepe answered, after waving his hand.

Domingo cursed. "I warned him not to be held up."

Just then there was a call from Pozoblanco.

"Rubio? Where the hell are you?" Domingo said.

Rubio said something. A satisfied smile appeared on Domingo's face. "Very good!" the captain answered him with a satisfied tone of voice. He quickly called Kolman.

The dusty Hispano-Suiza, going up on the sidewalk, stopped near the school building. Rubio got out first without a hat, in a military uniform, clean shaven, with two pistols, one large one in a wooden holster, the second, a small one in his belt. The other four partisans poured out behind him.

Their friends rushed to meet them. There were happy cries and embraces. Even Domingo could not refrain from expressions of delight. He hugged them all in turn. Pepe said, "Look! Suitcases! Just like a tourist!" Taking one of them Pepe added with surprise, "It's heavy!"

The entire group gathered in Domingo's office. Then Kolman and Rudolf drove up.

"What's with these suitcases?" Rudolf asked.

"Nothing good!" Rubio answered. He opened them, one after the other. In one was the uniform of a rebel major, a Michelin road map, a bunch of snapshots, toilet articles, and books.

Rudolf and Kolman began to examine the maps and documents. On the maps, the military situation was marked with colored pencils. Among the documents were manuscript materials written in illegible handwriting.

In the other, there was a Telefunken portable radio receiver and a portfolio with documents, a captain's uniform, and two field pouches, one with maps and the second with maps and documents.

"Well now, Rubio, tell comrade Kolman what you were doing behind rebel lines," Domingo said.

"Please spare me from this," Rubio implored. "My business is to drive, to work, to capture prisoners. Let Riego tell about everything, he saw and knows everything and knows how to tell a story. He's a teacher."

All eyes turned to Antonio Riego. Like Rubio, he had been a participant in the Teruel mission and had already been behind enemy lines on the southern front. Franco's insurrection had found him in Toledo, where he enlisted in the militia. He had been wounded in the hand and, with the wound still unhealed, went into battle with Captain Domingo's group. Riego understood politics very well and acted as Domingo's commissar and propagandist. He also wrote poems that were not too bad. He read them infrequently but with feeling.

"Okay, Antonio, report!" Domingo turned to the blushing intelligence agent, and only then did he notice that the handle of a second pistol stuck out of the pocket of Riego's pants.

Antonio began to speak, and I translated his story for Kolman, who took notes.

"We reached the Cordoba–Espiel road without any mishaps. It was a dark night, neither moon nor stars. There was only the faint rumble of Fascist night bombers flying out of the Cordoba airfield in the black heights. Then a train appeared, three lights and sparks from the funnel of the locomotive, and closer along the unseen road, car headlights flashed clearly. It was so peaceful, that, even sitting about one hundred meters from the road, we felt safe. We rested, had a bite to eat, and waited for a single car, but only columns were moving and, even then, very rarely."

Riego stopped and looked at Rubio.

"We had to wait a long time," Rubio emphasized.

"And so we waited!" put in Pedro Gomez, the youngest and tallest participant in the mission.

"Finally the lights of a single car appeared in the distance. It was approaching quickly. 'Let's go!' Rubio hurried us up, and we went right up to the road. In the uniform of an enemy officer, Rubio went right out onto the highway. He blinked his red flashlight directly at the approaching car. Everything was done just like in training at Valencia, the same way Rubio captured the fuel truck at Teruel. The car stopped. The headlights went out, but the light inside the limousine was on. There were three men in it.

" 'What's the matter?' the passenger who was sitting next to the driver asked rudely.

" 'Document check!'

" 'Can't you see our *salvoconducto* (safe conduct pass) on the window?' " someone said angrily from the limousine. A door slammed, and before we knew it, the car was off."

"It's too bad, we let such a prize get away," Gomez put in. "A Buick. Some colonel was riding in it."

"For a day, we hid in the bushes on the mountain slope. The man on duty noted when and what kind of vehicles were passing.

"In the course of the day, four trains with soldiers passed to the north, one passenger and three freights, possibly with ammunition. One had fuel. We watched but could do nothing. We needed a vehicle, but in daytime, we could do nothing more than count them."

"Finally night came again," Riego continued. "This time we went to the road right after dark. A column of trucks passed, then we saw the headlights of a lone vehicle coming from the direction of Cordoba. "

Riego paused so I could translate, then continued, "Rubio ordered me to run to meet the vehicle and give the blue signal if it was a car or a truck with no soldiers. I managed to run about a hundred meters as an ambulance came up even with me. I gave the halt signal and noticed that a red signal began to swing in reply."

"The ambulance was stopping," Rubio began, "I ran up and demanded their documents.

" 'We are an ambulance, we have a pass. You saw the column passed ahead of us, we're a little behind, we're catching up,' the driver answered. Next to him sat a sleeping medical assistant.

" 'Very good!' I answered and asked, 'Where are you going?'

" 'Pozoblanco.' "

"We took the car," Rubio continued. "No one showed any resistance. I sat behind the wheel, Riego was with me, and the rest were in the back with the driver, the medical assistant, and two orderlies. These are not tongues I decided, and we went on further toward Pozoblanco. We safely passed the control point near Villaharta."

"It was terrible," Riego put in. "At the control point the guard gave us the stop signal, but Rubio kept his head and gave a long blast of the horn and passed by. It's good that the column had already gone ahead of us."

"Before getting to Espiel," Rubio continued, "I turned west. The column, as the driver and the medical assistant confirmed, was going to Pozoblanco, and we went behind the lines. We drove about fifteen kilometers. We encountered solitary vehicles. It's obvious that partisans have not been on these roads, I thought, and decided to exchange our ambulance for a car. I parked the ambulance by the side of the road and waited. Now it was already easier to operate—I was not standing alone on the road to signal stop, I was next to a stopped ambulance. We let a pair of cars pass. They were not what we needed, and we couldn't immediately overpower two of them at once. At last, a solitary vehicle appeared, and our observer gave the blue signal. I went out on the road and stopped the car with a red light. The boys came up. Three Fascists didn't show any resistance. Then we drove on in two vehicles. We pulled off the side of the highway. We interrogated the passengers. We left them by the side of the road and went again on the highway."

"Before we got to Belmez," Riego began, "we had to ditch the captured vehicles in the Guaduamo River and take the day off in the Sierra de los Santos. There was plenty to eat. We rested peacefully on our day off. About three hours after nightfall, we approached the crossing guard near Belmez. At first he took us for Franco's rebels, but when Rubio took off his officer's raincoat, the guard and his wife gave us a surprised look and could not even say a word. 'Don't be afraid,' Rubio said, 'we are Republican intelligence agents.' When the guard was convinced that we were really who we said we were, he began to tell us everything we needed to know. Even his wife helped to explain where and with what cargo the trains were going, what kind of troops there were and where they were positioned, and the proper road procedure. We promised to stop in again on our return trip, but we became absorbed with the desire to go to Merida. Well, that didn't work out so we captured another pair of vehicles and drove around on the roads behind enemy lines. We talked to people, then came back."

"Well, how are the people doing?" Domingo asked.

"Worse than during the monarchy," Riego answered. "All the large estates are back in the hands of the landlords, and most of the peasants are wage laborers or tenants again. The rebels have turned the paradise 'country of olives'[1] into hell—large rent payments, taxes, low wages for heavy labor, and complete lack of rights—they can pick you up and torture you on the basis of denunciations."

[1]Andalusia has the largest plantations of olive trees in Spain.

"But the landlords and the leaders of the Falangists[2] are settled in far from the front lines," Rubio put in. "They have no confidence in their own troops."

"They mobilize and impress the mobilized from other regions," Riego continued. "The Falangists have many propagandists, especially among the clergy, and the landowners are afraid of losing their incomes. The Italian Fascists and the German National Socialists have even tried their hands at counterintelligence on Spanish soil. Because of that, we had to be careful. We went to populated areas only in the evening. By not hiding the fact that we were Republican intelligence agents, we learned everything we needed to know, and no one would take anything for provisions. Everyone was asking, 'When will they drive out the interventionists?' "

Riego paused and continued, "True, in Ornachueloz we ran into a fugitive priest. We knocked on the window of a small house on the outskirts. The light of a lamp showed through the shutter. 'Who's there?' a pretty confident and commanding voice called. 'Yours,' I answered. We exchanged greetings, and they opened the door for us. We went in and were stupefied. In the room was a Catholic priest and two armed men, clearly Falangists. It was good that we were wearing the raincoats of rebel officers. The conversation was brief. We were not prepared for a spiritual discussion. The meeting was a surprise for both sides."

"It was evident," Rubio said, "that the priest and his drinking buddies were not sure that we were who we said we were."

" 'We have no more wine, I'll run to the neighbors right away and bring a couple of bottles of great sherry,' one of the Falangists said.

" 'You can go later,' I answered. I drew my pistol and shouted, 'hands up!' The Falangists kept their heads and

---

[2] The Falange is the Spanish Fascist party.

raised their hands. We took their weapons and their documents, and they begged us not to kill them. But we couldn't take them with us, and the priest had to remain tied up. We asked him about the road to Palamos and went, of course, in the other direction."

The group seized several vehicles but brought back documents instead of captive tongues.

Rubio did not have time to get to Merida, nor was Ustaros's group able to make its way to Seville to find Rosalia's daughters.

The next day, Domingo's group and Rudolf took some dummy explosives and were supposed to drive in a few cars on a practical training exercise on a railroad bridge across the Guadalquivir River.

They worked at the exercises until late in the evening, then they said good-bye to the guard and left for Jaen. When they got to the crossing, they discovered that it was closed, and the signal was red, but they could neither see nor hear a train. The vehicles stopped. Suddenly the threatening cry *"Manos arriba!,"* hands up.

"What are you yelling about!" we answered from the car, "Don't you see we're on your side?"

There were shouts and curses, then about eight anarchists surrounded the car in which we were riding. They told us to get out and follow them to the station where the commander of an anarchist column was located. They did not take our arms, but we went under such a strong guard that any resistance was useless.

Domingo cursed the guards, saying that everything had been agreed to by the front headquarters, that the Russian partisan-engineer Rudolf worked with them.

We soon found ourselves in the office of the chief of the small way station. Inside the room, it was murky from tobacco smoke. Behind the table sat a short soldier with a

black-and-red bandanna, the collar of his blouse was unbut-
toned. Seeing us, the anarchist stood and without greeting
us, asked, "Who gave you permission for an exercise on the
bridge?"

"Front headquarters!" Domingo answered.

"No one can give permission without me. This bridge is
under my protection," the anarchist said angrily. Then pointing at me, he asked, "Where is this *señorita* from?"

"She's an interpreter for the Russian comrade—military
engineer—Louisa," Domingo answered quickly.

"Do you have documents?" the anarchist commander asked
the leader of the team which had brought us to the station.

"I don't know; I didn't check."

"There they are," I answered. I showed him my pass from
the headquarters of the southern front, which allowed me to
travel night or day in the front area.

The anarchist commander carefully read through the
pass, looked at it in the light, as if trying to detect in it a for-
gery and turning he said more politely, "Please be seated,
señorita!"

"Why and with whom were you shooting on the bridge?"
the anarchist asked Domingo.

"There were no shots of any kind. That was detonators
exploding."

The anarchist requested Rudolf's documents. After
carefully studying them, the commander asked, "You, Wolf—
you came from Germany?"

"No, from Poland!" Rudolf answered.

"But 'Wolf,' that is a purely German name!"

"It may be," Rudolf agreed, "but I don't even know German."

The duty officer finally called front headquarters, where
they reaffirmed that Domingo's group was permitted to conduct exercises on the bridge across the Guadalquivir.

"Everything is settled, but next time don't show up without my agreement and without my representative on the bridge," the commander of the anarchist column said in parting.

After that, we conducted practical exercises on the roads more carefully.

The Matador

There were many interesting people in Domingo Ungria's special battalion. Members of the international brigade fought in it who, it seemed, had come through fire and water on every continent. But the backbone of the battalion consisted of Spaniards. They quickly mastered the art of partisan warfare, the techniques and tactics of sabotage behind enemy lines. Among them, only Domingo was a military man. And even though he had achieved officer's rank, he could not stand to serve in the royal army and had emigrated to France where he worked in the Party underground.

The remaining soldiers were peaceful people before the rebellion, workers of almost all specialties, from common laborer to drivers, electricians, mechanics, builders, and miners, and among the latter, sappers. There were many peasants from Andalusia, Extremadura, Old and New Castile, and men from Valencia and Catalonia.

In Jaen, the former matador, Enrique Gomez, joined Domingo. He was an excellent soldier in the battalion at the battle of Granada. He was born, grew up, and worked in Navarre, where he became a matador. His parents had a large family but little land. Enrique was the oldest and had not yet learned to read and write when he went to work as a shepherd for a former matador who had been mutilated by a bull's horn in Pamplona at the end of the *fiesta*.[1] The herdsman loved to read and taught Gomez to read and write. Little Enrique fell in love with poems and stories about matadors. They grazed young bulls, and Enrique loved the strong, harsh-tempered animals.

"I hated matadors, picadors, and especially *banderilleros*,[2] who plunge the beautiful but painful *banderillas* into the animals," Enrique told us. "You know the poor little bulls have done nothing bad, but they torment them so."

Gomez touched a rib, which had healed, and continued, "But the former matador detected talent in me, and I finally went to work at *La Plaza de Toros*.[3] I helped the matador, I studied, and finally became one myself."

And the former matador waved his hand as the Spaniards do.

"But I loved and still love bulls, I was sorry for them; I knew their habits, I believed I would come out the victor, I escaped the sharp movements, and I spared my bulls for the final blow. I dealt it when the public wanted it. I knew how to work close to the horns of the bull; I would tire him, but not enervate him. When required, I even performed tricks. But as the critics wrote, 'He always worked precisely, easily, as if he has business not with an enraged bull but with a hornless cow.' "

Enrique again touched the broken ribs and continued, "At Pamplona exactly two years ago, at the *fiesta*, I had a little to drink, and decided to show the craftsmanship of the old school—accuracy of movement at the time of maximum risk. Everything was going perfectly, the bull was ready for the final blow, and he had done everything that I had asked of him. But just then, when the crowd silently followed my work and the behavior of the bull, among the spectators there was one of my enemies. He shouted with all his might,

[1] Holiday
[2] Participants in a bullfight who stick into the bull *banderillas* (metal lances) with small colored flags.
[3] The arena where bullfights take place.

'Fool! what are you doing?' Just for a second, my attention slackened. I felt pain in my left side. Warm blood flowed along my body, but I had enough strength to kill the bull. I fell alongside. Fortunately the bull broke only two ribs and didn't injure any internal organs."

"And you gave up your dangerous trade?" I asked.

"No! The public loved my work. They increased my salary—and I was already able to provide for my father's family and to travel on holiday with my younger sisters and brothers, who love to see the wide world. But February came, and the popular wave swept over me. I was not only a matador but also a propagandist. I read a great deal. I understood that the peasants and workers had no other way except the one the Communist party shows them. I went along this road.

"The rebellion found me in Seville, and I fought on the barricades, but the deceitful Moroccans and the rebels were victorious. After I saw the business of the rebel generals and officers, the savagery of the Falange, I could no longer kill bulls. Now I kill only those who raised the rebellion, who want to turn the people into slaves once again. I kill them without any pity. I came to Domingo's detachment because here it is not necessary to wait for an enemy attack or for an order to assume the offensive, we go behind rebel lines ourselves and blow up their trains and vehicles, and we hit them from ambush.

"An enemy train reminds me of the excited body of a bull or a fairy-tale dragon. But, instead of a blow of the sword, I pull the cord of a string fuse, and I see the bright flash, then hear the sound of the explosion and the hiss of falling debris. That takes the place of applause. I leave satisfied, knowing that one more train won't be arriving at the front."

"Enrique!" We heard Marquez call. "Come here!" The

matador excused himself and ran, his feet hardly touching the ground. Strength and dexterity are everywhere, I thought.

Gomez had a notebook with a portrait and verses of his favorite poet, Federico Garcia Lorca, who had been killed by the Fascists. In it were his notes about vehicles and trains he had destroyed.

Enrique Gomez was distinguished for his abilities as an intelligence agent and as a master of the capture or silencing of enemy sentries. In the detachment, he was nicknamed the Tiger of Navarre.

In his free time, the Tiger told stories about his work in the arena and about celebrated matadors.

"The success of a matador, his life," he said, "depends not only on his skill and the quality of the bulls but also on the spectators. Their shouts can spoil the mood, forcing you to repeat a trick!"

The former matador reflected for a moment and asked, "Louisa, have you seen a bullfight, and how did you like it?"

"Yes, once I watched, but not to the end. I couldn't bear it. My day was ruined."

It happened like this. Before our departure from Valencia to the southern front, Domingo got tickets to the *corrida* for the whole detachment. We left after breakfast, happy, orderly, and satisfied—with the exception of Rudolf, who had no stomach for the *corrida*.

The closer we got to *La Plaza de Toros* the larger the crowd became.

Along the street in a continuous stream, almost running, hurrying and passing each other, the noisy crowd went by us in the direction of the arena. Uneasy, excited by the unusual circumstances, thirsting for the spectacle, the people were very colorful in bright holiday dress.

All around us there were happy exclamations; joyous cries and greetings. The women's handsome faces gleamed, and they wore elegant hairdos. Bright, colorful contemporary dresses mixed with traditional costumes and their numerous wide ruffles. The women carried multicolored fans and wore airy shawls of lace, which fluttered as they walked quickly. Valuable earrings and necklaces reflected the sunlight. The men were dressed with taste; their serene suits and red ties standing out against the women's colorful dress.

In the air was the smell of expensive cigarettes and women's perfumes.

But here was the large, circular building of ticket offices. Over the small windows were signs, *"Sol, Sol!"* and *"Sombra, Sombra,"*[4] around which people thronged, hoping in vain to obtain a last-minute ticket. Domingo explained that, "Even in the past, there were not enough seats for the people of Valencia, and now there are many thousands of evacuees from Madrid and from cities occupied by the Fascists."

We flowed into the stream of humanity and slowly moved up to the entrance to the grandstand. Some of our group had thought to wear large, peaked hats in order not to be blinded by the sun. And, of course, everyone was in high spirits.

Suddenly abuse and noise were heard: some anarchists were attempting to force their way from the sunny side to the shade. But in vain; the crowd stood in defense of order, and the trespassers had to return to their own seats. Like most of the people, we showed up a long time before the start of the performance to make sure that we could occupy our seats. We sat not far from the aisle in the ninth row on concrete benches covered with dust. Foresighted Rosalia carefully spread a red kerchief on it.

---

[4]"Sun, Sun" and "Shade, Shade."

Finally, the stands were filling up. Music was playing. After the Republican hymn, they played revolutionary songs, and after them, *"La Cucaracha."* Then people in black-and-red neckties—more anarchists—began to occupy "free" places. Alongside the advertisements, everywhere there were slogans and appeals. Across the way from us *"No pasaran!"*[5] was painted in bright red letters.

Behind the barrier, the large clean sandy area, rolled flat and carefully swept, looked yellow.

The grandstand was already half full, the spectators had spread out, even in the aisles, and there were many soldiers in the audience as well as elderly men and women, young boys and girls, and even children. And all around us, the audience was buzzing, stirring, like a gigantic restless beehive.

On the opposite side in the passageway, the matadors' assistants appeared with baskets on their shoulders. Near the barrier, they unrolled the crimson *muletas* and put them on sticks, preparing them to be used.

All eyes turned to the entrance to the arena. The tension with which the people await the matador became obvious.

Finally the orchestra played the march for which everyone was waiting. The applause resounded, and the matadors appeared in the arena. Behind them, three men carried crimson cloths. Behind them, on lean ponies, were picadors with long lances, and farther still, a team of mules and attendants, whose duty was to clean up the dead animals.

The audience buzzed loudly, shouting out the names of the favorite matadors, who occasionally gave a measured bow toward their admirers. There were three of them.

The first, a rangy man, strong in appearance, seemed very young. He had on a short black velvet sleeveless jacket

[5]They shall not pass!

with a white vest and also short black trousers. He wore slippers on his feet and high gaiters. On his head was a black beret.

The matador was clearly nervous. He appeared tired and significantly older than the other two.

Domingo told me his name and surname, adding, "He used to be a celebrity, but he had bad luck. He barely survived."

The orchestra continued to play. For a moment, everything became quiet. They let the bull into the arena. From a distance, he seemed a small, lean little bull. The animal looked around, puzzled at the colorful crowd, at the orchestra, and the man with the crimson cloth. He did not want to attack anyone, but in his neck they stuck a red *banderilla,* and then another and a third. It's hard to imagine what unbearable pain they must have caused him. He shook his head, attempting to shake himself free of the agonizing shafts, but the movement just made the *banderillas* hurt him more. He was beside himself, and they teased him with the red cloths, bright like the patches of blood on the black coat of the little bull.

Finally the enraged martyr threw himself at his torturer, who jumped aside and stuck yet another *banderilla* into the neck of the poor animal.

Out of his mind from the pain, the bull attacked his inquisitor again . . . and again received a new *banderilla.*

If the bull had been rubber, then all the colorful shafts might only be decoration, but the bull was alive, and it suffered inconceivable torment. Finally, he threw himself once more at the matador who, with a deft thrust of the sword to the skull, killed his victim. Thunderous applause resounded and flowers were thrown into the arena. The matador bowed, and the workers dragged the dead bull from the arena with the team of mules. Then, as the orchestra played, a single cloud in the clear sky covered the sun.

"This is bad! Very bad!" Domingo said. "When the sun doesn't shine the *corrida* is ruined. The sun inspires the matador and calms the audience."

"Yes," Rosalia said. "Without the sun, you can play football, but there can't be a good *corrida* without the sun; even the spectators become gloomy.

So this is a *corrida!* I thought. A bullfight is not an entertainment but a terrible spectacle.

In many places, we had seen good but poorly dressed little boys playing *toreador* for hours, teasing not bulls but other little boys, who held in front of themselves a wooden bull's head on a stick.

"The profession of *toreador* in Spain is a romantic and dangerous one," Enrique said. "Only a few lucky ones manage to make a career of it, to become famous. Every year, dozens, maybe even hundreds of *toreadores,* die or are crippled; only a handful attain glory like movie stars in Hollywood or France."

Rudolf and I went outside as the spectators yelled and whistled.

In reality *corrida* was not a "fight" but the "murder" of bulls after agonizing torture.

After dinner, we went out into the city to a cafe, where we sat in the shade in wicker chairs. Lovers put money into the jukebox, and music was heard. The war went on; little boys were selling newspapers, shouting out the latest news. Along with reports from the fronts, they cried out about the death of a matador.

"Religion and bullfights are opium for the people," Marquez observed.

The former matador said, "Instead of waving a red *muleta,* it is much more pleasant to wave the red light of a lantern to stop a carful of rebels, to show it where it must park, and having put a hand on the hood, to request that they turn on a light and present their documents."

* * *

Domingo's unit had a mounted platoon, and in his free time, Enrique Gomez sometimes went there to display his horsemanship, but he refused to transfer to the cavalry.

"I have been a *picador.* I saw how the bull stuck horns in these unlucky animals; I always felt sorry for these poor, innocent steeds. I did not join to work as a *picador.* Besides, in our business, mines are needed to blow up trains, not horses."

Once the group commanded by Enrique Gomez returned from a mission with two beautiful cavalry horses. Gomez rode on one, and on the other they carried Jimenez, a wounded demolitions man.

"A cavalry patrol ran into our ambush," Gomez reported to Marquez. "We destroyed it, and these horses came over to our side, they didn't run away."

Gomez gave the horses to the mounted platoon, but he continued sorties as a foot soldier.

Andujar Tragedy

In March 1937, the enemy conducted an offensive on the southern front, attempting to capture an important crossroads, the city of Pozoblanco.

One warm, sunny March day, as we drove from Jaen to our base in Villa Nueva de Cordoba through a stream of refugees, we came out on the Linares–Andujar road. Suddenly we heard muffled explosions, and soon, we could see Italian airplanes in the clear sky. Two or three minutes later, we heard several powerful explosions, and in front of us, a growing cloud of dust rose over the city.

When we arrived in Andujar[1], which we could not go around on our trip from Jaen to Villa Nueva de Cordoba, the town was unrecognizable. Only ruins remained of many of the old buildings. The streets were littered with piles of bricks and stones, and gaping craters made travel difficult. Mothers screamed desperately searching for their children, and children were crying because they had lost their parents. Next to a dead peasant lay a severely wounded donkey, which tried to stand but kept slipping in its own blood.

Near a half-destroyed two-story house people with crowbars, shovels, and homemade levers were trying to clear rubble; from the ruins of the house, the weeping of a child

[1]A small town seventy kilometers east of Cordoba, on the north bank of the Guadalquivir, famous for the manufacture of pots.

could be heard and, from time to time, the heart-rending screams and moans of a woman.

Finally Jimenez, secretary of the Andujar Committee of the Communist party, shouted "That's enough!" He was covered with dust, and with a shove, he was going into the opening that had been cleared in the rubble. Everyone waited anxiously.

Suddenly the moans and lamentations under the ruins stopped, and from the narrow opening between the stones, Jimenez held out a sobbing boy, three or four years old. Then, from behind the child, an old woman appeared. She was crying.

Last to leave was the filthy Jimenez. "Help me carry out the child's mother," he said in a strained voice. "She's dead."

I was working at an improvised first-aid post with a very limited number of medical staff. They brought us the severely wounded who often were in need of complex operations; they also brought us those for whom a bandage was sufficient.

The doctors, their assistants, and the nurses worked tirelessly, selflessly, and under a great deal of pressure, but there were not enough of them, and many of the wounded had to wait a long time for their turn. I remember one ten- or twelve-year-old boy, both of whose legs were broken below the knee. His face was deathly pale, his forehead sweating. He had lost a lot of blood and needed a transfusion quickly, but he did not complain about the pain, just called for his mother, not knowing that she was dead.

It is difficult to describe all the horrors we encountered in the hastily organized field hospital that filled with wounded during the air raids of the enemy air force.

Many were left crippled, without arms, without legs. They carried many away covered with white sheets.

After a couple of hours, first aid had been given to all those who needed it.

For a long time after everything I had seen and lived through that day, I could not calm down. It was hard to recall the unfortunate, maimed people, but even harder to recall the children mutilated for life or orphaned!

For two hours, our car carried the wounded and the dead. The driver of Rudolf's car, Vicente, made five trips. During the same time, Pepe transported eight severely wounded children and women to the hospital. Two of the children died.

Meeting in Pozoblanco

In March 1937, the enemy managed to come close to Pozoblanco.

"Louisa! Please come with me to the commander," Kolman said to me, "I need to discuss a very important matter with him that I cannot do with my guard." He sometimes called his interpreters, his "guard."

"But Rudolf and Domingo aren't here, and I'm in charge of everything."

"I'll take full responsibility. Get ready; I'll come by in ten minutes," Kolman answered decisively.

And so we went to the headquarters of the front. The guardsman sat next to the driver and the colonel and I in the back seat.

In Andujar, Perez Salas was not at headquarters. Kolman and I went to see some officers we knew in the headquarters and began to discuss the military situation.

"The situation is very difficult," one of the officers observed, "the commander is in Pozoblanco. As far as we know, he has decided to abandon the city. Almost all of the population has already been evacuated."

"But in Jaen they are mobilizing all transport, and in the morning, reserves will arrive in Pozoblanco"—I was translating Kolman's words—"The capture of Pozoblanco by the rebels puts an important crossroads at their disposal and opens the way to the mines, mercury, tin, lead, and other minerals that are so necessary to the Republic." Kolman was addressing the chief of staff.

"We know all that, but we are threatened with encirclement, and the enemy has a definite superiority of strength," the chief of staff answered.

"Maybe we should report to the commander by teletype that reinforcements will arrive in the morning," Kolman suggested.

"It would be a waste of time! We have already reported. The commander decided to abandon Pozoblanco, and it's useless to try to speak to him about this question," the chief of staff added sadly.

Although he knew Perez Salas's stubbornness, Kolman decided to go to Pozoblanco.

"Let's go, Louisa. We will try to convince him that reinforcements will come tomorrow morning and that we must hold the city until their arrival."

Kolman's tireless, always happy driver, Emilio, confidently drove the car that night along the mountain road through the stream of refugees from Pozoblanco.

Suddenly the car stopped. In front of us stood a stubborn donkey, two large baskets hanging from his sides with a child in each one. The donkey did not want to turn, the children were crying. Their mother had tears in her eyes.

Cows were lowing, sheep bleating, the people plodding along dejectedly. It was sad and painful to watch the people, who had abandoned everything where they had lived until the invasion of the rebels. They left their shelter, their goods, everything, and trying to save themselves, they walked far away into the unknown behind the lines of the Republican forces. At least the refugees were well received everywhere. People shared everything with them. I saw that frequently in Valencia, Murcia, in Jaen, and Linares.

We arrived in Pozoblanco late at night. The half destroyed and deserted city was completely dark. Not very far to the west, machine-gun fire disturbed the night silence.

It was not easy to find the commander in the deserted city. We eventually located the headquarters of one of the battalions in a half-basement of a two-story stone building. Near the headquarters, several cars and a truck were parked. Fortunately, one of the officers inside recognized Colonel Kolman and assigned us a soldier who knew where the commander was. As we were about to leave, they brought two rebel prisoners under guard into the headquarters. Even though Colonel Kolman was in a hurry to get to Perez Salas, he could not resist the temptation to interrogate the prisoners quickly. "It is very important to clarify the situation behind enemy lines before my discussion with the commander," he said. I translated his request.

"Please go ahead," the officer, whom we knew, politely answered.

We began the interrogation. The first prisoner had a tired and frightened look. His uniform was dirty and torn, his face covered with black bristles. He was illiterate, and I had considerable difficulty in conducting the interrogation. Kolman wanted to know as completely and exactly as possible the number, personnel, arms, positions, and mood of the enemy soldiers.

We often had to ask further questions to clarify the prisoner's answers. Kolman was nervous, he was looking at his watch.

"That's probably enough," I said finally, "we'll learn nothing more from him."

The adviser agreed. The first prisoner was led out, the second brought in. He was either a corporal or a junior officer, and he answered our questions confidently and clearly had knowledge of the situation. He pointed out on a map the position of subunits and supply depots. Like the first prisoner, he emphasized that he hated the Fascists, especially the arrogant Germans. Kolman was satisfied with these statements.

"Well, now let's go see Perez Salas," he said when the interrogation was finished.

"The enemy is exhausted by the fighting, the offensive surge of his forces at Pozoblanco has already long ago run short," Wilhelm Ivanovich said. "In the morning, reinforcements will arrive, so we've got to convince Perez Salas to hold the city until their arrival. It's most important that we not immediately get a negative answer. The colonel is stubborn, and that's why we'll begin from afar."

Walking around the ruins, we went into a building with a cupola. It must have been a monastery or a Catholic church. Inside, one small electric light bulb burned dimly in a large hall. Fifteen or twenty wounded soldiers and Republican officers lay on stretchers and cots. A few of them moaned softly. The stuffy air was saturated with the smell of blood and medicine. They led us across the hall to the commander's office, where we found him sitting by the fireplace. Somewhat indifferently, he stood and came to meet us. "*Señorita!* It's dangerous to come here so late," he said as he let go of my hand. When he was greeting Kolman, Perez Salas's smile became an expression of indifference.

Wilhelm Ivanovich felt the cold reception and could not decide whether to speak to the heart of the matter. "Louisa, help me," he whispered as they brought coffee. After sipping from it, I moved closer to the fireplace, took the iron pivot used as a poker, and adjusting the flue, said, "I love to sit by the fireplace! This, *Señor* Colonel, reminds me of a Nenets' fire in a *chum,* a tent made of poles and deerskins with an opening on top to allow the smoke out."

"What kind of people are the Nenets?" the commander asked. His attitude had become more lively.

I told him. Then we spoke about the theater, about literature. Kolman told us about Latvia, and I talked about Leningrad and again about the north. We drank more coffee and time passed. Listening to our stories, Col. Perez Salas warmed up a bit. During a pause he observed, "*Señora* Louisa, you speak such good literary language, as if you lived a long time in Spain. Where did you master Spanish?"

"I studied at the Institute, worked as an interpreter, and read Spanish literature."

"Well done! You see your knowledge has proved to be useful." Perez Salas smiled mysteriously and continued, "How ignorant I was when I thought only polar bears and bearded men live in Russia. It turns out that there are also beautiful girls there. It's amusing that they learn foreign languages in the big cities and then live in the capital."

Well, I thought, the ice is broken.

Seizing the moment as he began to add a log to the fire, I whispered to Kolman, "Let's try it."

Wilhelm Ivanovich understood. He began to speak.

The conversation was conducted as if we were at home. Perez Salas heard Kolman out then asked, "Can you guarantee that reinforcements will arrive tomorrow?"

"They will come without fail. In Jaen, they are gathering all available transport," Kolman answered.

To my surprise, Perez Salas agreed not to abandon Pozoblanco, and in our presence, he issued the order to hold the city at all costs.

We sat talking with the commander until morning. The night was troubled and dark and from the neighboring hall, the sounds of the wounded could occasionally be heard. The telephone rang often, officers came with reports.

When we finally left the commander, Kolman thanked me repeatedly, then said, "Now it is probably clear to you that you must transfer to me for good. Very often I can't do anything with my interpreters when I have to speak with the commander—and not only with him but with his chief of staff as well."

"It doesn't have anything to do with me, the colonel believed that reinforcements will arrive in the morning without fail."

Silently we walked to the car.

"Emilio! *Vamos* to Jaen!" Kolman said, waking the driver.

Emilio yawned and stretched for a few minutes, then sat behind the wheel. Suddenly, we heard the heartrending rumble of approaching enemy aircraft.

"It's a little early!" Emilio said, starting the engine.

But we did not have time to leave before the bombing began. The sound of a powerful explosion came from behind the house that stood across from the headquarters. The car shook. About ten meters away, a large piece of tile roof fell and broke into pieces, and fragments ricocheted from the hood of the car.

Six planes bombed from a low altitude with impunity, then flew away.

We were lucky. The bombs fell all around us, but our car was not damaged, except for a few dents in the hood. During the bombing, we stayed in the car and afterward went to see Perez Salas.

"The commander already knows that the reinforcements have passed through Villa Nueva de Cordoba," the officer on duty told us.

About thirty minutes later, the reinforcements arrived.

"Very good! Just in time!" Perez Salas said, after listening to the report of the dusty, sleepy, but satisfied battalion commander.

"Just in time!" Kolman affirmed, greeting Valenzuela. "An hour earlier, they would have come under the bombing; any later and the commander would have changed his order about holding the city."

Just then in front of the headquarters, we heard horns honking.

"Something else happen?" Kolman asked.

I didn't have time to ask before an officer popped into the room and shouted happily, "One of ours knocked down an Italian plane; we captured the pilot and brought him here."

The young, well-fed, clean-shaven pilot was pale and clearly frightened. He reminded me of the insolent young Germans we had met at dinner in Paris before our departure. The restaurant we'd eaten in was not far from the Soviet embassy. The Germans who sat down at the neighboring table evidently understood a little bit of Russian. They were going to Spain and took Porokhnyak and the tank officer, Pavel, for pilots, too, recommending to them that they go back home.

We began to interrogate the prisoner. He understood Spanish very well, but answered in a mixture of Italian and Spanish, and I did not understand it all. His unit was stationed near Cordoba.

"Russian planes are better," he finally said, then he added, "and devils fly them!"

During those difficult March days, Pozoblanco held. The enemy was thrown out of the city, and Domingo's detachment performed well; its groups captured prisoners and obtained important intelligence data, derailed enemy trains, and blew up vehicles, disrupting work behind enemy lines and forcing the rebels to waste their strength and resources protecting their communications.

The members of the international brigades—the Yugoslavs, Czechoslovaks, Poles, Finns, Italians, Hungarians—played a large role in Domingo's detachment. But Germans, Austrians, and Russian emigres did not work out for us. Germans had little success behind enemy lines. Hardened in the class struggle, they arrived in Spain to fight against the Fascists. I had heard that they fought well at the front. They studied well, but they did not learn how to work well in small groups behind enemy lines; they fell into ambushes and ran into enemy patrols. One of them blew off two fingers with an electrical detonator.

As a result of this, Rudolf consulted with Domingo and they decided to honor the German comrades' request, taking them back to Albacete. The Austrians, who were young but ill-suited for action behind enemy lines, also asked to go back to their brigade.

The tall, lean, and very strong Finns proved to be fearless saboteurs, mastering techniques and tactics. They were excellent at orienting themselves in unknown areas without compass or map. The Spanish comrades said the Finns were like fish in water when they were behind enemy lines.

"Very courageous and intelligent saboteurs!" Marquez said about them. They had made sorties against the rebel lines of communication with him.

After returning from the rear and getting their hands on some money, the Finns were transformed. They drank a lot, made a lot of noise, or disappeared to no one knows where. Because they did not know Spanish, they were often arrested when drunk.

Rudolf talked to them more than once, saying that if they could not do without alcohol, they should just get drunk and go to sleep. They'd agree. But after the next routine raid behind rebel lines, they'd get drunk again and make a row.

"Outstanding fighters!" Juan Grande said about the Finns, "but they know no limits when it comes to drinking." We finally had to let them go.

Yugoslavs, Poles, Hungarians, Italians, and Slovaks all operated calmly and confidently behind Fascist lines.

We also had three Russian emigrants, Alexander, Fyodor, and Mikhail, two of whom were tall, one short. All of them reported to us in the uniform of the international brigades.

Even though they spoke French well and soon could speak not badly with the Spaniards, Rudolf never took them with him. They seemed to me to be most unfortunate men. They were taken from Russia when they were young children, not because their parents were not rich but because they had served in the Tsarist army.

"They got into the White Army because they had little class consciousness, and on account of complete stupidity, they fled Russia," said Mikhail, the short one.

"We had our share of trouble there in France. French workers look down on us, they call us Whites, but what kind of Whites can we be, when the only wealth we have is our hands? And on top of that, the princes and barons among the emigrants try to involve us in their political schemes."

"We want to go back to our motherland so much that we decided to come to Spain and fight to prove that we are not Whites but real Reds," Alexander said.

The third one, Fyodor, had received a higher education in France but was forced to be a worker. "There's just not enough work," he complained. "I tried to set up my own business, I invested all of my savings, went into debt, and got burned. So I went to work as a longshoreman, then as a crane operator. I see a Soviet ship in port, and my heart fills up, that's how much I wanted to be in Russia. The motherland pulls me," he said, "but you have to prove that you're not a White."

So they fought against the rebels and their German and Italian allies. They fought desperately to win trust and receive permission to return to the motherland. Fyodor and Alexander died in Spain, but I don't know what happened to Mikhail.

Even Living Next to a Convent Didn't Help

After a night of rain, a warm sunny day was especially pleasant. Everything was going well. The adult population of Jaen worked, the children studied or played, each one worked at their own place. Sastre, Rosalina, and other Spanish comrades were finishing up a regular batch of mines in the kitchen when suddenly there was a loud explosion. We didn't understand right away what was going on, since there hadn't been an air raid warning. As it turned out, enemy aircraft had suddenly flown from behind the mountains and begun to bomb the city from low altitude. That was so unexpected that we did not have time to turn off the kerosene stove on which we'd been heating pitch. When one of the bombs landed on the building next door, our house shuddered, the wall cracked from the shaking, the kerosene stove fell on the floor, and before we could come to our senses, the floor was in flames and a hot mixture of kerosene and pitch was flowing along the corridor, which had bedrooms off both sides. In two rooms the situation was extremely dangerous because we kept crates of dynamite under the beds. The apartment filled with smoke. Not knowing what to do, Rosalina wailed desperately, but the efficient Sastre grabbed a pot and ran to the faucet. No water! The rest rushed about in fright, not knowing what to do.

"Get blankets and cover the fire with them," I shouted in

a voice that was not my own. I had two boxes of explosives under my bed. One of the men ran up with a fire extinguisher, but it did not work. Even so, after a few minutes, all of the blankets we had in the apartment were on the floor, pungent smoke seeping through them, but the fire was out. Then we put out the smoldering hot spots one after another. And all that time, the bombing continued, but at least the bombs were falling somewhere else.

In the apartment, it was dark from smoke and dust, and outside, we could hear the explosions of the bombs and the roar of the airplanes. We did not know what to do, and could not decide whether to abandon the house.

When the bombing ended and the dust settled, we saw ruined buildings, gaping craters, glass and broken bricks on the roadway, fallen poles, tangled wires, dead and wounded people, and mules. Only the convent was completely whole.

Leaving Rosalina alone in the room, we ran over to the building of our partisan school. It was intact. I immediately went with the assistant of the man on duty to the Party Provincial Committee.

Committee secretary Valenzuela sent all the school staff to the area of greatest destruction, where beautiful buildings, which had stood for hundreds of years, had been reduced to rubble. From underneath the rubble we heard heartrending moans and the cries of the seriously wounded. Those we could locate, we pulled out from under the ruins and gave first aid.

The personnel of the special battalion displayed resourcefulness, courage, and valor while burrowing in the ruins to rescue the victims and to render first aid. Ignoring the possibility of a second attack, the local people also worked selflessly, and before nightfall, all of the most urgent tasks were done.

Domingo and Rudolf were, of course, not there. There never seemed to be bombings when they were around.

Even though not a single bomb had landed on one of our buildings, I decided that it would be best to take the explosives and mines out of the city. We spent the night in an olive grove. In the morning, the sun came out, and it became hot as it usually is in Andalusia in the spring, and we returned to the city. We cleaned up the kitchen and put everything back in order. The water supply had been restored by then, so Sastre and his assistants began to assemble mines.

The next day, Valenzuela came to see us at the school. He'd had a sleepless night so he had dark yellow patches under his eyes, but he was composed as usual. "Louisa, I never expected that we would complete our rescue work so quickly." He wiped the sweat from his face and continued, "Extraordinary people! They all worked!"

The workers of the Provincial Party Committee were often guests at our school, and we owed a good deal of our success to their very active participation and help. Everything that could be obtained in the province, the school had in sufficient quantity. And materials that could not be found in Jaen, we received from other cities with the assistance of the Provincial Party Committee.

Unforgettable Meetings

One day in March 1937, Colonel Kolman called me. "Louisa, come over here right away! The top brass have come from Valencia."

"Hello, Louisa!" the man who came out to meet me said in greeting. Wearing a zippered Spanish jacket, he was an imposing and obviously military man with a fine-featured face. "I'm happy to give you the good news, they have recommended you for a second order, the Order of the Red Banner."

"I serve the Soviet Union," I answered.

"Well, now let's wash up!" suggested Kolman and led us into the room, where Conchita had set a beautiful table.

The chief who had come, "Comrade Grigorovich," who was G. M. Shtern, conducted himself so that everyone felt free in his presence as if among good friends.

"But why are they awarding me a second order, and Rudolf Wolf has none? You know he's done so many things that you just cannot leave him without an award."

"They also recommended him, and you can tell him that. I am very sorry that he is not in Jaen because I have heard a lot about him but have never seen him."

We raised a toast to the motherland, for the quick and complete defeat of the rebels and Fascist interventionists. Then, unexpectedly Grigorovich asked me, "Louisa, what do you think of the possibility of your translating for Colonel Kolman? You know how hard it is for him. Rudolf can get around even without interpreters."

The prospect of the transfer tempted me; I liked to work with the energetic and very attractive Colonel Kolman, but I could not imagine my being in Spain outside the collective of partisan saboteurs, and they were used to me. I was taken aback and said nothing.

"New work doesn't suit you?" Grigorovich asked, watching me kindly.

"I didn't expect this. I am so accustomed to my fighting friends that I can't imagine parting with them. Please leave me with the detachment, and when it is really necessary, I will go with Colonel Kolman as his interpreter," I answered, surprising myself with my courage.

"You have problems with your staff, Comrade Kolman," Shtern noted. "Up until now you haven't been able to get Louisa to work for you."

"I understand you," Grigorii Mikhailovich said, turning to me. "I am in complete agreement with you. It's good that you are so attached to your collective. Well, we will honor your request, and won't tear you away from the partisans, but when your help is really needed by Wilhelm Ivanovich, you will help him!"

I clearly saw the hurt face of Colonel Kolman, but I was happy that I would not be reassigned. We sat and talked for a long time. Grigorii Mikhailovich summarized the international situation for us, then the situation in Spain.

Finally Grigorovich proposed a toast, "For those who, disregarding their own life, repel the enemy! The motherland will not forget those who fought against fascism in Spain. On January first, seventeen Soviet pilots and tank of-

ficers were awarded the highest recognition, Hero of the Soviet Union, for courage shown in the defense of Madrid. Together with a detachment of people's militia, soldiers of the
Republican Army and of the international brigades defended
Madrid against the interventionists and reactionaries. We
still have much fighting ahead of us, but we look bravely to
the future.

"The flower of the proletariate fights in the international
brigades. Many have perished in battle against the Fascists,
but their service is great, and the Spanish people will not
forget their sacrifice, nor will the workers of all the world."

Saying good-bye, General Grigorovich once again con-
gratulated me on the forthcoming award. Then he said,
"There are less than eight months until the celebration of the
twentieth anniversary of the Great October Revolution. We
hope that by that time the rebels will be defeated and we
will get together to celebrate this important date under more
festive circumstances."

But his wishes, unfortunately, were not realized. The defeat of the Fascists and interventionists did not work out.

Soon after Grigorovich's departure from Jaen, Rudolf
told me that Tumanyan and Ksanti (Khadzhi Mamsurov—
the senior adviser on partisan warfare) were coming for a
few days. We had been expecting Ksanti for a long time, but
the fact that Tumanyan was coming with him was news to
us. We didn't even know that he was in Spain.

During his stay in Madrid, Domingo Ungria had met
with Ksanti and gave him Rudolf's detailed report on the
work that we had done on the southern front. Ksanti supported the proposal for the creation of a special battalion
and did everything he could to help the captain.

When he came back from Madrid, Domingo was delighted
with Ksanti. "A very good comrade! Attentive, calm, and he

understands this business because he's been behind enemy lines many times." Domingo was delighted.

By that time, Ksanti's military deeds were already well known. Besides his direct participation in the defense of Madrid, he had headed a detachment in sorties behind enemy lines. Ksanti directed the majority of partisan detachments and special groups, among which was our detachment, later a special battalion.

Ksanti sent several comrades to Domingo's detachment for an exchange of experience; among them was the Yugoslav Toma Chachich, a brave, disciplined, and charming comrade.

In fact Ksanti did visit Domingo's battalion soon with G. L. Tumanyan, who had sent me and Rudolf to Spain.

G. L. Tumanyan and Khadzhi Mamsurov familiarized themselves with the battalion's training, affairs, and personnel. They inspected the workshop/laboratory where we made mines and hand grenades, approving both the workshop and the workmen.

They also wanted to visit the base northwest of Adamuz, and to my surprise, neither Rudolf nor Domingo tried to talk them out of it. So, after visiting the battalion base in Villa Nueva de Cordoba, they made the trip with Jan Tikhii and Ivan Krbovanets along as interpreters. I stayed at the lighthouse with a small group to assure the safety of our guests' return from behind enemy lines.

To the relief of those who were left at the lighthouse, after inspecting the secret base, G. L. Tumanyan and Kh. Mamsurov returned the next morning, tired but satisfied with what they had seen.

By the time of my meeting with Ksanti, I knew a great deal about him from the stories of those who had gone behind enemy lines with him. Khadzhi Dzhuorovich never said anything about his own military deeds, but he said a lot about the coura-geous defenders of Madrid, about the boldness and initiative of those who completed important military missions under difficult circumstances. They said that Ksanti had a sharp ear and knew how to get his bearings quickly in the difficult con-ditions behind enemy lines. Members of Domingo Ungria's detachment were also convinced of this when they went be-hind rebel lines to the base near Cordoba with Mamsurov and Tumanyan. Domingo's little Antonio was especially delighted by Mamsurov's arrival. He was fascinated not only that Ksanti knew how to ride a horse but how the horse obeyed him—now carrying the horseman like the wind, now prancing calmly.

In the middle of May, I had met with Ksanti for the sec-ond time, in Valencia. He had just returned from Barcelona, where he had gone with Rudolf. Soon after their arrival there had been an anarchist putsch in Barcelona. They left when the Republican troops had gained control of the situa-tion in the city and the rebels' hopes for anarchist assistance were not realized, but on the streets there were still separate hot spots of resistance by anarchist bands.

Magnetic Mines

After returning from the mission to the secret base northwest of Adamuz, Ksanti said to Rudolf, "You make many kinds of mines but there's one that you don't have, a mine that can be quickly placed on a fuel tank, an airplane, or a locomotive and which will stick to the target to be destroyed."

"Yes," Rudolf said, "that is more difficult, and we really have no such thing."

"You know mines like that are needed very much," Gai Lazarevich said. "Try to make them."

The Provincial Committee had people capable of penetrating the railroad stations and even the airfields of the enemy, but neither they nor our school had the necessary means to make possible the destruction of material resources and putting airplanes, locomotives, and fuel tanks out of action without being detected or without leaving any trail. Mines which could be stuck to targets, could be set quickly, and which would not fall off during movement, were something we really needed.

Even Sastre, always a happy master of invention, lost sleep over this. We conducted many experiments and tried all kinds of sticky chemical substances, but we were disappointed. We tried concocting new ones, but with no more success. I don't remember now who first suggested using magnets. We managed to get them from the schools.

I remember the joy of the workers in the workshop when they saw how the little magnets held the charge the saboteurs needed. We had many kinds of delayed-action fuses that were suitable for use in magnetic mines, and could delay detonation from a few minutes to several hours. But in all of Jaen, we had only enough magnets for a couple of dozen mines. So Sastre suggested we ask the committee to obtain more for us.

Comrade Aroca, the secretary of the Party Provincial Committee, listened to Sastre's request and came to the workshop himself. After examining a homemade mine, he stuck it to a metal cupboard, took it off and looked at Sastre and then at Domingo, and said, "Remarkable! We will get magnets, and not like these—better ones!"

He immediately wrote a letter to Barcelona and, after a week, brought the first large batch of magnets from Catalonia. They were smaller than the ones we'd gotten from the school but significantly stronger. Two of them could reliably hold a mine with a charge of four kilograms.

In 1942 in the USSR, at the Higher Operations School for Special Tasks, where del Castillo and Domingo were, small English magnetic mines appeared.

"Swindlers! Why are they called *English*?" said Domingo indignantly as he examined their fine construction. "These are just an improved variation of our Jaen magnetic mine."

Later, during World War II and the partisan struggle against the Nazi armies on the territory of the Soviet Union, our Spanish comrades encountered metal PV-42 "frogs," which were also mass produced by the English. "Ours was better, safer and more reliable even though it was larger in size," they said. Those who used it first in Spain had a reason to be proud.

Thus, at the initiative of Ksanti, Tumanyan, and the Party Provincial Committee, one of the problems of increasing the strength of our strikes was solved. With the aid of magnetic mines, many fuel tanks, railroad cars, and locomotives were destroyed, and during World War II many airplanes and trains with fuel and lubricants, ammunition, and enemy troops were destroyed by them. Those mines were used by partisans and members of the underground in all of the countries occupied by the enemy. And the first of those they used in far-off Spain.

Hornets' Nest

Not far from Andujar, on a high mountain behind Republican lines, was the monastery *La Virgen de la Cabeza* ("The Monastery of the Head of the Virgin"). While retreating at the end of 1936, rebels occupied it—police and their families—and they often conducted daring sorties from it. The few Republican attempts to eliminate that hornets' nest had not been crowned with success; thick walls, solid vaults, and the hard to cross, open approaches assured the garrison a reliable defense. Artillery barrages, bombing from the air, and attempts to take the monastery by storm had not brought the desired results. Ammunition, arms, and provisions were dropped to the rebel garrison by Fascist planes, but sometimes the resupply fell on the positions of the Republican troops.

During the preparations for a new storming of the monastery, I had to go with Rudolf and later also with Kolman to the command post of the battalion that besieged the monastery stronghold. The first time, when Rudolf, Domingo, Sastre, and I went, a traffic controller stopped us and warned us it was dangerous to continue by car since the area was exposed to enemy fire, and it was better to walk about a kilometer a little below the road.

"But they're driving on the road!" Rudolf said, pointing at the tracks of a car that had passed not long before.

"There are those who drive and those who abandon their

cars and go on foot. About three days ago the Fascists hit a Fiat, and we managed to drag it out only after dark. If they had spotlights in the monastery, we wouldn't be able to pass even at night," the talkative traffic controller said. Even so, Domingo, Rudolf, and Sastre decided to rely on their Ford.

Quickly picking up speed, Pepe drove his Ford into the dangerous sector of the road. The rebels remained silent. About one and a half kilometers of open space separated us from the monastery. When we had crossed more than halfway, I was horrified to see little puffs of dust kick up in front of us on the monastery's side of the road. Pepe also saw them, but he squeezed to the opposite edge of the road as he continued to drive at high speed. When he'd left the dangerous ground behind, Pepe stopped, wiped the sweat from his forehead and said in a tired voice, "We made it!"

The battalion commander, a smart, elderly captain, already knew the reason for the visit by Domingo and Rudolf, and he met us warmly.

"I'm sick of this hornets' nest! I can't do anything with my battalion. The rascals are on the mountain, and you can't go any closer, and at night they conduct forays, they hunt for sheep," the battalion commander complained.

"Why, for what?" Rudolf asked.

"For sheep, they have problems with their food."

"Well, well," Rudolf said. Clearly he was thinking of something. "Can we get a closer look at this lair?"

"We might, but the forward observation post is almost a kilometer away."

It took us about twenty minutes to get to it, bending low in the trenches in places, and behind a rocky ridge. Through the binoculars the monastery seemed very close. The marks of the shells that had fallen on the walls, the cave-ins made by the aerial bombardment, and the gun ports were visible in the walls. Gilded crosses shone in the sun.

"Hornets' nest, and we can't smoke them out! There is nothing! If we could bring up a good charge of dynamite, we could blow it up," I translated the battalion commander's words when he finished his examination of the monastery.

"Unfortunately, that option is very difficult," Rudolf noted, and Domingo agreed with him.

"You mean your demolitions men are powerless, too?" the battalion commander asked with bitterness and obvious disappointment.

"Why powerless? Give me a moment to think," Rudolf answered.

We returned to the command post in silence and began to get ready for the road.

"You will have to wait until dinner. In the monastery, they are already expecting your car. These snakes also have outstanding marksmen, but they won't shoot during dinner because they are occupied with their meal," the battalion commander said.

"It's still a long time until dinner, but we can slip out, that's for sure," said Rudolf. "Look! Pepe has already re-painted the car the color of the road." Rudolf pointed at the Ford, where a satisfied Pepe continued to paint.

We said good-bye, and Pepe drove the car along the dangerous sector. It felt like at any moment they would cut us down from the monastery. Pepe also seemed to be thinking about this, increasing speed until he was finally at full throttle. The monastery remained silent.

At the traffic control point, the controller stopped us, then said with surprise, "Forgive me! I didn't recognize you. I was wondering where this car came from."

*   *   *

After a few days, Kolman also planned to go to the command post of the battalion that was besieging the monastery. He asked me to go with him, and I agreed.

In contrast to the small, calm Pepe, Kolman's driver, Emilio, had a sense of humor and loved to joke. He had already passed across the dangerous sector of the road in front of the monastery more than once, and laughed after learning how Pepe had repainted his car before leaving the command post.

"Even without such adornment it is hard to see our car from a distance. The monastery is large, and the car is small, it seems farther away," Emilio said.

They stopped us at the control point, but the traffic controller greeted the driver like an old friend, "Have a good trip, Emilio!"

"With your prayers!" he answered.

Emilio drove across the dangerous section as if shot from a cannon. He had passed halfway across when suddenly, in front of us, it looked like some kind of animal was running ahead of us, raising dust. Emilio slammed on the brakes, almost going into the ditch, and then sped ahead. We saw no more columns of dust on the road ahead of us.

"Machine gun," Kolman said.

By then Emilio was already reducing speed as he drove up to the command post.

"*Señor* Colonel!" the captain said to Kolman. "Well, you come yourself. I understand this is necessary, but why do you have to risk the *señorita*?"

Rather than translate the battalion commander's words, I answered him myself.

"There is nothing dangerous about this. You know they are far away!"

"Yes, it is far away, but bullets can fly even farther," the captain answered.

Kolman talked with the battalion commander, and I translated. The battalion commander was complaining about the fatigue of his men, who were fed up with the fortress. Then Kolman gave the battalion commander the list of signals to be used with the Republican Air Force, and the plan for positioning the battalion.

The captain did not understand everything right away, and for a long time, I had to translate Colonel Kolman's explanations. With the battalion commander's aid, Wilhelm Ivanovich learned the positions of the battalion subunits that were providing information about the composition and conduct of the rebel garrison. He spoke about reserves, camouflage, discipline, the system of firing, and other pressure on the enemy garrison, the constant military preparedness, about the trenches and barriers. It was hard to translate Kolman's conversation with the battalion commander, incomparably more complicated than Rudolf's negotiations and discussions.

We were waiting for Perez Salas, but eventually they called to say he would not be coming. Kolman and the battalion commander, one officer, and two soldiers decided on the spot to establish the position of several subunits. Kolman changed his civilian pants; they brought me a military uniform. It suited me, but the pants were a bit short.

Bending over, we followed the path, and about the last twenty meters we had to crawl Cossack style.

"It's no use for a platoon to hold here, better for it to move forward fifty or one hundred meters to the north," Kolman advised and the battalion commander agreed.

"Abandoned positions can be used to deceive the enemy," Wilhelm Ivanovich said. "Why don't you use dummies for this?"

"Good!" agreed the battalion commander. "We'll try it."

We returned along the same path but apparently less carefully; a bullet suddenly ricocheted from a rock and we threw ourselves down, waited for a moment, then crawled farther.

We left at the dinner break. A sniper of some sort shot at the car as we reached the end of the road, but this time Emilio calmly and skillfully swerved. For some reason, I did not think about the danger. Maybe because I was working all the time translating everything that Kolman was saying, or maybe because I was confident that everything would turn out all right and our driver would maneuver in time. But when we reached safety, I looked at the mountains, and it seemed to me that we had lost our way. I was used to seeing the mountains with brown, fantastically carved dark canyons. But after the rain, the color of the mountains changed, and they became an unrecognizable yellowish red. But Emilio had driven us to the right road.

As I later learned from Domingo, Rudolf and the demolitions men had thought of a way to smoke the rebels out of the monastery.

"We followed them for a long time," he told me, "deciding how to destroy the garrison without ourselves getting close to the monastery walls. Finally we figured it out. The rebels in the monastery badly need provisions and ammunition; that is why they shoot so feebly at the cars that cross the dangerous section by day." I was obviously interested, and Domingo paused, pleased that I was waiting for him to tell the rest.

"We used mules. We loaded one with two boxes of ammunition, and when he came under fire, the rider jumped off and hid. The rebels didn't shoot the animal, and it calmly went off the road and began to nibble on the grass. This all happened toward evening. In the morning to our great pleasure, the mule was gone. Evidently they led him away to the monastery. Two days later, near evening, another mule carried two boxes. Only this time the load was special. The animal had been raised in the monastery and the battalion captured it by following a group of rebels who had carried out a foray from the hornets' nest."

"So you gave them another mule?"

"We gave them not only the mule but also two boxes, one with a twenty-kilogram mine. The mule was led by the same mule driver. They shot at him, and the soldier hid in the rocks. Left to its own devices the animal apparently recognized its pasture and calmly headed toward the monastery walls. The driver even shot in its direction a few times to drive it toward the monastery.

"It got dark. We waited and eventually lost hope. But about ten o'clock in the evening a powerful explosion rocked the monastery.

"After an hour, enemy aircraft appeared over the fortress, and our antiaircraft cannon and machine guns opened fire. That forced the pilots to drop parachutes from high altitude so the majority of the supplies were carried into positions controlled by the Republican battalion, or on the open ground in front of the fortress, where the rebels could not go.

"Then *our* planes bombed the fortress! In the morning, over the walls of the formerly impregnable rebel citadel, the long-awaited white flags were raised. The hornets' nest was no more.

"So the Andalusian mule worked no worse than the Trojan horse; the mine exploded when the rebels attempted to open the box."

"The mine was concealed in a well-built metal box. That caused a lot of curious men to gather around it. Some prisoners told us that, 'We thought it was something valuable, and our leaders took it with them to their quarters. When they attempted to open the box, the mine exploded.' All the ringleaders were killed, and without them, and with so many wounded, the remaining men decided to give up."

At a New Base

When Domingo's detachment was designated a special battalion and became eligible for all types of allowances, the commander had to write orders and keep accounts according to form and also to present reports. A battalion staff was necessary, and Domingo had only one staff worker, Esperanza, a short round-faced girl with glasses. She composed lists, distribution registers for uniforms and monetary allowances, and accounted for food, but there was no one to present the accounts and reports. At the same time, the scope of the sabotage work also was increasing. Staff workers were needed, but none of our troops was suited to such work. Rudolf went to Albacete and brought back with him a small group of men from the international brigades, among them a Capt. Lyubo Ilich. He knew French very well, understood Spanish and could put together the accounts and reports, and Domingo agreed to appoint him chief of the battalion staff, but Rudolf was already planning to create special brigades and was preparing Ilich for the post of commander of the second battalion, so he often involved the captain in direct participation in operations.

Ilich did not waste any time, he worked and studied, drawing on the experience of the others. He was precise, decisive, tactful, and calm in the most difficult conditions.

He quickly mastered the codes, sabotage techniques, and

tactics and soon simply took root in the Battalion *Especial*. In a short time, when Rudolf and Domingo were leaving, they left Captain Ilich in charge. They began to form a second battalion. Now one of the battalions was designated for action behind enemy lines in the area of the southern front and the second for action on other fronts, where circumstances required. There were sufficient rations, and there was also captured equipment.

By this time, Battalion *Especial* on the southern front had several bases behind enemy lines where the necessary resources and forces for strikes on communications and other objectives were sent. Domingo's saboteurs already knew the area and the routes to the most important enemy targets very well, and on instructions of the Provincial Committee, they established connections with people who were enlisted for sabotage and conducting propaganda.

Bases in the enemy rear were set up in the mountains, masked by thick high vegetation, far from populated areas, within ten or twelve kilometers of the front line, where both sides usually had fighting contact only along the important roads and the rest of the area between them was covered by patrols and, less often, by ambushes.

As a rule, the saboteurs of Domingo's battalion stayed at those bases as long as they were sure that the rebels did not know about their existence. When leaving, the command did everything necessary to erase all trace of their stay. But the enemy sometimes found signs of the saboteurs' stay, and for this reason, the saboteurs tried not to return to the old bases. Instead, they took up positions near them and watched closely in order to capture enemy spies or soldiers for interrogations.

In early April 1937, in Jaen it was already very hot and many men from the international brigades who were not used to the heat were tormented during the day by the hot air, the flow of which, after heating up on the scorching stone and asphalt, rose in a noticeable blue mirage.

On one such day, Kolman's radio operator, N. I. Mironov, came into the battalion headquarters with his partner the cipher clerk, I. A. Garbar. As usual the affable Nikolai Mironov had a camera hanging on a small strap. Well, I thought, he's come to take some pictures. But from the appearance of Ivan Alekseevich Garbar, which was more serious than usual, I knew that they had not come for that.

We greeted each other. Ivan Alekseevich wiped his face with a large handkerchief and said, "I have an urgent coded message for Rudolf from Kolman!"

"But he's not here! He's in Villa Nueva de Cordoba," I answered.

"How can I speak with him?" Garbar asked.

"Let's try the phone."

While the man on duty called Villa Nueva de Cordoba, Mironov maneuvered to take a picture of me and Garbar with the fence of the convent in the background.

"Rudolf is not in Villa Nueva. He went with Domingo to Pozoblanco and will return at the end of the day."

"This can't be postponed," Garbar said.

"If it is so urgent, then we can be in Villa Nueva de Cordoba in two hours."

"We'd go with you, but we can't. It's almost time for our scheduled transmission," Nikolai Ivanovich said. "We're tied up." He wiped sweat from his round, smiling face.

We called Kolman, and he told them to entrust the message to me. I left immediately for Villa Nueva de Cordoba together with two of our Spaniards who had been resting after a mission.

It was past noon, but the sun was still almost at its zenith. Pepe drove the car quickly but carefully as warm, refreshing air blew through the open windows. Peasants were working in the field, and it seemed so peaceful that it would have been easy to forget that a war was going on if not for the camouflaged cars coming toward us and the control points near populated areas.

At our base in Villa Nueva de Cordoba, dinner had just been finished, but no one was resting; the men were preparing for a sortie. Rudolf and Domingo arrived an hour or two before dark.

"It's wonderful that you're here, Louisa," Rudolf said. "We're going out to a new base; there's a lot of mail there, and no one to translate. Tikhii and Juan Pequeño are getting ready for an assignment, and anyway, they avoid these translations the way the devil avoids incense."

"I have an urgent message," I interrupted.

Rudolf took it, read through it, and said, "Get ready! You must go to the base without fail."

He wrote an answer to Kolman at once.

"Everything is clear. Today the groups are going out to complete the job."

"Encode this and transmit it to the man on duty then get ready." Half an hour later, we were already on the way.

I prepared to read and translate the mail, which had been taken out of our secret mail boxes that Domingo and the saboteurs of the battalion maintained for communication with members of the underground, intelligence agents, and saboteurs in Cordoba, at the airfields, and train stations. The mail boxes saved us from having to organize meetings with people who were working in the enemy rear. Our intelligence agents put coded intelligence information and reports about completed work in a designated place where you could go unnoticed. Couriers then retrieved the reports and brought new assignments, instructions, orders, and sometimes necessary materials.

When Rudolf and Domingo were at the base behind enemy lines, they studied the information that had been received on the spot and often made new assignments at once. Domingo listened to Rudolf's advice, but for him to get that advice, I had to be there to translate the reports since, even with Domingo's help, Rudolf did not understand completely what was written in the messages. He had tried to enlist Juan Grande for this task, but Juan did not know how to read handwritten text. Ivan Kharish and Jan Tikhii sometimes helped Rudolf, but they found the work difficult. This time we expected important and urgent intelligence information, and that is why Rudolf took me to the base.

Many years have passed since then, but even now I remember well how our chief—Ksanti (Khadzhi Mamsurov)—prohibited Rudolf and me going behind enemy lines except for when it was necessary to quickly assimilate and immediately answer mail that had come from our secret agents. Studying the mail at the hidden base often was simply necessary since that saved up to two days, and circumstances often demanded quick decision. The command and staff of the battalion headquarters, which had only just been organized, still did not have the necessary knowledge and experience and had to learn through practice, often behind enemy lines, how Ksanti had done this and taught others to do. Following his advice, Rudolf worked this way too.

After dark, Domingo, Rudolf, Marquez, Tikhii, Buitrago, and I, and twelve men with heavily loaded mules, parted with our patrols that covered the Adamuz–Villa Nueva de Cordoba road, and got under way. The front was quiet, and only occasionally, somewhere far away, to our right, west of Pozoblanco, was there the rare short exchange of gunfire.

We walked for a long time and, as always, carefully. At last, we began to dodge like rabbits. This meant that we covered our tracks on the approach to the base.

We descended lower and lower, and finally, we saw the

calm mirror of the reservoir. We stopped on the bank. It was quiet, and only the constant roar of the falling water was heard on the left.

We quickly took the packs off the mules and sent the animals back with the guides. So that the tracks would not be seen we tied a large broom to the mule that was going last.

"Well now let's build our boat quickly," said Marquez. The men began to swarm around in the dark, some lowered the goods into the water in rubber bags, others set up a large canvas boat. In about five minutes, the boat was ready; eight men took their places in it. The first group pushed off and disappeared.

Waiting was tedious. It was silent. More than twenty minutes had passed when the boat returned.

"Everything is all right!" Jose Puertas, the short commander of the group, reported.

"Let's go!" Domingo said to me, and we sat in the rocking boat. The last to sit was Marquez. In his hands, he held the rope from the raft which was made up of our cargo.

Tikhii and three other strong saboteurs began to row, and we slowly started out. Our men waited for us on the west bank. Everyone got out, and Tikhii headed back to the eastern bank.

Finally everyone gathered. We began to move uphill on a steep path; things that we could not take right away were hidden on the bank. Several times, men returned for them, and at last, everything was collected at the base. After checking the guard, Domingo and Rudolf said good-night to me.

But they did not let me sleep long; early in the morning, they brought the mail—reports and maps of the disposition of enemy guards at the airfield, Fascist newspapers, and orders.

"Louisa, please translate this document immediately,"

Rudolf requested, handing me two sheets written in a large uneven hand. Evidently it had been written by a hardworking but little-educated man.

I began to read and translate, and I was captivated by it, a fine eyewitness account. After finishing the translation, I gave it to Rudolf, the original to Domingo, and they began to study them.

The report described a new control point on the Cordoba–Seville road and the procedures there. The building had been repaired, and an underground patriot who had taken part in the repair was connected with Battalion *Especial*.

"We need to send a group there right away!" Domingo suggested.

"A group? Too dangerous! It's an unnecessary risk!" Rudolf said. "Better to provide a delayed-action mine and Maria herself can place it on the target. The explosion will happen when she's not there, and she'll be beyond suspicion."

"Okay! I agree!" Domingo answered.

I translated a few more documents before I got a chance to look around the new base. It was surrounded by spreading trees, from which hung beautiful sweet pods. A large quantity of them covered the ground.

"Excellent food for mules!" Domingo said. He was totally indifferent to them.

The rays of the sun passed through the crown of the tall, spreading trees; on the soft, green grass you could see flowers and insects.

"Look, what a beautiful reservoir, it is so clean and tranquil!" the captain said, pointing down to where, like a silver mirror, an artificial lake formed by the dam of a hydroelectric station stretched into the distance.

"All the olives have already been harvested, and no one

will come here; there's no reason to!" Domingo said in an attempt to calm me, seeing that I was pensive.

In the very hot midday at the base in the mountains, we enjoyed the cool clean air while the groups of Buitrago, Tikhii, and his friend Marquez prepared for a simultaneous sortie against enemy communications. They had to take with them everything necessary for the mission, and to pack it carefully so that it would be at hand, complete and comfortable for carrying. Before leaving on the mission, the men of the groups had to study the route, to assign duties, and to plan who and how one must act in various unexpected situations.

When it was still early in the morning, the tireless Marquez prepared his group for regular sabotage. He did everything carefully. He also paid attention to his men. Marquez loved to get ready ahead of time so there would be a few hours to rest before going out on an operation.

After finishing his preparations, he stretched out on the ground and began to read *Mundo Obrero.*[1] Marquez had great physical strength and excellent fitness. The straight lines of his face seemed from a distance as if they were carved from granite. He was not tall, and he wore his black hair combed back. He walked softly, noiselessly, on the balls of his feet; he never parted with his pistol, cleaned and took care of it often. Marquez had been a fisherman, now he caught not fish but trains and vehicles. He made excellent, light, collapsible boats from bamboo and canvas or other waterproof fabric. He was proud of having participated in the battle against the rebels at Cadiz. He had been with the Republican forces when he fell in with Domingo's detachment and joined the Communist party. Marquez had never yet failed to complete an assignment, but

[1] *Worker's World,* the newspaper of the Central Committee of the Communist party of Spain.

they had not always been carried out to *his* satisfaction. He never exaggerated the results of the demolitions he set off and often reported, "There were explosions, but the results are unknown."

His motto was "Get to the target unseen and without needless risk. Set the mine, hide it, get out!"

Marquez went deep behind rebel lines with his group, mined strongly guarded objectives, and attacked automobile columns. His group carried out raids on protected objectives, which were always a surprise, carefully prepared, and successful and, as a rule, without loss on his side.

After preparing everything for a mission, Jan Tikhii did physical exercises.

"As if he needs it! He's tall and fit, and he's full of energy. Now he's standing on his hands!" Marquez said one day while watching Jan. On an operation to destroy a bridge north of Cordoba, Jan carried the wounded Manuel more than two hundred meters in his arms, like a baby, even though Manuel weighed more than seventy kilograms.

He himself selected men for the group who were physically strong, especially those capable of marching quickly day and night. He involved them in his exercise program and trained them in different kinds of hand-to-hand combat.

His group had gathered for an operation, and was positioned on the slope of the mountain that was next to the hydroelectric station. Through the crown of trees, the lake could be made out.

After learning the layout of the base and having breakfast, I set to work again translating dispatches, reports, and articles from rebel newspapers. In the evening, a messenger left with delayed-action mines for Maria.

"Louisa!" Rudolf said to me, "today, I have to leave the base, and you will have to stay here a bit longer. Here, as you know, it is pretty quiet. I'll contact Ksanti, report to him the new intelligence information and return."

Domingo and Rudolf summoned Marquez and Tikhii.

"Judging from the reports, the situation has changed," Rudolf said. "There are reasons to delay the departure of our groups on this mission. Today, I am going to Villa Nueva de Cordoba; I will make contact with the command, and then communicate the decision by radio. I will try to return to the base tomorrow night."

Before dark, one of the groups left to complete an assignment that Kolman had requested. When it was out of sight, Rudolf headed to the east with Pedro Buitrago's group, which had just completed a routine mission.

"So tomorrow listen to our transmission without fail," he reminded me and Domingo.

The night passed uneventfully. In the morning, we listened to the radio for the prearranged transmission, which confirmed the departure of the groups of the elder Buitrago and Tikhii, according to plan.

"It's a shame," Domingo remarked, "that we can hear and understand but we can't answer." We had receivers but no transmitters.

A Punitive Force

We were just having breakfast when the man on duty came running up. "Comrade Captain! Five trucks of soldiers and an armored car are coming to the hydroelectric station."

"Where did you see them?" the captain asked.

"There they are!" he said handing over the binoculars.

Domingo looked, and I froze as his face turned red.

Tikhii got his binoculars, too.

"Uninvited guests are coming to see us," he said softly. "Too bad it is so early. Look, Louisa!"

I took the binoculars and saw six vehicles, which had turned off the road to the hydroelectric station, and which were slowly crawling up the mountain.

"Stop work. Give the alarm and get everyone together," Domingo ordered the man on duty. He went out of sight. There was no audible alarm, but very soon everyone had stopped work, seized their weapons and all necessities, then quickly assembled by groups under the huge trees.

"It's very early!" Domingo swore. "Look!" he said to Tikhii, pointing to a vehicle that had stopped next to the collapsed remains of a small bridge. The trucks were positioned at the side of the road, stopped under the trees, camouflaged. More than a hundred enemy soldiers poured out of them. From the mountain, they seemed like toys.

The sun had not yet reached its zenith. I glanced at my

watch. Domingo automatically did the same, then looked at the sky, where he saw thin, high clouds. It was 11:42.

"Could it be that Alex fell into their hands and couldn't hold out? Could he do this?" Domingo said softly, having gathered the commanders of the groups.

The American Alex had been missing for about a week after an unsuccessful attempt to destroy a bridge.

I pictured in my mind the meticulous, happy, short American, who had quickly mastered Spanish and who more than once reproached Rudolf in my presence for not being able to learn to speak Spanish. Alex was brave, but physically weak. Could they have caught him and beat him? I thought. I immediately concluded that Alex was not the kind to betray his own.

"No! Alex didn't give us away!" Marquez said softly and confidently.

"How do you know?" asked Fyodor, the former White.

"Look! They didn't come here looking for us, they just want to rebuild the bridge on the road to the oil-processing factory. They're collecting rocks and sawing trees," Marquez calmly noted.

The men below seemed small and harmless, but we saw the straight rows of rifles that they had placed on the ground. In the distance more vehicles appeared. "Could it be that they are coming here and not to the hydroelectric station?"

I still didn't realize the danger hanging over the detachment. We only numbered about fifty men and had only two machine guns. The rest were armed with rifles, pistols, and grenades. Within two kilometers were well-armed rebel forces twice the size of ours that could quickly be increased in case of a clash. From Cordoba to the wrecked bridge was no more than thirty kilometers—less than a forty-minute drive. From the bridge to our lines was an hour's march. Apparently the men of the detachment understood this very well.

Through the binoculars, the group commanders watched the five new vehicles that had just appeared. They, too, turned toward the wrecked bridge.

"We need to be ready to get away quickly," Domingo said.

The cars drove up to the bridge, and two soldiers with dogs jumped out of one of them.

"Dogs! This is even worse!" the captain observed. This time he did not even swear.

A platoon or so of the enemy moved up the mountain toward the abandoned oil-processing factory. The dogs pulled forward, and their handlers increased their pace.

"Good! Very good! Let them go to our former base, there are booby traps there," Domingo said. And a little more calmly, we continued to observe the rebels who had gathered at the bridge. Some were restoring the bridge, and others were resting. Two airplanes appeared in the sky from the direction of Cordoba. Luckily, they flew east of the reservoir, and that meant that they could not see us.

The sun was still high in the sky when the platoon with the dogs began to come down from the oil-processing factory into the valley. By then, the work on the bridge was stopped. The vehicles, full of soldiers, left their cover and headed toward the hydroelectric station. After driving up to the dam, they stopped, the soldiers hid in the forest on the east bank, and we lost sight of them.

"We'll leave," Domingo decided.

After concealing in well-camouflaged hiding places everything that it was impossible to take with us, the detachment moved out, going up the mountain, dodging so that, after we made about half a kilometer up the slope of the mountain in one direction, we almost went back again. Marquez stayed behind with one of his assistants to set trip-wire mines with very fine threads that were colored like grass.

We continued to retreat up the mountain, getting farther away from the hydroelectric station. We eventually stopped under the cover of huge spreading trees. Below and to the east of us was the long, smooth lake, across which lay our route to Republican Army positions.

The sky was becoming more cloudy.

"The dogs and soldiers are at the crossing," the man on duty reported. They could be clearly seen through the binoculars on the east bank of the reservoir.

Domingo looked at the sky then at his watch. "It's still almost six hours until dark! Very bad!"

The soldiers who had been walking along the lake shore suddenly stopped. Possibly they had found our crossing place and went no farther. A part of their group with a dog broke off and headed toward the hydroelectric station. The rest entered the woods.

After an hour or two, high-speed boats appeared on the reservoir. They passed by our crossing place, turned around, and put in on the east shore, where we had seen the soldiers earlier.

"They found it, the snakes!" Domingo said, handing me the binoculars.

Then one of the boats crossed the lake and put in on the western shore. We were less than a kilometer from the boat and could see how the one who was apparently the commander gesticulated. The motor of the second boat started, and it headed to the western shore. There were five men and a dog, and once ashore, the dog clearly found our trail. It seemed as if the sun just hung at its zenith. But the soldiers did not risk coming up the mountain. The boats went up the reservoir about two kilometers, and returned to the hydroelectric station.

We expected a punitive force to show up, but there was none.

"It will soon be dinner time! Now they won't be here earlier than 1600 hours. Let's fortify our own strength," Marquez suggested. In spite of the danger, he was in a good mood.

"Let them eat then follow the fresh trail, that we wouldn't go on again! I didn't prepare a present for them for nothing!" he said, looking at his assistants.

"Even though it's a little early, let's eat!" Domingo said, and everyone except the guards started eating dinner.

After dinner, everyone sanitized the area and cammied up while Pedro, Marquez, and Tikhii, and others made delayed-action grenades from the meat cans.

Some time later, we suddenly heard a loud explosion.

It was so loud that it sounded like one of the bombs that had exploded near us in Jaen.

Domingo called me over, and on the mountain slope where Marquez had set the mine, I saw a black-brown spot, and the breeze carried a huge cloud of dust along the slope. Right of the hole, in it's immediate proximity, lay the remains of those who had not long ago been rebels and dogs, farther off lay the bodies of others who had been killed, the wounded were crawling away, and still farther, in numbness and bewilderment, stood those who had escaped injury.

"Remarkable! Looks like they wiped out nine or ten," someone said, his approval directed to Marquez and his assistants.

"There are a couple of more presents down there, but they won't be going any farther for a while. Too bad," Marquez said. "Comrade Captain! Let's finish off the rest!" Domingo just threatened him with a fist. "Not one shot! Nothing to give us away!"

"But look, that tall, lean one is standing behind," Marquez said.

"He's standing too far away, the snake," said Domingo.

"Should I try to take him out with the machine gun?" There was no stopping Marquez.

"No, we can't give ourselves away!"

Apparently expecting an attack, the rebels who were still alive lay down.

"We could destroy the platoon completely, but those who remain at the hydroelectric station would hear the shots, and in an hour, the enemy could have an entire battalion searching for us, and a second one from Cordoba, and then even airplanes. And before dark, they'd have us so completely surrounded that even at night we couldn't get home."

"Look over there. They're still moving," Domingo showed me. "By the time they sort things out, it will be night, and our trail will get cold."

Eventually the rebel soldiers grew bolder and, no longer fearing a partisan attack, began to treat their wounded, but two, apparently sent by one of the commanders, ran down.

"The sun has gone down!" Domingo noted with satisfaction.

"Good! Very good! Its time for our patrol!" Tikhii said.

"Wait a minute! What patrol?" said Domingo.

"The one you assigned us! You go to Adamuz, and we'll go to the railroad! That's all!" Marquez said.

"Wait a minute!" Domingo affirmed his decision. "Until reinforcements have arrived, we will retreat, so the enemy won't be able to detect us." He ordered them to prepare to go.

"Set a couple of good surprises that will be heard when they come this way, and let's go!" the captain ordered Marquez.

About ten minutes later, the detachment began to withdraw to the north. And just in time. Soon the two boats again appeared on the reservoir, and a little later two airplanes flew over us at low altitude, but they did not notice us, or they were only conducting reconnaissance; they just turned sharply and flew a little farther to the west.

"They didn't see us. It could be we can see them better from down here than they can see us from up there," Marquez said.

Moving with difficulty along the mountain, we marched about two kilometers as the sun sunk lower on the horizon.

"Rest!" commanded Domingo.

We spread out under trees which cast long shadows.

"Time to go! Otherwise we will lose the night!" the tall Buitrago, who until then remained unnoticed, said to the captain.

"Okay! Go! Day after tomorrow turn south of Obejo across the front line right at the lighthouse," Domingo agreed.

Buitrago and Tikhii's groups said good-bye and headed directly west. I knew them well, and Tikhii and Buitrago were like my brothers.

"Give this to my wife!" Antonio said to me, handing me a packet with a letter and a red flower he'd plucked while on the march in the forest.

"I'll give it to her," I said.

"I don't have anyone to send something to and nothing to send. So take this two hundred pesetas! Give it to someone you find who needs it!" said the elderly Andalusian from Buitrago's group after he slipped his very shabby small purse into my hand.

"Give this note to Esperanza," Tikhii requested. He was not indifferent to the young Spanish girl in glasses.

The groups left. My heart was heavy, as if I had lost something.

"Let's go!" Domingo said when the groups were out of

sight. "Everything will be okay. These guys won't go wrong," he added, apparently noticing that I was sad.

The captain led us north along a forest path. No one followed us. The airplanes were no longer flying over us. Night was falling, and everyone's mood improved. There was even some quiet joking.

A Forced Swim

I had not noticed how dusk had sneaked up on us as we headed toward the reservoir.

"They won't forget us," Marquez said as he pointed at the bright searchlight of the slowly moving boat.

"We will wait until it goes back to the other side! Be ready to sprint!"

We began the well-practiced motions to put together the canvas boat.

I was prepared to swim. I packed my field bag, outer clothing, and pistol in a rubber sack, inflated it, and tied it tightly. Then everything was ready for crossing to the other side, and those who couldn't swim were sitting in the boat when the patrol boat turned and headed our way.

"Quickly! Quickly! Pull the boat into the bushes," Domingo said.

We managed to conceal ourselves in the brush before the searchlight began to search the shore. We had to wait while the boat made another run, heading by us in the direction of the dam.

"Let's go! Louisa, you climb into the boat," Domingo commanded.

"Those who don't swim well should sit in the boat; I won't have any difficulty crossing this lake, especially with a float like my bag," I answered.

"You can swim across, but you'll catch cold, too. Sit!" Domingo said. I did not argue.

I took the rudder, and two stronger but unskilled men began to row. We had barely managed to go twenty-five meters when we noticed that the boat had begun to leak. We started to look for the hole by feel and found it, but we couldn't plug the leak, and more water was coming in.

The thin canvas had apparently worn out from carrying it from place to place, and it became clear that we were not going to cross the lake in the boat. In order to lessen the pressure, I jumped into the water and suggested that everyone who could swim should do the same, holding on to the inflated rubber bags. One man cautiously lowered himself into the water, then a second and a third. Two, who did not know how to swim, gradually sank into the water with the boat. It turned out that one young Andalusian had not inflated his bag, and the second was afraid of getting a cramp and would not abandon the boat.

"Salvador! Take my bag!" I said to the young Andalusian. "Take it! Hold on! You won't drown!" I tied his heavy bag to the boat, which was still floating.

Salvador had grown up where there was no place and no time to learn to swim. He held my bag strongly in his hand, but from time to time he'd flip over, and I had to help hold him out of the water so that he would not choke.

It was impossible for us to shout for attention, so those who knew how to swim moved farther away from the boat without noticing what had happened. The cold of the water penetrated the body. With the men holding on to it, the half-sunken boat moved forward very slowly. If the enemy launch should appear, things could turn very bad. For me, it quickly became clear that those clutching to the boat could not make it to shore under their own power.

"Hold on to the boat and the floats!" I said quickly, and gathering all my strength, I sprinted to catch up to those who knew how to swim. When I reached them, I said, "There's a leak in the boat! The men can hardly hold on in the water!"

Domingo, Marquez, and the others stopped, treaded water.

"Back! Marquez and the other strong swimmers, follow me!" the captain commanded. Then he added, "The rest get to shore and wait for us there!"

Meanwhile, the boat was almost motionless. "Put the floats under the canvas!" I advised. I had experience in rescue work on the waters of the Mezen.

Domingo did not understand at first, but when I showed him, slipping his bag under the canvas floor of the boat, he understood, then quickly pulled toward the shore.

Marquez also hid his float and made it fast to the boat, the bottom of which was already up over the water, supported by the rubber bags.

Soon, one after another, the other good swimmers came dragging the inflated bags after them. They slid them under the boat's frame, onto which all of the ones who did not know how to swim were holding. Just as it seemed that we were already out of danger, the enemy launch near the dam turned around, and its running lights caught our attention. Luckily, the crew did not notice us, so the launch was proceeding slowly along the shore.

"Hurry up! Faster!" Domingo said hoarsely. Finally, Marquez tied a line to the boat's frame, and unwinding the skein, he swam quickly.

Soon we were all pulling the boat, and it quickly edged closer to the shore, dragging with it those who were holding on to the frame. Finally it ground ashore.

"Quickly get the bags and follow me!" Domingo ordered.

While we were sorting out the bags, the launch was coming closer, its powerful searchlight probing the reservoir and its shores.[1]

When we had gone up a little way on the bank and were in pretty thick bushes, the captain ordered us to stop. In front of us was a bare slope.

We stopped. In spite of the warm night, the swim had given us chills; we began to shiver. The searchlight felt its way along the banks and finally reached us, passing through the brush that concealed us. The launch drifted slowly past, and it seemed to me that they had to see us. But the launch went by, and we found ourselves in the dark again. Just then in the mountains on the other side of the reservoir, the rumble of a distant explosion was heard.

The small, homemade, delayed-action mine we left behind had done its part, distracting the enemy.

"Forward! Follow me!" Domingo commanded, standing up in his wet undershorts, and all of us, half-naked, continued upslope. When we could no longer make out the surface of the water, we stopped to get dressed.

I went to one side, took my clothes from the bag, dried myself off and got dressed in dry clothing, which felt warm and comfortable. By then, Domingo was passing out shots of twenty or twenty-five grams (about an ounce) of cognac from the emergency rations.

"Drink to my salvation!" Salvador said, giving me his portion.

"Thanks! Warm yourself. You definitely have to learn to swim!"

"Well, have a sip at least, and I'll learn to swim! I'll

---

[1]The reservoir supplied water to the hydroelectric station and the irrigation system.

learn, I promise! Just drink a little!" Just then a second de-layed-action grenade[2] exploded on the other shore.

"Now they won't bother us," Marquez said.

And so it was. The nearby launch went to help the other cover the far shore. It was a beautiful spectacle, and most important, it cheered up our group.

It was not the first time the special battalion had used delayed-action grenades, and without doubt the enemy knew about them, but the explosions always delayed and dis-tracted them. And so it happened this time. Soon we heard shots.

"Let's leave them the boat as a present!" Marquez suggested.

Domingo understood immediately. "Only add a little more TNT so that just a memory will be left of the launch."

Marquez took the TNT and fuses, and disappeared with his group into the dark.

On the other shore, shots occasionally rang out. Time passed slowly, and Domingo started to get nervous. "What's holding him up?" the captain said.

Marquez noiselessly emerged from the darkness and re-ported, "We left them a good-size present. They won't be of-fended!"

By then the searchlight beams were searching our bank. Eventually they illuminated the place where we had left the water.

We watched to see what would happen next.

---

[2]The homemade grenade consisted of a container with from seventy to two hundred grams of nails or other metal objects, a blasting cap, a fuse five or ten centimeters long that burned at about one centimeter per second and that smoldered at about one centimeter per minute. A cover protected the grenade from the rain. Such a grenade exploded about ten to thirty minutes after the fuse was lit, and with an oxygen delay mechanism, any time from about five minutes to five or six hours.

The searchlight probed through the area along the shore, and as we expected, the launch slowly headed toward the half-submerged canvas boat. We were confident that the rebel soldiers would not try to follow us in the dark. The members of the punitive force were afraid of the dark; it was always our ally.

Suddenly the bright spot on the shore disappeared; the earth shook, a fountain of water shot up, and the enemy had one less launch. The crew of the second launch, evidently not understanding what had happened, used its searchlight to detect its lost partner.

Domingo hugged Marquez in the dark. We went on our way. After a few minutes, a far-off explosion was heard, and then disorderly shooting was heard.

"There are three more that still have to explode," the captain noted. "They will go off toward morning. A very good and reliable way to hit these bastards."

We marched toward our lines.

Undoubtedly, what had happened at the reservoir would result in increased vigilance, which might lead to our small group being noticed before it could cross to the Republican Army position. We knew that, so we moved more carefully than usual, stopping often to listen. We had delayed-action grenades ready to use if we needed them while retreating.

We knew that at the very same time, Rudolf ought to be returning to the base with a small group and might go to the reservoir, where there were probably a lot of nervous enemy soldiers.

We hoped that Rudolf's group, having heard the explosions and the shooting, would not attempt to cross the reservoir and would not fall into a trap.

Just a little farther, and we would be out from behind enemy lines.

But here the point patrol stopped.

"Patrol!" Marquez whispered in my ear.

In fact, I could clearly hear footsteps in front of us. We froze. Now everything depended on whether they would notice us or not. The patrol moved slowly. We were flat on the ground, and I could hear my heart beating.

Several uneasy minutes passed. At last, it was clear that the patrol had passed. We rested briefly, then moved on, slowly and cautiously.

We crossed the front line unobserved and, after safely going behind our own lines, started out to find Rudolf, but the battalion commander in whose sector we had crossed the front informed us that, "Rudolf crossed the front, going out with a group right after dark."

From time to time across the front, we heard exchanges of gunfire.

"Today it's unquiet in this sector," the battalion commander continued. "The rebels are nervous."

"Of course they are," Domingo answered. "They spotted some saboteurs near the hydroelectric station and lost some people and a launch."

We should have alerted Rudolf and his group in time! I thought, but the lack of two-way communications was the problem. We could not alert Rudolf, nor meet him as he was returning, and his group could walk into our base and fall into an enemy ambush.

Domingo was quiet for some time, thinking.

"What will we do?" I asked.

"By my calculations, Rudolf must have reached the reservoir by now. We can do nothing," Domingo answered bitterly.

After sending the men to the base at Villa Nueva de Cordoba, Marquez, Domingo, and I remained at the battalion command post where our group had crossed the front line.

The night was quiet and warm. Small clouds drifted slowly across the starry sky. At the front, it had become calm. From the battalion commander, we learned that Rudolf's group might have time to return that night. The forward posts were alerted to let it pass through.

Domingo was so exhausted that he fell asleep sitting up. Marquez paid attention to everything, and having excellent vision and outstanding hearing, he caught everything that went on around us. But I could not sleep. Now I was beginning to understand that Rudolf meant more to me than I had been conscious of.

Before dawn, he returned along another path. When I learned this, it was like a mountain had been pushed off my shoulders.

We met his group on the way to the command post and rushed to hug one another, like people after a long separation.

"What happened to the base?" Rudolf asked first.

"Later, first tell us how you escaped the trap," Domingo asked him.

"If there hadn't been explosions and shootings, we might have been caught. They alerted us to be careful. We went to the shore and thought everything over very carefully. We were afraid that you were cut off, but we had no communications and could do nothing. In any case, we decided to distract the rebels from the base so we set seven delayed-action grenades on the eastern bank. When they began to go off, the rebels fired at the shore from the launch. We watched from the side. Finally the game with the launch ended, and it became quiet around the old base, so we decided to return."

"And I was wondering all this time," said Domingo, "why there were so many explosions. I thought maybe the rebels had begun an artillery barrage, but it was just you adding more grenades?"

"Yes," Rudolf said, "now tell us what happened at the base?"

At that time we didn't know that there had been fourteen soldiers on the launch, with a captain in charge, and that Marquez's mine had killed them all. Intelligence agents told us that the next day at the reservoir the rebels were fishing out the remains of the crew.

We returned to Villa Nueva de Cordoba when the sun was already high and the heat had penetrated into the stone buildings. A few of the men were complaining about the heat, but for me it was cold; I shivered.

Alone Behind Enemy Lines

In my youth, I often had to swim and work in the coldest water; in the fall, we gathered cranberries in the marsh and, in the summer, cloud berries. More than once, I fell into hidden pits in the marsh or into the river and got all wet. Then I usually had to walk several kilometers for a change into dry clothing, sometimes in pretty cold weather. Many times I had caught fish with a dragnet in water that seemed unbearably cold. But the hardest thing was working on floating logs that had run aground.

We labored for hours in icy water, and sometimes I got cramps in my legs.

Then, tired and shivering, we got out of the water and ran all the way home so that we did not freeze. For many of us, that kind of work left its traces. Some of us had constant pains in our legs, others came down with rheumatism, and some got pneumonia.

My legs hurt, too, but I continued to work.

I had not expected that the night swim in the mountain lake would lay me up in bed, but the next day I not only had pains in my legs but a general feeling of lethargy. Toward evening, my temperature rose sharply, and Pepe took me to the doctor in Jaen, who had already treated Rudolf for radiculitis, a disease of the spinal nerves, and

when he had been wounded by the explosion of the detonator.

"With your condition, such cold baths are contraindi-
cated," the experienced doctor said affectionately. I had
known Frederico del Castillo since the first days of my
arrival on the southern front. He was an excellent comrade,
a member of the Jaen Party Provincial Committee. Just his
presence made me feel better.

"It's nothing; it will pass," he reassured me, having
looked at the thermometer and written a prescription for
medicine.

"You need treatment if you're not to take a turn for the
worse. Summer is just beginning. You would be better off in
a cool pine forest in the Soviet Union. There you have many
beautiful places. One day the war will be over, and I'll come
to visit you without fail," the doctor said. Visiting the Soviet
Union was his cherished dream.

But Colonel Kolman took a different approach. "You had
to go with the partisans! You took a swim. Enough! Say
good-bye to your saboteurs and come work for me; you
won't take any cold baths working with me."

Many people came to see me while I was sick. After Kolman, Domingo and Alex arrived together.

The American had lost a lot of weight, but remained the
same cheerful fellow.

"Sit down and tell me where you got lost for a whole
week? What happened to you?"

"In a word, bad luck," Alex said. He sat on a chair and
seemed even smaller.

"Well, report in proper order! Then Louisa will tell you if
it was bad luck or not," Domingo suggested.

"We didn't manage to blow up the bridge," Alex said.
"The rebels detected us, and we had to retreat. It was dark. I
was one of the last people in the file. I tripped, fell, and hurt

my right leg so badly that I could not stand up right away. I guess I fell alongside the path so no one noticed me. When I finally managed to stand up, no one was around. Somewhere behind me, the pursuit was shooting up the woods, and they set off some flares. My leg hurt a lot, but even so, I tried to catch up to the group. I got lost. My leg ached.

"I hoped to get farther away from the bridge before dawn. Morning found me in an olive grove where the trees were so sparse that it was like standing in an open field. Even worse luck, the highway was close by. Well, I thought, this is the end."

"An unenviable situation," Domingo said.

"Studying the area, I noticed a stone fence less than a meter high, and it was covered with greenery. There wasn't anything any better in the vicinity, so I decided to try to reach it. Luckily, thorns grow in places like that, and the brush was pretty thick. I got to the tallest bush and got scratched all over. I lay down to take care of my leg, which was swollen below the knee, and the pain got worse when I moved it. I had to cut my *alpargatas.* I wanted to sleep, but I couldn't on account of the pain in my leg. While I lay there I noticed that the olives had all fallen off the trees, but no one had gathered them. It was as if everyone had died. Sometimes I could hear heavily loaded trucks pass on the road.

"All day, it was like I was in hell, my leg hurt, and there was nobody to help. At dusk, I saw two peasants walking along the fence. From time to time, they pressed up against the fence. Possibly they were listening and watching.

"Well, I thought, they can discover me this way. But after waiting a bit, the unknown men rushed under the trees and began to gather olives . . . it meant they were expropriating from the feudal lords what was theirs, I thought. I tried to walk, but my leg was as if it belonged to someone else. I decided to ask for help.

"I shouted, but no one answered. The peasants froze on the spot."

Alex paused; I prompted him; I wanted to know what happened next!

"Soon I heard footsteps, but at first I couldn't figure out which way the peasants were going. Then one of them asked, " 'Where are you?'

" 'Here behind the fence!'

Using all my strength, and overcoming great pain, I crawled out of the bushes. A bent old man came up to me.

" 'What happened?'

" 'I hurt my right leg and can't walk.'

" 'Who are you and where are you from?' the second one asked in a soft voice.

My outer clothes looked like a rebel's, but underneath I was wearing the uniform of a Republican Army sergeant. I'd had all day to think about my answer to this question.

" 'I'm a conscript. I'm going home,' I said in a bad Castillian accent, knowing that southerners from Andalusia wouldn't understand.

" 'You decided to escape?' the bent one asked in an approving voice.

" 'Yes!' I agreed. 'But I fell, hurt my leg, and can't walk.'

" 'What will we do, Antonio?'

" 'Have to ask my brother. We'll report this to him,' the second one answered.

" 'Wait here. We'll get the olives. We'll take them and come back for you,' the old man said.

"The peasants gathered the olives, treated me to some, and left.

"An hour passed. Time went very slowly, my leg ached, and no one came.

"From the tone of the conversation, I believed that they would not turn me in. I wasn't afraid of this. I was worried that someone would notice them. You know they were gathering olives on the landlord's land.

"I heard steps approaching from a distance. Someone was coming cautiously and stopping from time to time. I readied my pistol and a grenade, but there was no cause to be afraid. Three men brought a homemade stretcher and quietly—stopping every once in a while to listen—they carried me.

"We probably walked about an hour to get to a village. When houses could be seen against the sky, they put the stretcher down on the ground. Two remained with me, and the third went somewhere.

" 'We can go,' he said when he returned, and they carried me almost at a run about a hundred meters along a street and into a courtyard and then into a room where, in the light of a weak kerosene lamp, I saw an old woman and a beautiful girl, who had set the table.

" 'What's wrong with your leg?' the first woman asked.

" 'I fell, hurt it!'

" 'Well, show me!'

"I was uncomfortable about taking off my pants in the presence of the girl. The elderly woman noticed this. " 'Take it off! Take it off! She won't look!'

"I obeyed her. After seeing the swelling, the woman shook her head, felt the leg carefully, and clucked her tongue. " 'You will have to bear this. Don't cry out. It is forbidden! They might hear.'

" 'Enrique, help me!' she said, and a strong young boy walked in.

" 'Take the leg like this!'—she showed him—'and hold it so it won't fall,' the energetic woman commanded. Then, with the aid of the boy, she pulled my foot so hard that I almost lost consciousness from the pain, but I didn't cry out.

" 'Patience, little son, now everything will be all right!' my savior said.

"They fed me and hid me in the garret in straw. I quickly fell asleep. When I woke up, for a time, I didn't know where I was. My leg hurt less, and the swelling was down. I came out of hiding. All around it was quiet and partially dark. I heard movement and froze in place. Someone was coming up to the garret.

"The girl I had seen in the house was creeping up to me. '*Señor,* here's some food and dishes. Don't leave here!' she said to me and softly stole away.

"I ate and fell asleep again. I woke up when it was already dark, and the pain in my leg had noticeably subsided.

"I violated the orders of my rescuers, and crawled out of the straw, but the garret was too low to allow me to stand.

"In the hellish darkness the girl again crept toward me with a new portion of boiled beans in a lot of olive oil, with a piece of cheese—it wasn't cottage cheese or sheep's-milk cheese.

" 'You crawled out, naughty boy,' she said. 'Crawl back into your hiding place and don't come out!' Then she added, 'When it's time, I'll come for you myself. My name is Conchita.'

"The days and nights flowed together, slowly, one after the other. Already I could step on my right leg. I got ready to thank my hosts and leave. But suddenly I heard someone I didn't know coming.

" 'No, *señor*, it is very bad to sleep here. The mice have set up here. They have fouled up the place. There's no cat. We will make up a comfortable bed for you in our room. You will be okay there,' Conchita was saying. I admit, I was not indifferent to her.

"Suddenly the beam of a flashlight slid along the garret. My heart leapt and the blood pounded in my temples.

"A man crawled into the garret, shined the light around once again and said, 'There's no smell here. Make us a bed on this straw.'

" 'Good, *señor*, now in the meantime I invite you to come to the table,' the girl answered.

"The new arrival went away, but I wasn't pleased with the prospect of sleeping with a stranger.

"Again I heard someone coming up. Enrique cautiously approached me.

" 'Soldiers have come to the village. Three will spend the night with us. Quickly! Come down after me,' he said. Taking the dishes, he silently withdrew.

" 'Good-night, *señor*. It's time to rest. Everything will look better in the morning.' Conchita was already bidding good-night to the surprise guests.

"After an hour, she came out to me, told me that I had to go to the front line, and gave me a bundle with food. I started to thank Conchita, then I hugged her!

" 'Leave! But don't forget our house when you return!' she said as I was going. For some reason just then I automatically moved my hand along my cheek. I was horrified. Bristles! I realized what I must look like to her. I wanted to shave, to return and kiss her."

Alex became quiet. I realized how difficult it had been to tell this story. .

There Are Various Kinds
of Saboteurs

"Anna, may I come in?" I heard Valenzuela's familiar voice behind the door.

"Yes, please, come in."

"Comrade saboteurs, you'll have to do something quick," he said. "That Quiepo de Llano is going to mine all our trains and vehicles. The general has started to take action." Valenzuela paused and looked at the surprised Domingo.

"Yes, Gen. Quiepo de Llano isn't just full of hot air!" Valenzuela continued. "Remember his threat on the radio that for each wrecked train behind his lines, he would organize ten wrecks behind our lines, for each automobile destroyed by mines or ambush he would destroy ten of ours."

"We remember! I heard it myself," Domingo said.

I had not personally heard the radio broadcast, but I knew about it from Domingo and others.

"Have the Fascist saboteurs already blown up one of our trains?" Domingo asked in a serious tone, even with a noticeable sense of alarm.

"No, they have not yet blown one up, but they have already dispatched rebel saboteurs, even supplied them with mines with wheel fuses," the secretary of the Provincial Committee said.

"Have we caught saboteurs or found mines?" Alex asked.

"We caught two, and two came in on their own to the Linares station."

"Good! Please give us all the details," Domingo said.

"Yesterday, about midnight, two teenagers came to the Linares station. One, Joaquin, is fifteen, and the second, Benito, all of twelve. They asked for the senior officer. 'Where are you going?' the *miliciano* (militia man) on duty asked. 'We don't want to go anywhere,' the older boy answered. 'We need to see the senior officer. We are from the Fascists from Cordoba.'

" 'I'll take care of it myself. Come with me, rest until morning and then I'll take you to the committee that handles it,' the *miliciano* suggested.

" 'But we have mines for trains!' the younger said shyly.

" 'Well then show me what you have for mines!' ordered the arm of the law.

"The boys began to untie the bundle of clothes they were carrying, which had until then appeared innocent. When he saw dynamite and wires, the *miliciano* grabbed his pistol and shouted, " 'Hands up! Bandits!'

"The unlucky saboteurs raised their hands and left the mines on the duty officer's table.

"With one hand the *miliciano* held the pistol on the quaking teenagers, with the other he knocked hard on the wall and yelled, 'Get up, you devils! Quick, get up!'

"Two reserve *milicianos,* who had been sleeping in the next room, ran in.

" 'Why are you yelling? Can't you handle two punks by yourself?' one of them asked.

" 'Look! Be careful, that's dynamite!'

"They searched the boys and found neither documents nor weapons. In the morning, they delivered them to Jaen, and this is what they said.

"The rebels had arrested them and their parents soon after the capture of Cordoba. They held them in an overcrowded prison, where they went hungry. Many were shot. A month ago, some major came and selected several boys. The wardens began to feed them better and said, 'Soon all of Spain will be free of Communists and other devils. In order to earn a pardon for your family, you children have to go behind the lines to the Reds and carry out a simple assignment.' What sort of assignment they did not say. Many boys did not agree to take part. But these two and twelve others agreed. They were separated from the others and began to get better rations. A priest talked with them. They talked with soldiers and civilians. Everyone was trying to convince them that children had to contribute to the struggle against the godless Communists who had sold Spain out to the Russian Bolsheviks, who were already destroying the country. They frightened the boys, deceived them, and trained them while carefully observing their behavior. Those who looked suspicious, they removed from the team, and their fate is not known.

"The rest they treated well, fed well, and didn't spare the wine. They taught them to carry out arson and to set simple dynamite charges on railroads in the dark of night. The boys mastered those arts and could quickly set mines day or night. Then they were sent south of Andujar, to blow up a train near Linares. But the boys decided not to complete the mission, and to find the chief *miliciano*. In the morning, the *milicianos* came across two other kids who had buried their mines and were drinking coffee. At first they denied they were saboteurs, but later they acknowledged it; their mines have already been found. The militia is still looking for other saboteurs," Valenzuela said.

Domingo asked, "What are you thinking of doing with these saboteurs?"

"That's why I came to seek your advice," the secretary answered. Everyone was silent. "Really what could be done with teenagers?"

"And what would they like to do?" I asked.

"Joaquin requests to be sent to the army, Benito wants to work as a metal worker, and the other two, who are also twelve or thirteen, just want any kind of work. All the boys ask that it be announced that they were caught on the railroad and shot, then maybe their families will be freed."

"That's not a bad idea," Domingo said. "Maybe we should also announce that they blew up a train?"

"We shouldn't do that!" Alex said. "The Fascists have agents, and if they discover the deception, they will shoot the boys' families."

"But it's not a great expense to blow up the track in two or three places near Linares, to cover for the boys," Domingo suggested.

"Well, and what about you, Louisa, what do you think?" the secretary asked me.

"Not having seen these unfortunate boys, and not having talked with them, it's hard to say."

"Perhaps, we could take the one who requested to go to the army into the detachment so he could become one of our saboteurs?" the captain proposed. After some discussion, Alex, I, and the others supported him.

Later I learned that when they proposed to Joaquin that he join the partisans, he thought about it and answered, "Where will I be a partisan? They will catch me and shoot me and my sister and mother, too."

"But what if you will be a partisan with me?" Domingo proposed to him.

The boy looked at the captain distrustfully and said, "No, *señor* officer, I don't need to join the partisans, they'll catch you right away!"

"Oh you, you're so easily frightened!"

"No, I am not easily frightened. But I know the Fascists have a lot of security, and they catch many partisans!"

"Have you seen any of those that were captured?"

"No, I haven't, but that's what they write; that's what they say."

"Who writes, and who says?"

"The newspapers write; the major who chose us said; he said a lot, and that guy who taught us to set mines did, too."

"Who is this who taught you to place mines?"

" *'El Dinamito'* they call him. Yes, and his boss also said so."

"Who is his boss?"

"This tall guy, and when he speaks, he speaks hoarsely."

"What is his name?"

"I don't know, *señor* boss! He is a large *señor,* he smells of spirits, the hair on his head is in waves, his fingernails are long. He says that he himself was an anarchist with the Republicans, then he went over to his own. They promised him great rewards."

"So!" Domingo said, stretching out the word, looking intently at the boy. "Remember this! The Fascist newspapers lie, the major and the other bandits are wrong!" and as if rapping out the words he continued, "It isn't partisans sitting in rebel prisons, only unlucky people like your brothers and sisters and your parents. The Fascists are liars! They have learned how to lie!" The captain finished, slapping Joaquin on the back.

"So it's a lie that they capture many partisans?" the boy asked.

"Lies, and the kind meant for fools!" Domingo answered. "We have been going behind Fascist lines for more than a month, and they haven't caught any of us. Perhaps you've heard that we blew up the train with the Italian airmen?"

"Of course! Who hasn't heard of it. Everyone heard, but they said that all the criminals were caught!" Joaquin answered.

"Lies! Not only were they not caught, but they continue to derail rebel trains!" Domingo blurted out.

"Then take me; I know how to set mines, take me! I will take revenge on the skunks for everything they have done!"

We took Joaquin into the detachment, but told no one where he had come from so that enemy agents would not find out. At night, as misinformation, we conducted two explosions on the road to Linares, causing no disruption of traffic; trains only rarely ran on that line.

In Valencia

"The doctor is getting insistent about your health," Rudolf said one day after returning from a routine raid.

"What does that mean?" I asked.

"Go to Valencia, for proper treatment and rest," he answered.

"If you don't send me away, I won't hurry."

So I remained in Jaen, but Frederico del Castillo listened to me attentively, then said, "You must begin treatment as soon as possible. Medicine in the Soviet Union is better. You have so many beautiful places for summer vacation and for treatment of your illness. Go and get treatment, Louisa. Rest, and then come back to us with renewed strength."

Rudolf raised no objection to the doctor.

"Wait a little while, and we will go together, but for now come work for me," Wilhelm Ivanovich Kolman said, when I said good-bye to him before my departure from Jaen. "I won't make you swim in mountain lakes, and you won't get sick."

I did not want to leave. Before my eyes, ordinary soldiers had turned into officers of groups, platoons, companies, and battalions. For a short time the great strength of proletarian internationalism turned into a single family composed of Yugoslavs, Spaniards, Slovaks, Czechs, Italians, Poles, and Bulgarians. And they all demonstrated courage, bravery, resourcefulness, sharpness of wit, and when necessary, intelligence, in the struggle with the enemy. They learned to make and use perfect technique behind enemy lines, to conduct intelligence, to establish communications with people in rebel-occupied territory—almost without losses on our side.

It was difficult to part with little Pepe, reckless Rubio, cheerful and calm Marquez, and many, many others, but just two days later, I was in Valencia.

The difficult revolution was going on. Valencia, the temporary capital of Republican Spain, overcrowded with refugees from Madrid and other places, was like a barometer of conditions at the front and for the situation in the country.

The rout of Italian Fascists at the battle of Guadalajara in March caused rejoicing among the people, and the victory was connected with the March Plenum of the Central Committee of the Spanish Communist party, which had advanced the slogan "Win the War," and with demands for establishment of order in the rear of the Republican Army, and also for a change to aggressive action at the fronts.

After life at the front, Valencia seemed strange, nearly incomprehensible. The enemy was in Teruel threatening to cut off Catalonia, and in a number of places, the anarchists and others continued to commit outrages. The result of the treacherous policies of England, the United States, and even France, which had taken part in the blockade of the Republic and which had encouraged the intervention of Fascist Italy and Germany, was being felt. But, just as in peacetime, after dinner, girls and soldiers strolled along the streets, and the streetside cafes were filled with diners, among whom soldiers predominated.

Some fought at the front, worked in factories and plants,

in the fields, and in the mines, but others found the means and the time to dine in restaurants on the shores of the radiant Mediterranean Sea, where music played while the waiters poured wine and served food that had little in common with the rations of soldiers and workers.

I arrived in Valencia on the eve of the proclamation of the Republic. The provisional capital was constantly threatened by regular attacks. But that morning, the city was brightly decorated with flags, red banners, posters, and flowers. Somehow lost among them were the black-and-red banners of the anarchists.

There were even more flowers than usual. They were raised in the area not only for the decoration of Valencia and Madrid but for export abroad; the blockade had deprived hundreds of people of making a living that way.

In the evening, there was a festive gathering in the Alcazar Theater to which many Soviet people were invited. I went with comrades, going early so we could visit with friends before the meeting.

In spite of the threat of air raid, a large crowd milled about in front of the theater. We met our friends, talked, and by the time we decided to go in, it turned out that the theater was already overcrowded, and we were left outside to listen through the loudspeakers. But we heard a call from the crowd, *"Nuestros amigos rusos! Los camaradas sovieticos!"*[1] and a Spaniard with a red bandanna came up to us and led us into the theater.

The huge hall was rumbling. More than half of those present carried rifles or pistols. More and more new people came in, sitting on the steps, in the aisles, and on the win-

[1]Our Russian friends! Soviet comrades!

dow ledges. It reminded me of the stories about the days of the first celebrations of Great October in the large cities of the Soviet Union!

Then the rumble began to grow quiet, movement stopped, and there was thunderous applause. The members of the presidium marched onto the stage.

The audience reacted enthusiastically to the words of orators who were clearly expressing thoughts with which they agreed. They applauded loudly when there was a speech about Republican victory, and they shouted indignantly when they spoke about the despicable activities of traitors, about the savagery of Fascists.

I translated the words of the orators for my comrades. Then when one of the speakers said that there were Russians present, I did not have time to translate before friendly applause resounded, everyone stood up, loudly calling, *Viva Rusia! Vivan nuestros amigos sovieticos!* In this way, the Spaniards in the hall of the theater expressed their feelings toward our Soviet motherland, toward our people. The meeting was not long.

When we left the theater, the crowd greeted us again, hugged us, and presented us with flowers. Suddenly a Spanish captain, with a large pistol in his belt, rushed toward one of the Soviet comrades. They hugged like brothers meeting after a long separation.

"This captain saved the life of a Soviet tank officer!" said one of our comrades who was standing next to us.

In Valencia, the doctors were very attentive to me. They gave me all kinds of medicine and ordered X rays. After examining them, the therapist said, "You need treatment, and the sooner the better."

But the pills and medicines helped me, or maybe it was

just that I had been able to rest at the Valencia partisan school, that had been organized by the Central Committee of the Spanish Communist party after our meeting with Jose Diaz. Two of Rudolf's first students were still there as instructors, training the partisan saboteurs and making the equipment they needed.

"Don't hurry to leave, Louisa! Our army is growing, and we are establishing order on the home front. When we beat the Fascist scum, you will go home victorious," said Pedro, one of our six first "old men." On the other hand, the cook, an old woman who had escaped from Toledo, advised me to rest in Valencia.

Lieutenant Garcia, the chief of the Valencia school, declared, "We won't let her go anywhere; we'll treat her." He had been sent to Valencia by Domingo after training in Jaen.

Go or stay? At home, my young daughter and family waited for me. And no matter how good the work was in Spain and how beautiful the country was, I still missed my motherland.

"There is nothing to think about. You have done your work. That's enough. Now it is necessary to get treatment," my friend Nora Chegodayeva said. During the half year of her stay in Spain, she had worked on almost all of the fronts and was so involved that literally her entire life was the war. In spite of the hard, sometimes very dangerous work, she looked cheerful, bubbling with life, young and beautiful.

"I didn't leave in time," said her adviser, N. N. Voronov. "The colonel who replaced me was killed on the front near Andujar, and I had to wait for a second replacement. I am pretty tired. Go, Louisa. And when you get to the Soviet Union, kiss the first policeman you see for me. I miss the motherland so much! Be sure to kiss him."

Even though Voronov was joking, his yearning for the soil of the motherland was clear. No matter how beautiful Spain, no matter how attached to the partisans or Domingo I was, our room in the dormitory on Gogol Boulevard seemed nicer to me than the cozy little house in the outskirts of Valencia.

Then, unexpectedly, they called me to decide the question of sending Soviet people from Spain to the motherland.

The comrade to whom they had sent me addressed me for the first time by my true given name and patronymic, "Anna Kornilovna, have you ever traveled by sea?"

"Yes, on the White Sea from Mezen to Archangelsk and back. I can take the rolling, but I don't like it."

"Were you very seasick?"

"No!"

"Very good. If you survived the White then you will feel wonderful on the Mediterranean and . . . you will carry out an important assignment."

"What kind of assignment?"

"A critical assignment! A military assignment. As interpreter, you will help Comrade Serebryannikov accompany the ship to a particular place. If the ship comes under attack and the Fascists attempt to search it, you must prevent the enemy's capturing a certain case with important documents. Now go for your photograph."

The next day they showed me my passport. They had turned me into a Bulgarian. Seeing my puzzlement, the chief said, "Now citizen"—he called me by the new surname, name and patronymic—"please memorize this biography." He gave me three sheets of typescript.

For two days, I studied my new biography. On the third day, they examined me.

"Evidently you haven't been to Bulgaria in a long time, since you know your native land so poorly?"

"I have never been there!"

"How can that be; where were you born?"

"In Bulgaria . . ."

"So you must have been there?"

"But I don't remember anything. They took me to the Soviet Union when I was still a baby."

They asked me many more questions and after the discussion said, "Even if they question you in your sleep, you must not forget that you were born in Bulgaria, that your parents took you to the USSR when you were still a baby, and that on account of this, you don't know the Bulgarian language."

At last, I had learned my new biography by heart. After a week, I said good-bye to my friends in Valencia and went on to Cartagena.

The day was sunny and hot. I could go to Cartagena by two roads, along the sea through Alicante or through Murcia. I chose the latter where I had arranged to meet Domingo and Rudolf. About thirty kilometers from Valencia, we saw hundreds of peasants near the water distribution system on the old canal. The crowd was buzzing.

"This is how they decide disputes about water distribution," Pepe said. "Without irrigation, most Spanish land is dry and hard, cracked like the face of an old peasant. But the land yields great harvests if you give it water. In the past there were *tribunalas de las Aguas*[2], which were ruled by the landlords. Now the people themselves decide questions of

[2] Water courts.

water distribution for irrigating the orchards, gardens, and fields."

After dinner, we arrived in Murcia, the main city of the province of the same name. It spread over the center of a huge oasis, which was supplied water by canals from the Segura River. I had been in this garden city once before, but then it was spring, and it was especially beautiful.

My last meeting with Rudolf and Domingo was short but seemed even shorter to me. They were going to Madrid and "on the way" they had come to Murcia.

"We will clear Spain of Fascists, and I will come to the Soviet Union for sure," Domingo assured me. "If the war drags on, come back again!"

The meeting with Rudolf caused me only pain. The men are staying, and I am leaving, I thought. But it was too late to change my mind, everything had been finally and irrevocably decided!

In spite of the difficulties of returning by sea when Republican Spain was blockaded, I was drawn to the motherland. There is good reason that we in the northern Soviet Union say, "He who hasn't gone to sea, hasn't seen sorrow." But I was afraid to be late, so early in the morning, I left for Cartagena, a city of a hundred thousand with a beautiful natural harbor and the main base of the Spanish Navy. Near the city there were deposits of iron ore, zinc, and lead. There were many small mines and also large factories. The port, city, and railway junction of Cartagena were covered by antiaircraft artillery, the muzzles of which were noticeable despite their camouflage.

For five hundred years before our era, Cartagena had been called New Carthage, a strongpoint and the home port of Carthaginians who by that time had displaced the Greeks.

The city looked very businesslike, and few festive people were seen. The population of the city port was on a warlike footing, on alert.

In Cartagena, they gave me the suitcase with the especially important mail and carefully instructed me about what I was to do if the rebels or Fascist interventionists attempted to capture the ship.

Nine Days at Sea

Our command ordered N. N. Serebryannikov to keep an eye on the course of the steamship. "The captain, and part of the crew, are not reliable—they're anarchists. You won't get along with him," the comrade told me in parting after he gave me my passport. "Even though they are in the Republican Navy, many of them could desert to the enemy in difficult conditions and try to sell the ship and all its contents. You need to be alert. Don't under any circumstances allow a change in the assigned course, and in case of hostile attack or betrayal by the crew, don't let them get the suitcase with the secret documents."

They alerted me once more, "Help Comrade Serebryannikov!"

The instructions were finished. We said good-bye and were getting ready to sail when suddenly there was an air-raid alarm. Soon we heard powerful explosions, and the steamship shook from the bombs falling in the bay, but none of them fell on our ship. Then the bombardment ended, and the all clear sounded.

"According to the schedule it is time for us to sail," Serebryannikov said. I translated his words for the captain.

The captain listened attentively, smiled pleasantly, and answered, "We will wait a little bit longer!"

"Why wait for another air raid! We are not protected by

some magic charm! We must do everything on time. We can't delay; we don't want our ship seen near the Republican coast at dawn—then no camouflage would save us." I was translating as Serebryannikov spoke.

"Okay, let's go!" the captain finally said.

We left the port in the dark. "We are going very slowly," Serebryannikov said, when I stood with him on the captain's bridge.

I translated for the captain. He waved his hand and spoke with bitterness. "The *Magellonez* is not a passenger express, just an old freighter, and what's more the hull hasn't been scraped clean of the mussels that grow on it. It is impossible to go faster."

The ship was really slow, and later we watched impatiently as other vessels passed us, even local coastal traffic. The first day was especially demanding. The interventionists and rebels blockaded the coast of Spain, and in a decrepit ship, we had to break through the blockade of hostile ships to gain the coast of Algeria.

Serebryannikov neither slept nor rested, fearing that the captain or his crew (more anarchists) would turn in to rebel Morocco.

Dressed in very different civilian clothes, the passengers walked out on the deck when there were no other ships close by. Apparently by nationality, they stood in small groups and talked. Some spoke in a language that was somewhat similar to Spanish, that was the smallest group—Romanians. Others spoke in a language completely incomprehensible to me, and as a rule, they smoked intricate pipes while they were standing. Most of all, there were people of Slavic origins. The latter completely stopped their conversations when anyone walked near.

Suddenly a boat was approaching from behind, on our

course, and it was clearly going to overtake us. The anxiety on N. N. Serebryannikov's face was growing. He was married to the binoculars, now looking at the ship that was approaching us, now intently observing what was happening on the sea in the other directions. "It's definitely overtaking us!" he said with alarm, putting down the binoculars for a moment.

The captain also looked anxiously at the ship.

"I think it's military," he said in an agitated voice and then, turning to Nikolai Nikolaevich Serebryannikov, added, "My friend, Captain, order the passengers to leave the deck quickly."

"Even though there are no signs that an enemy military vessel is following us, I will have my passengers leave the deck until further orders," Nikolai Nikolaevich answered. The deck was cleared.

The large, fast ship, passengers visible on deck, quickly grew closer.

"No! It's not military," the captain said.

"The ship is bigger than ours and may be under control of Fascists, so be prepared, Louisa. If they try to board, quickly make sure you throw the contents of the suitcase into the ship's furnace."

The captain was nervous, and I noticed that Serebryannikov absentmindedly touched the pocket in which he carried his pistol.

At last the ship overhauled us on the right, overtook us, and passed by. Nothing happened. Yet another danger was over.

When we could no longer see the passengers on the ship without binoculars, Serebryannikov said, "Let the passengers come out."

I no longer remember how many times ships we met overtook us, or passed us by, but each time, our passengers had to leave the deck and hide in the hold, and I got ready to destroy the secret documents.

Fascist planes occasionally flew over us, and we rode out some heavy seas, but Nikolai Nikolaevich Serebryannikov who was responsible for the ship's arriving according to plan, was invariably on the bridge.

"Time for you to rest, Louisa," he said to me more than once and sent me to my cabin. For some reason, we did not use my new surname, probably because Serebryannikov took custody of my personal weapon and documents when I arrived aboard, and my identity card and travel pass for the southern front were in the name of Louisa Kurting.

In the small cabin, I could not fall asleep for a long time. The ship rolled violently in the rough sea, my head began to ache, and I could not sleep. I took a powder for my headache and went to the porthole. Through the thick glass, the shadow of the ship, cast by the moon, was visible. And I was reminded of a moonlit night in the taiga, in a *malitsa*[1] and in an enormous sheepskin *sovik*[2], in felt boots with high leather tops. I was riding in a low, wide sledge. The road was long, the night frosty. Admiring the moon, I fell asleep. I was awakened by a bump; I glanced around and was horrified, I was lying on the snow. As before, the moon shone above. The frost penetrated to the skin. I had been left alone at night in the taiga. I had so much clothing and shoes that I could not stand up, I could not even turn over. It was terrible, very terrible! How could the driver not notice that I had fallen? Was it possible that, before he found me, wolves would get to me? How horrible! But then I heard the clattering of horses hooves on the frozen snow crust.

---

[1] A *malitsa* is a kind of *shuba* or overcoat, put on from the head, with wool underneath like regular *shubas*.
[2] A *sovik* is a *shuba* or overcoat of deerskin with the wool outside, worn across the head.

"Anna, oh, Anna!" my driver was shouting.

I responded to his call, and he picked me up and put me in the sledge.

Someone was knocking on the door in alarm.

"*Señorita! Señorita!*" Mario, a short sailor from Barcelona, shouted. "Some kind of ship is coming up on us. The Russian captain asks you to come to the captain's bridge!"

From the bridge, we could see a military vessel of unknown nationality fast approaching. He turned on a searchlight, and we could see that they were looking for someone in its narrow beams.

After about fifteen minutes, our ship came under the blinding beam of the searchlight. Once again, I prepared for the worst, for the capture of the boat by Italian Fascist pirates. We sailed in waters where they blatantly operated.

Half an hour of tension, half an hour of anxiety, and to our joy, the ship went to the north, toward the coast of Italy.

At last, everyone who was roused by the alarm went to rest.

When our "tub" had moved away from Sicily, two airplanes appeared from the north. At first they circled over a large tanker that was going on our left to the west, and then they headed toward us.

The deck was empty. This time the captain was calm, or he appeared unafraid. The airplanes with Italian markings were very low over us but flew by, apparently because they saw the boxes of oranges.

"What low life! They are not afraid to fly low over our unarmed vessels, but how they flee like cowards from Soviet planes," said Mario. He was young, adept, and strong, and though he wore the black-and-red necktie, he was, by his own convictions, Red.

"Russian flyers are brave," he continued with great emotion. This was said with such conviction that it was hard to believe that he was an anarchist. Mario supported his passion with facts.

"I saw it myself. Eight Fascist planes flew against Cartagena, and only three Russians went up against them. The Fascists saw them and dropped their bombs where they fell into the sea and then disappeared. Cowards!" And he expressively waved his hand, in complete contempt and hatred of the Fascist pilots.

Among the crew were reserved men with black-and-red neckties, but even they smiled warmly at the passengers, to whom they were unaccustomed.

From time to time, we found ourselves in swells. We rocked violently and lost our appetite. At those times, Mario brought me lemons and oranges.

When we were sailing toward the Dardanelles, he came to my cabin. The weather was fantastic. The sun had already set.

"*Camarada!* I love Russian people very much, your people, who could create such good airplanes, have such brave soldiers as your pilots, tank drivers, and machine gunners. I would like very much to sail on your ships together with your brave sailors."

But he had no chance to transfer to the Soviet Navy, and I could not help him.

We did not take notice when we sailed through the Dardanelles, but we passed through the Bosporus during the day.

Under the warm rays of the sun, along the coast of the Bosporus the tall minarets, churches, and beautiful buildings of Istanbul could be seen.

The very narrow strait was filled with a large quantity of ships and a still larger quantity of boats.

But we could not take a good look at the natural beauty or the beautiful city, we hid behind the boxes so that no one would notice us from the shore or from the ships and boats.

On signal, our ship stopped and a launch headed out toward us. All passengers, even Serebryannikov, rushed into the hold on command and hid there behind the boxes of oranges.

Meanwhile, the control officers came onto the ship from the launch. I do not know what they discussed with the captain or how they checked the documents, but I heard very well how the Turks came down into the hold and how the captain said that he was hauling oranges. Well, I thought, if they begin a detailed examination of the hold, they'll find us and then there will be a big problem, and near the sea and the motherland. Fortunately, the control officers went up out of the hold.

After a few minutes, the ship started off.

"You're going!" Serebryannikov called loudly and joyously, "we're home."

At last we were in our own native Black Sea, which did not seem to be black; its water was a pleasant blue color.

"So, Louisa, we're home!" Nikolai Nikolaevich said. A warm, satisfied smile broke out on his face, and he went to rest after nine days of anxiety and alarm.

The behavior of our passengers changed. The sound of loud Russian speech was heard. I learned that many of them were the first volunteers who had been replaced.

We arrived on Soviet soil in Feodosiya on a warm spring day.

It is hard to convey our joy. We had returned home, to the motherland!

I remembered the order of Nikolai Nikolaevich Voronov and Nora Chegodayeva, to kiss the first militiaman I saw, but decided not to fulfill it when I saw in port a well-built sergeant in the uniform of a peace officer. He was on duty.

I found my sister at home. My daughter was not there, but from the appearance of the room and how happy Shura was with my arrival, I knew that everything was all right at home.

My daughter came in; she was red in the face; evidently she had run far. She already knew that I was in Spain, and when she calmed down from the unexpected meeting she said, "Mama! Tell me what is going on in Spain, what did you do?" But I could not tell her anything about my work then.

In the People's Commissariat for Public Education

In late fall 1937, I returned home after medical treatment. The day was overcast and cold. I was on Gogolevskii Boulevard. The trees had already lost their leaves, and the benches on the boulevard were empty. The pedestrians were wrapping themselves against the cold; as always, they were hurrying somewhere.

When I arrived at the entrance to our house, I unexpectedly encountered the rector of the Lenin International School, K. I. Kirsanova.

"Hello, Klavdiya Ivanovna. What is the matter with you?" I could not restrain myself; in front of me stood a haggard, pale woman, whom I had adored, captivated by her tact and simplicity.

Instead of an answer, tears shone in the eyes of Klavdiya Ivanovna.

"Don't ask! The others will tell you!" she said softly and began to cry.

I never could have imagined that the cheerful woman who had served continuously as rector of the Lenin International School since its founding in 1920, who was sensitive to the needs of others, could be so depressed.

I still did not understand what had happened, and I addressed the woman, who was clearly agitated by great bitterness. "Klavdiya Ivanovna, perhaps I can help with something?"

"Thank you, Comrade Obruchaeva, there is nothing you can do to help now. Only believe me, that I was, am, and to the end of my days will be a Bolshevik." Klavdiya Ivanovna wiped her tears with a handkerchief and added, "You probably know that they closed our school?"

From friends who worked at the Lenin International School, I already knew about that, but no one understood what had provoked the closing. I did not even ask Klavdia Ivanovna about it, just said, "Yes, I know!"

"They liquidated not only the school. Don't worry, there is work enough for all. Some went to the Red International of Trade Unions, others to the Central Committee of the Bolshevik party," Kirsanova answered.

Several other acquaintances from the Lenin school came up, the conversation ended, and we said good-bye.

Mainly workers of our school lived in the building. I learned that Klavdiya Ivanovna had been excluded from the Party for connections with "enemies of the people."

About another week passed, and I put in an application to the People's Commissariat for Public Education with a request to go to work in one of the Spanish children's homes.

"We have a great need for workers," said the person who led me in the personnel department of People's Commissariat for Public Education. "There is a vacancy for an interpreter in the children's home in Obninsk. If that suits you, fill out the application, and we will give it to the administration."

It took me a long time to complete the application, to add references. I took down the telephone number of the home's personnel department, but no one called. Even so, soon I was summoned to the People's Commissariat for Public Education.

"Today the people's commissar will receive you," they told me in the personnel department.

Can it be, I thought, that the people's commissar himself speaks with the workers of children's schools?

After a few minutes, the director of the personnel department and I were already in the commissar's reception room. Up until then, I had never spoken with a people's commissar, so I was very nervous.

A bell rang, and the secretary went into the people's commissar's office and then came out and said, "Pyotr Andreevich invites you to come into his office."

I was very worried as I went into the office behind the director.

The people's commissar of public education, Pyotr Andreevich Tyurkin, greeted us, asked us to sit, sat himself and, looking at the application, began, "I read, Anna Kornilovna, your declaration and application and decided to speak with you." The people's commissar paused and glancing at me, continued, "You are requesting a job in a Spanish children's home?"

"Yes! I know Spanish, I know the country and the people, and for that reason, I think I can serve as an interpreter or a teacher in a Spanish children's home."

The people's commissar smiled mysteriously.

"Interpreters are not a problem for us. We need people for a bigger task," he pronounced thoughtfully. "We have talked it over and have decided to offer you the post of head of the administration of children's schools and special schools."

It seemed improbable that they were offering me, an interpreter, the post of head of an entire administration, a job about which I knew nothing. I found I could not answer right away.

Seeing my confusion, Pyotr Andreevich smiled.

"What are you thinking about? What's bothering you?"

"Comrade People's Commissar," I began, "I beg you to give me a job in a Spanish children's school, a job more in keeping with my knowledge and experience."

"Well, what do you mean, Comrade Obruchaeva?" the people's commissar began. "At the present time we are promoting worthy comrades into important leadership positions. You fought in Spain, you are the holder of an Order of the Red Star, you have excellent service and Party references."

"Comrade People's Commissar, I have never worked in administration, and I can't imagine what one must do there. I haven't had to manage anyone, and I beg you to spare me from such a promotion so that I won't let you down," I answered. I feared that I had been too straightforward.

"Anna Kornilovna, don't be frightened, we will help you to learn the job. In the administration, there are good, experienced people, but they need a leader."

"No, Comrade People's Commissar, there is a Russian saying, "Stick to your own knitting."

"There is also another saying," the people's commissar interrupted me. "A cat may look at a king." Don't think about refusing; you are a member of the Bolshevik party, which now demands from us great effort with all our strength and the daring promotion of young personnel."

Everything that the people's commissar said to me seemed as if in a dream; it was hard to believe that that kind of meeting could happen in the daylight.

It seemed to me that the people's commissar, who had devoted so much time to me personally, and even more to my application, which had been given to the personnel department, would finally get angry and dismiss me, but nothing of the kind happened.

"Comrade Obruchaeva!" Pyotr Andreevich began calmly.

"We will appoint you all the same, to the executive post of head of the administration of children's homes and special schools, and you will go to work. All the proper conditions will have been created for you."

He stood up. Clearly, he would not listen to any more objections. And what was said was said in such a tone that I decided, What will be, will be.

Almost the entire night, I did not sleep. My thoughts would give me no rest; I worried about my future job, no detail of which I had so much as imagined.

I awoke still tired, and I returned to the People's Commissariat for Public Education.

I went to the head of the personnel department as we had agreed. He accompanied me to the office of the director of the Administration of Children's Homes and Special Schools and introduced me to the staff. There were about twelve people in all in the administration.

After meeting all of them I was left alone with the secretary, Comrade Aleksandrova.

The elderly secretary, with graying hair, whose name and patronymic I have unfortunately forgotten, placed a whole pile of all kinds of files on the table for me, and said, "Anna Kornilovna! Here is the morning mail and outgoing documents."

"Help me examine the papers!" I said to the secretary.

"Read through the incoming mail, make decisions, and add instructions. The mail that is going out over your name you sign, but if it's for the signature of the people's commissar you stamp it. If it requires information or any one of the staff, call them through me or directly by telephone. You have the latest list of them on the table under the glass."

I glanced at the thick files and such a sadness seized me that I thought I would cry. But there was nothing to be done. I had to read them.

What wasn't in this morning's mail? Here they exposed "enemies of the people," there a boy ran away, incidents, requests, demands . . . there was less outgoing mail, but even that was a mystery to me.

I could make no decisions; everything was unfamiliar to me. I called the secretary.

"I beg you," I called her by her name and patronymic, "help me get started."

The large quantity of uncompleted incoming mail was the result of the long-standing lack of a head of the administration. Those who were on temporary appointment were not making decisions. On some of the documents, I saw the written instructions of my predecessor Comrade Gasilov, who had already been declared an enemy of the people, and that is why no one paid attention to his decisions.

All day visitors arrived, and telephone calls interfered with work. Only the night remained for reading incoming documents.

The secretary and I left after midnight. I had a headache and the biggest problem was the oppressive weight of the backbreaking work. Everything was completely new to me. At first I thought that the "special" schools trained "specialists," but it turned out that they were schools for the deaf and mute, the blind, and other children who were impossible to teach in the common schools.

The staff presented me with lists of the leading workers of the special schools and children's homes, indicating when each of the present staff had assumed the current position and who had held the positions before the incumbents. I learned that in 1937 more than four-fifths of all directors and their deputies had been removed.

The majority of the newly appointed workers did not have the necessary knowledge or related experience, and that is why the condition of the homes and schools, and the education of the children in them, significantly worsened in 1937. It turned out that it was not only me who had been forced to work without knowledge of the job.

The next day was even harder. Beginning very early in the morning, the directors of the special schools and children's homes, workers of my administration, and representatives of the local administrations came to me.

And it was like that every day. It was a good thing that the secretary was experienced and that, to the extent of her powers, she helped me to sort through the papers, but even with her help, I could not handle the flood.

The more I got into the job, trying to cope with the duties placed upon me, the more convinced I became that I was not prepared for the position. I arrived early in the morning, spent hours at the administration and in meetings until late at night, but often I could not even get through all the incoming mail, on which I had to write instructions. Sometimes I signed outgoing mail composed by my executives without being confident that it was correct.

The people's commissar worked even more, but even he did not manage to get everything done on time. Very important problems that only he could solve were not solved only because he did not have time for them. And he did not have time because many questions that could be decided in the field were not decided there, since the purges had left no experienced, qualified staff of leaders, and the young Communists promoted into important positions still had not mastered their rights and responsibilities and, of course, had not had proper training.

Worst of all was to have to deal with those who were "temporarily acting" or even "acting" in certain posts. They were not thinking about tomorrow but only about not making any mistakes. At that time, there were quite a few people like that.

The large number of planned and ad hoc meetings also interfered with work. At these meetings there was a great deal of talk about "vigilance" against enemies of the people, wreckers, etc., which sometimes led to unjustified suspiciousness.

Under those conditions I was chosen to be a member of the Party Committee of the People's Commissariat—in spite of my declining the nomination—and my work increased even more.

Nadezhda Konstantinovna Krupskaya

Soon after I began work in the People's Commissariat for Public Education, completely unexpectedly, Deputy People's Commissar Nadezhda Konstantinovna Krupskaya invited me to her office. I remembered how we had talked about her warmly in far-off Spain.

I often had heard about her modesty, accessibility, and simplicity. I wanted to meet with her and talk, but when I went to her office I was worried all the same. How could I not be worried, I was going to see the person who had walked the great path along with Vladimir Ilich Lenin.

I went in and introduced myself. We exchanged greetings.

"Please, Comrade Obruchaeva," said Nadezhda Konstantinovna in a quiet voice, indicating a chair.

"Forgive me for taking you from your work, but I want to talk with you about the children's homes and the special schools," she began, looking at me intently with large golden-gray eyes. On her face was a friendly smile. My shyness and worry disappeared.

Nadezhda Konstantinovna had taken an active interest in the organization of the children's homes and the special schools, the course of study, work, and daily routine. She asked what the children did in their free time, and how things were going with the job placement of pupils who, because of age, could no longer be in the children's homes.

"Well now we have gotten to know each other," Nadezhda Konstantinovna said, evidently satisfied with my answers. "When you need my help in anything, don't be shy, come to see me."

"Nadezhda Konstantinovna, things are going badly with personnel at the children's homes and special schools."

"Yes, I know," Krupskaya agreed. "Right now, many children's homes and special schools have turned into passageways. There is great turnover of staff. Almost none of the directors who worked many years and dedicated their entire conscious lives to the rearing of children remain. There are many moral and material difficulties, but one must work under all conditions. The children don't have parents, a collective is needed to replace the family. The children are our future, our replacements!"

We parted, and I felt much better as a result of our conversation.

About two weeks later, Nadezhda Konstantinovna called me again. That time I wasn't worried, and went calmly into her modest office. She wore a worn, but clean and well-pressed, dark blue dress, with a closed collar and long sleeves. She had on worn, low-heeled slippers.

"Comrade Obruchaeva!" Krupskaya began, "I have invited you to tell me about the Spanish children. How do they feel here with us?"

"They are still not accustomed to us, even though our people are doing everything so that the Spaniards in our children's homes feel as if they were in their own mother's house and so that they would be convinced that they have found a second motherland."

"What about the teachers, do they speak Spanish?"

"This is very difficult. Few study Spanish in our country.

Another difficulty is our winter. Right now, even in Odessa, there is cold such as they never have in most regions of Spain. Many Spanish children have seen snow for the first time here."

Nadezhda Konstantinovna listened attentively, and when I spoke of the first snow the Spanish children had seen in the Soviet Union, she smiled.

"Not long ago they told me about one such case," Krupskaya began. "It was in the Leningrad Children's Home. The first snow fell at night, and during the day the Spanish children had already begun to play in the snow. They called the children to dinner. Many children filled their pockets with snow. After taking off their coats they went into the dining room, then it was quiet time. While the children slept, one of the teachers went into the cloakroom and was surprised by the huge puddles. Drops of water were still falling from the pockets of many of the coats."

Nadezhda Konstantinovna paused. I had heard the story, but I expected that Krupskaya would say something more.

"When the children woke up," Krupskaya continued, "there were no puddles on the floor; the staff had wiped them up. Only wet coat pockets and flaps remained to remind them of the snow. When they learned that the snow had melted, the children were very sad."

"There are also difficulties with textbooks, Nadezhda Konstantinovna," I said. "There are no Spanish books. We translate Russian books into Spanish."

"It is a difficult problem, and of course, it requires time," Krupskaya agreed. "But what about resources?"

"The All Union Central Trade Council will provide resources; it allocates funds both for translation and publication of textbooks."

"How about teachers?"

"In each Spanish children's home there are a few Spanish teachers to teach Spanish language and literature, but most of the teachers are ours, the majority of whom do not know Spanish and conduct lessons through interpreters, which is very difficult."

"What are the prospects for personnel?" Krupskaya asked.

"The Central Committee of the Bolshevik party and the Central Committee of the Communist Youth League have devoted a great deal of attention to the Spanish children's homes. They have sent good Party members, teachers from the Communist Youth League, doctors, and tutors to work in the homes. The chief of the department for Spanish children's homes, Comrade I. P. Semenov was himself raised in a children's home, and he knows all the problems and habits of orphans. He loves children very much and is often in the children's homes himself."

"What about food?" Nadezhda Konstantinovna asked.

"At first, this was also a problem. Our managers and cooks did not know Spanish food. They cooked everything in olive oil, but the Spanish children were used to a kind of olive oil we don't have. Now they have become accustomed to our food. It is much more difficult with the medical service."

"Why?"

"Many of the children arrived covered with scabs and sores. They were literally taken out from under bombardment. Many babies lost not only their parents, but also their brothers and sisters. There were cases where the brother landed in one children's home and the sister in another, and our workers had to seek them out and get them back together."

After discussion of matters related to the special schools, Nadezhda Konstantinovna asked, "Comrade Obruchaeva, they told me not long ago that you were born and raised in the Mezenskii area of Archangelsk Province."

"Yes," I said.

"Was your last visit there a long time ago?"

"In 1929, I went away to school, and have not been back since, even though my mother and sisters are still in the village of Dorogorskoe."

"You should visit your relatives, it isn't good to be separated from the land where you first saw light," Krupskaya said with reproach.

"I would be happy to go, but I can't find the time. It's far away. It takes a week to get from Archangelsk to our village of Dorogorskoe and more than a week on the way back. So I'd spend almost all my vacation on the road."

"The tsarist government certainly knew where to exile the revolutionaries," Nadezhda Konstantinovna observed.

"Yes, there were quite a few exiles in our village! They taught the local people a great deal, even to mow grass with a scythe, (before them, we cut it with *gorbushas*[1]). Yes, the politicals educated us!"

"People such as Inessa Armand, Voroshilov, Popov, Serafimovich, Moiseenko, Yasvitskii, and others did a lot of work in exile."

"Inessa Armand and Popov told us a lot about your severe region. It was not without reason that Governor Englehardt, after a trip to Mezen in 1897, had to acknowledge that all of the county seats of Archangelsk Province were generally unattractive, but the saddest of all the 'wooden ones' at that time was Mezen."

Thus it was half a century ago. Now it is fashionable to go from Moscow to Mezen by plane for a day. The city has

[1] A curved scythe with which they did not mow, but they cut the grass from the shoulder.

grown, gotten prettier. Now they no longer burn fat or torches to drive the night's darkness from the streets.

During my next meeting with Nadezhda Konstantinovna, I made a request.

"Nadezhda Konstantinovna, I don't have the necessary experience. I have neither the strength nor the knowledge for the job. Help me change jobs if only to become an inspector for the Spanish children's homes."

"Anna Kornilovna, I understand you, but I am afraid that I can't help you."

Nadezhda Konstantinovna was upset, and I no longer dared to say anything more on the subject.

I met many more times with Nadezhda Konstantinovna. We spoke a great deal about the practical needs of the schools. Not having children of her own, she devoted a great deal of attention to the children in her care, especially to orphans.

More than thirty years have passed since my meetings with Nadezhda Konstantinovna, but the image of that charming, sympathetic, and sensitive, highly erudite militant friend of Lenin has remained in my memory my entire life.

With the Spaniards Again

I could not stand the stress. The lack of sleep, the lack of confidence in the correctness of the decisions I made, the continuing arrests of the leading workers in the field, and in the apparatus of the People's Commissariat were depressing.

Once again, the forced swim in the icy water and the cold nights in the mountains of Spain began to tell on me. I felt worse and worse. In the evening, my temperature rose. The doctors recommended treatment, but I had no time. Eventually, the people's commissar, an attentive man, noticed my unhealthy condition during one of our meetings.

"Are you sick, Anna Kornilovna?" he asked.

"Yes, the doctors say it is a relapse of the illness I got in Spain, and I must undergo systematic treatments, but I don't have time for them."

"I know. We will find a deputy, then it will be easier, and you can be treated, but go to the polyclinic right away."

"Comrade People's Commissar, I have worked four months without a deputy, buried in papers, but I am used to working with living people. I beg you to consider my request."

"Okay. We'll consider it, but now go to the polyclinic."

At the polyclinic, they reproached me for not coming sooner, and then it was necessary to begin everything from the beginning.

Soon the people's commissar designated me senior inspector of Spanish children's homes. With great joy I transferred my duties to my newly appointed chief, M. S. Shifrin. I was relieved. I could take my treatments and, at the same time, work not with papers but with children whose fathers were continuing the fight against the Fascists. There was a lot of work to be done in the small department, the kind of work that was within my powers, and quite often, I was leaving for home when others were returning from the theater.

Everyone worked hard, beginning with the people's commissar of public education, P. A. Tyurkin, and ending with the secretaries and inspectors. M. S. Shifrin, the newly appointed chief of the administration of special schools and children's homes, also worked a great deal, but even he could not manage to do everything. The solutions to many problems were delayed for long periods of time by the promotion of a great number of young personnel to positions for which, as a rule, they did not have the proper experience.

Working in the People's Commissariat of Public Education, I had occasion to speak with the people's commissar of public health, N. A. Semashko. As part of his duties as a member of the children's committee of the Central Committee, he continued the work of eliminating homelessness and neglect of children that had been begun by F. E. Dzerzhinskii. After the Civil War years, there had been many ragged, hungry, homeless children, who warmed themselves near the slag heaps from locomotives. By the late 1930s, the devastation, hunger, and neglect were behind us, but there were many difficulties with the children, especially the Spanish ones.

The people's commissar of public health was also overloaded with work. Now and then at some gathering or meeting at the People's Commissariat of Public Health, where

I also had to be, he inquired about the children's health, about the provision of medicines, and the work of medical personnel.

"It is a tough job, but necessary and honorable," Nikolai Aleksandrovich said one day. "Children are children," he continued. "They are our future, but working with them is full of surprises. Take any good children's home. By appearances, one must give a bonus to the leader and the serving personnel, and suddenly one silly little child has an emergency, and everything goes to pot. It means they were keen on showy achievements, but they weren't watching the details."

In general, my situation in the People's Commissariat of Education was not an easy one. At that time, I was the only woman who wore the Order of the Red Star. In those days, there were no ribbons that could be worn instead of the medal, and those who had won an award usually wore the medal.

A few award winners enjoyed special attention at the regional Party conferences in 1938, where I had the good fortune to be a delegate and to sit next to Nadezhda Konstantinovna Krupskaya.

One time, a Professor Feldberg came from Leningrad. He was the head of a scientific research institute on Jaures Quay, where they were working on eliminating speech defects among children, and preparing blind, deaf, and mute children for work.

After arriving at the People's Commissariat of Education, Feldberg came to the office of the chief of the Administration of Children's Homes and Special Schools; he apparently did not know about the fate of my predecessor.

I saw an unknown man open the door. He looked in for a second and hurriedly left before I had time to come to my senses and invite him in.

Feldberg then walked to the special schools section and asked, "Where might I see the head of the Administration of Children's Homes and Special Schools?"

"In his office," someone said.

"But he's not there, some actress is sitting there."

"No, that's not an actress, that's our new chief."

After a short time, he came to my office. We got acquainted and began to discuss business.

On November 9, 1938, there was a party in Spanish Children's Home Number 7 (in Moscow on Pirogov Stroot) in celebration of the twenty-first anniversary of the Great October Revolution. The son of Dolores Ibarruri, the handsome young Ruben, attended the party. He sang ancient Asturian songs so well and with such enthusiasm, that those who knew Spanish sang with him. Mikhail Koltsov was there. He delivered a brilliant speech in Spanish and then translated it into Russian, and everyone present interrupted him often with loud applause.

Koltsov recognized me. He began to ask about Domingo and Rudolf.

"I am very interested in the participation of people from other countries in the fighting behind rebel lines," he said. "When Rudolf was there, Domingo's detachment had representatives of many peoples, all of whom took part in the war against the Fascists. I am gathering materials, and think that the time will soon come when we can speak publicly about it."

We were sitting in the dining room where the party was being held, and Mikhail Yefimovich made notes of the names and everything I said about Kharish, Tikhii, Alex, Krbovanets, and some others. But when I could not answer some of the questions, I said, "Of course, Rudolf knows more; he was in Spain longer, and he participated in operations at Madrid and Saragossa."

Mikhail Kolstov promised to come back again soon. But that meeting did not happen, and we learned that he was among those of whom we could no longer speak.

While I was working at the People's Commissariat of Education, my name changed from Obruchaeva to Starinova. But on the advice of my doctors, after ten months, I was forced to give up work at the People's Commissariat of Education.

News from Afar

Meeting with Spanish children who had been forced to abandon their country, I was all the more convinced that during my stay in Spain I had fallen in love with its people. I had forever left a part of my heart there.

In those years, the world closely followed events in Spain, where the war of a courageous people against fascism continued. The Soviet Union rendered moral and material aid to Republican Spain, but the blockade impeded and sharply reduced its size. All of this we knew and endured with bitterness.

On February 22, 1938, the rebels occupied Teruel. To a significant degree, that was the consequence of the program of the minister of national defense, Indalesio Prieto, who was opposed to the Communists and in every way tried to limit their role in the army, promoting undependable officers to the highest military posts. Some of them later went over to the rebels.

On April 3, Lerida, the main city of the province of the same name, fell. On April 8, the government was reorganized. Prieto was removed, and his post was occupied by Juan Negrin. The rebel offensive continued, and on April 15, they penetrated to the Mediterranean Sea, splitting Republican Spain into two parts, Catalonia and the south-central zone.

In the summer of 1938, the Fascists began a strong offensive against Valencia, but it was broken by the steadfastness of the Republican troops. At that time, Negrin's government received a large shipment of Soviet weapons, armed the Catalonian army, and on July 25, the "Army of the Ebro," under the command of Juan Modesto, forced the river Ebro over a wide front and swiftly moved to the south.

In Moscow, we read the reports about the victories of the Republican forces. The rebel offensive against Valencia was stopped. The operation on the Ebro continued until the middle of November 1938. The Republican Army's lack of arms and ammunition and the growing influx of Italian troops had led to the rebels' success in reestablishing their position, but the Ebro operation convincingly demonstrated that if there had been no blockade, and the Republican Army could have received what the Soviet Union could give, the rebels and their German and Italian allies would have been defeated.

The power of the Republican Army, and the maturity of its commanders had grown so much by that time, that Negrin's government decided to remove all foreign volunteers from the army, hoping that, by doing so, it would promote a reexamination of the policy of nonintervention and the removal of the blockade from Republican Spain.

At the beginning of December 1938, the evacuation of almost all volunteers from Republican Spain was completed. Their participation in the struggle against the rebels and Fascists was a real heroic feat, international aid in the defeat of Fascist intervention.

On December 23, a Fascist offensive began in Catalonia. The Republican forces repelled the Fascist attack, but the interventionists had great superiority in numbers and especially in military equipment, and arms and ammunition sent from the Soviet Union were held up in France.

On January 26, 1939, the interventionists occupied Barcelona. By the beginning of February, they had occupied Catalonia.

On February 9, Admiral Ubieta, under pressure from the English, surrendered Minorca, the Republican bastion on the Mediterranean Sea. On February 22, the English and French governments recognized Franco and severed diplomatic relations with the legitimate Republican government, and by that action delivered yet another stab in the back to the Spanish people.

Then the conspirators began to act. The commander of the Army of the Center, Col. Segismundo Casado, the leader of the Right Socialists, Julian Besteiro, and the commander of the IV Corps, the anarchist Cipriano Mera, headed the conspiracy. In the beginning of March 1939, the world learned of the treachery of Casado's group, which betrayed the Republic using parts of the IV Corps under the command of anarchists, and opened the front to the Fascists in spite of the heroic opposition of many patriots, mainly Communists.

At the end of March 1939, Republican Spain fell.

It was as if something had broken in my heart. I did not want to believe that the rebels had taken over Spain.

For thirty-two months the Spanish people heroically conducted an armed struggle against international fascism. The subversive activity of the anarchists, which ended in treachery, the conciliatory policy of the Right Socialists, the petty bourgeois parties, the policy of encouragement and de facto cooperation with the Fascist interventionists on the part of the governments of the United States, England, and France each left its own black mark.

Republican Spain fell, but the struggle of the Spanish

people, and the blood of Spanish and foreign volunteers who had come to help them, did not fall in vain. Plans for the quick enslavement of Spain were ruined. In Spain, the Fascists had received their first powerful armed rebuff.

In Spain, the volunteers of the international brigades gave everything to the struggle—their youth and their maturity, their knowledge and experience, their blood, their hopes and aspirations, and many even gave their lives. And they asked for nothing in return, neither honors nor awards. The surviving members of the international brigades used their experience in the struggle against fascism in the ranks of the resistance movement, in partisan warfare behind the lines of the Fascist occupiers during the Second World War, and in this way accelerated victory over the dark forces of fascism.

In November 1937, Rudolf Wolf returned from Spain and to his real identity, as Major I. G. Starinov. After four months, he became Colonel Starinov. It was especially hard for us to bear the fall of the Spanish Republic. Too much bound us to its heroic defenders.

In the second half of November 1939, Ilya Grigor'evich Starinov went on assignment to Leningrad. By that time, we had become husband and wife. In December, the war with Finland began. I remained at the firing range in Ilino, hoping that the war would be over quickly.

However, events developed differently than we had expected. The Finnish war took on the characteristics of protracted trench warfare. The enemy made a large quantity of their own types of mine, and Starinov organized the clearing of them. In February 1940, he was seriously wounded by a Finnish sniper, and only the skill of the Soviet surgeons saved his right arm and his life.

Since many of the Spanish comrades with whom we had fought behind rebel lines had succeeded in getting back to the Soviet Union, we sought them out, and they attempted to find us. But the operational security we had used in Spain worked against us. They knew me as Louisa Kurting, and Starinov as Rudolf Wolf. But Starinov eventually managed to find Domingo Ungria who was employed in Kharkov as a metal worker in a tractor factory, along with a group of former soldiers of the Spanish Republican Army.

In the summer of 1940, after Starinov got out of the hospital, we stopped in Kharkov on the way to the Caucasus. It is hard to talk about meeting with the man with whom we had begun our partisan path in far-off, beautiful, sunny Spain. Three years full of events, difficult experiences, demands, and hopes had passed.

We were interested in what had happened to the friends with whom we had conducted missions behind enemy lines, and who had participated in operations against rebel communications. Where were they now, our comrades in arms?

Domingo was his usual voluble self. "The Fascists, imperialists, and traitors of the Madrid junta of Casado caused the fall of the Republic. The Spanish people bore a huge loss, hundreds of thousands died in battle, hundreds of thousands are dying in the prisons, but those who fought behind enemy lines, the partisans, turned out to be invulnerable. We even helped to save hundreds of those who were threatened with inevitable death. We had to get to the USSR by way of Algeria."

Domingo told us about the fate of many of our friends. After we left Antonio Buitrago was deputy commander of a corps in Catalonia; others had become officers of special sabotage brigades. Ilich climbed the staff ladder and became chief of staff of the XIV Corps.

"Ivan Kharish became an adviser and senior instructor of one of the sabotage brigades. He was in action until the last days of the war. Tikhii, Marquez, Rubio, Salvador, and many others were killed in the final battles. The fate of Kharish and Ilich is not known."

"What about Alex?" Starinov asked.

"A very brave man. Many times he went behind enemy lines. He went to see Conchita. Her brother Enrique joined the partisans, and carried out intelligence missions. The members of the international brigades began to leave, but Alex did not want to leave without Conchita."

Starinov interrupted. "But how did Alex end the war?"

"He blew up a lot of trains and enemy vehicles and took part in a lot of ambushes," Domingo continued, "and in raids, but . . . he died in an uneven skirmish, in a defensive action, which had to hold during the retreat."

"And Conchita?" I asked.

"Conchita . . . stood with him, but the bullets didn't get her. After the treachery of Casada, she went with her group into the mountains."

"Remember the teenage saboteur, what's his name . . .?"

"How could I forget Joaquin? He became an outstanding saboteur. He paid the rebels back for everything, for his mother, his sister."

And so there were stories and reminiscences.

It was the first we had heard about the heavy losses of our friends in battle, we learned about new heroic deeds of the soldiers of the first Battalion *Especial,* but the fate of many of our friends who had crossed the border to France, and who were there in camps, remained unknown to us.

On June 22, 1941, The Great Fatherland War (World War II) began.

In October 1941, carrying out a special mission in Kharkov, I. G. Starinov found Domingo, Manuel Belda, and twenty other Spanish comrades, who wanted to join the ranks of the Red Army so that they could take active part in the war against Hitler. Starinov managed to enlist the whole group in a unit that he commanded. They all participated successfully in World War II's partisan struggle.

In February and March 1942, almost all of the Kharkov group took part in the "ice marches" behind enemy lines across Taganrog Bay.

In the course of the war, the number of former Republican soldiers under the command of Colonel Starinov quickly grew, and by the fall of 1942, exceeded two hundred men. Among them were Manuel Vasquez, Domingo Ungria, Francisco del Castillo, Joaquin Gomez, Jose Vieska, Cano Erminio, Rafael Estrela, Luiz Castillo, Chilo Mariano, and many others.

From the Spanish comrades, I learned about the death of our friend, first secretary of the Jaen Party Provincial Committee, Cristobal Valenzuela. His dream of coming to the Soviet Union after the war was not realized. Frederico del Castillo had been sentenced to life imprisonment in Spain; he languished in the Fascist torture chambers. Del Castillo eventually served twenty years in prison. He became ill with cancer and was released in 1959. But the governor of Jaen prohibited him from practicing medicine.

"You can put me back in prison," the doctor declared, "I can't ask for charity." The governor reconsidered his decision, and Frederico del Castillo not only rendered medical assistance to people but he also conducted important Party work. Skillfully maintaining secrecy, he began once more to work on agitation and propaganda. But his disease was merciless, and after a few months, the doctor-revolutionary died.

Unforgettable Meetings

Starinov again went to work on partisan activities, he organized and headed partisan schools, commanded special units, and after the formation of headquarters of the partisan movement, he worked in it. In the units and schools that he had occasion to command, there were inevitably Spanish comrades, among them Domingo Ungria and other participants in the joint struggle against fascism in Spain.

One Sunday, in the middle of August 1942, Dolores Ibbaruri and a group of the Central Committee of the Spanish Communist Party, famous officers of the Republican Army, came to the partisan school near Moscow, at Bykovo, which Starinov headed.

I played the parts of hostess and interpreter.

The guests were with our unit until late in the evening. Now, as if in a large moving picture, the men of the heroic struggle of the Spanish people against fascism pass by in my memory.

Soon after this meeting, groups began to leave for assignments behind enemy lines. The detachment of Francisco Gullion, which had many veterans of the first armed rebuff of fascism, participants in the ice marches across Taganrog Bay, participants in the battles of Smolensk, Kalinin, and in Belorussia, left for the Leningrad front to operate behind the lines of the Blue Division, which had been sent by Franco to help Hitler.

Two detachments, basically made up of former Republican soldiers left for the Caucasas.

All the detachments carried out their military assignments in very difficult conditions in the winter of 1942–1943. They acted resourcefully, boldly, and bravely, derailing troop trains and destroying enemy vehicles, attacking from ambush, and repelling the enemy assaults. The groups and detachments in which the Spanish comrades served caused great enemy losses, but they also suffered losses of their own.

In December 1942, Col. Khadzhi Mamsurov visited the school. At that time, he was one of the leading workers of the central headquarters of the partisan movement. Many of the Spaniards knew him simply as Ksanti, but they were all happy with his visit.

Over a cup of tea, I had a chance to reminisce with him about our activities in Spain. That was when Khadzhi Dzhourovich called Starinov "The Elusive Hero." It was the first time I had heard the expression.

We reminisced about Rubio and Marquez, about Francisco Gullion, about Jan Tikhii, Lyubo Ilich, Ivan Kharish, Ivan Krbovanets, Toma Chachich, and others. Khadzhi Umar Dzhourovich said, "As far as I know, Ilich and Kharish in March 1939, were in a camp for internees in France. What happened to them after that is unknown, but judging from the news from Yugoslavia and France many former soldiers from the sabotage units and subunits of the Spanish Republican Army are operating there."

Sabotage actions began in Yugoslavia beginning in the fall of 1941, and their number grew quickly. But at that time, it was difficult to determine exactly who was organizing them. We knew only that Yugoslav Communists were at the head of forces fighting against the occupying forces.

The meeting of Kh. D. Mamsurov with the former Republican soldiers at the school, where I. G. Starinov was the chief, left a deep impression on the partisan saboteurs, especially the Spanish comrades who personally knew him or knew about his heroic deeds.

Former Spanish Republicans fought along with men from Rostov, Kalinin, Smolensk, Ukraine, Belorussia, and later with men from Bryansk, and the Leningrad partisans. Some had a chance to destroy enemy troop trains and vehicles on the territory of Poland and Czechoslovakia. They were successful everywhere.

After returning to the motherland in 1937, I had a chance to see many of the Soviet comrades that I had met with in Spain. More often than the others, I saw Khadzhi Mamsurov. From major, he quickly rose to Brigadier General and after the war to Lieutenant General, but he remained the same simple, accessible, and humane man.

From the first days of the war, Mamsurov worked on the training and dispatching of partisans to the western and northwestern fronts. More than once, he went with groups behind enemy lines to mine roads, destroy columns of vehicles and even tanks from ambush.

On February 25, 1968, Khadzhi Mamsurov delivered a speech at a celebration of the fiftieth anniversary of the Soviet Army. Everyone was dazzled by his brilliant report, but on March 5, pitiless death tore Khadzhi Umar Dzhourovich from our ranks.

I last saw Vilgelm Ivanovich Kumelan (Kolman) in 1938, and it was thirty years later that I learned that he had died, a young general, in 1952.

In 1964, Starinov's memoir, *Mines Await Their Time,* was published. In it, he told the story of our fellow traveler to Spain, Pavel, the tank officer. All of those he wrote about had been located. Only the tank officer Pavel remained silent. Finally, in the spring of 1967, we received a long letter from Pavel, and at the end of December, Pavel Iosifovich Lipin came to visit us.

Thirty-one years had passed since our joint trip to Spain, but he was still the same cheerful Pavel. In Spain, he fought under the command of one of the first volunteer tank officers, Col. S. M. Krivoshein, he taught tank officers, and participated in the battle at Guadalajara.

In Spain, Pavel found a friend for life, Conchita, with whom he returned to the motherland. He fought against the Finns. World War II found him in Leningrad. Conchita and their young son were supposed to be evacuated, but they could not get away in time and had to remain in the besieged city. Eventually, Pavel managed to send Conchita to the Urals, and he himself went to battle again. On the approaches to the Volga, he was seriously wounded when a round went off in a tank, breaking Lipin's leg. His wounds not yet healed, Pavel discharged himself from the hospital and began to teach new tank drivers.

Pavel Iosifovich had already been retired a long time when we were reunited, but he continued to teach—no longer tank drivers but automobile drivers; he headed one of the schools in Leningrad.

Ivan Kharish—The Crusher

In 1944 Starinov learned that Ivan Kharish was not only alive but that he headed the diversionary service of the People's Liberation Army of Yugoslavia, where he was known as The Crusher.

I. G. Starinov sought a meeting with Ivan Kharish in 1944, when he worked in the headquarters of the chief of the Soviet military mission in Yugoslavia, then again after the reestablishment of friendly relations between the Soviet Union and Yugoslavia. Ivan Kharish wrote much and warmly about Rudolf in his memoirs, which were published in 1959 in Yugoslavia, and he had not even forgotten about me.

And so at last, Ivan Kharish was presented with a chance to invite Starinov to Yugoslavia to participate in marches along the roads of the great partisan actions, together with a group of Soviet pioneers, who were headed by the editor of the magazine *Pioneers' Truth*, N. M. Chernova.

In August and September 1957, Starinov visited Yugoslavia for twenty-four days. There he learned in detail about the military path of Ivan Kharish—Juan Pequeño—The Crusher, after he had landed in an internment camp. Lyubo Ilich and Ivan Kharish escaped from the camp at different times. Lyubo Ilich remained in France and entered the French resistance forces, where many other Spanish comrades from the XIV Partisan Corps also fought.

Having a lot of experience on the job, Ilich, who knew French very well, became chief of the operations section of the headquarters of all the armed forces of the resistance. In France, he was given the rank of general. After the war, Ilich went into the diplomatic service and, in 1967, was ambassador of the Socialist Federated Republic of Yugoslavia in Switzerland.

After escaping the camp, Ivan Kharish headed for his homeland, where he had not been for fourteen years. It is easy to say "he headed for." He decided to go through Germany. He did not have the necessary documents, so he usually passed himself off as someone in search of a job. He was an outstanding cabinetmaker, and his scheme was successful. Germany, which had by then attacked the Soviet Union, needed workers very much, and Kharish quickly found work in his trade. He worked so diligently that his boss was very satisfied. But Kharish was in a hurry to get to Yugoslavia so he could take part in the battle against the German occupation. So he told his boss that if the boss could get him documentation for a trip to Yugoslavia, he would return with other good workers.

In a week, the boss got the necessary documents for a trip to Yugoslavia for Kharish. Of course, once in his native Croatia, Ivan Kharish organized a small sabotage group, and on October 9, 1941, derailed his first troop train.

The echo of that explosion was heard not only in German-occupied Yugoslavia but far beyond its borders. Ivan Kharish continued to train saboteurs. With them, and single-handedly, he derailed enemy trains, destroyed bridges, and wiped out the personnel and equipment of the enemy.

Ivan Kharish, who had become Ilya Gromovnik, trained more than twenty-five hundred partisans in Yugoslavia alone. He taught Yugoslavs, Bulgarians, Hungarians, and Greeks, who carried out sabotage in Yugoslavia, Hungary, and Greece.

In his speeches, Ivan Kharish often said that he conducted sabotage with the aid of mines he had learned to make in Spain with Rudolf—Ilya Starinov. And he wrote about that in his memoirs and in newspaper pieces.

Gromovnik personally carried out more than two hundred significant acts of sabotage, destroyed trains, military equipment, and troops of the invaders, and among his attainments was the destruction of six enemy generals. His detachment alone carried out more than thirty-two hundred acts of sabotage. Several thousand acts of sabotage were conducted by saboteurs of other commands who had been trained by Kharish and his instructors.

The renowned saboteur, by 1957 brigadier general, Ivan Kharish was named a People's Hero of Yugoslavia and he was awarded many awards and medals by Republican Spain, Yugoslavia, and the Soviet Union.

Epilogue

Time is merciless. All the more often newspapers carry obituaries with the names of those dear to us. But the living preserve the memory of those who were killed and who died.

Where are they now, the partisans of the special battalion with whom I had occasion to practice partisan warfare in distant Spain?

On November 30, 1980, *Pravda* printed an article by V. Chernyshev, from Madrid, "Two friends served." One of the friends was lieutenant of the Soviet Army Francisco Castillo, who had removed mines from buildings on the streets of Berlin in May 1945. I knew him well. The second was the former chief of staff of one of the Republican divisions, major of the Spanish Republican Army, lieutenant of the Soviet Army, Manuel Alberdi, whom Starinov knew.

We have been bound by a strong friendship with Francisco del Castillo since 1937 when we worked under very difficult conditions. The command of the Spanish Republican Army not only underrated the possibilities of the partisan struggle behind enemy lines, some even hindered its development. The allotment given to us for the training of Domingo Ungria's group was not even equal to the normal allowance in the Spanish Republican Army, in spite of the fact that the group would be conducting intelligence operations behind enemy lines and had demonstrated a high level of military competence through successful sorties behind enemy lines at Teruel in December 1936. At the order of the Central Committee of the Spanish Communist party, the Communist officers of the unit put the group on allowances in the sector in which the groups were operating. Rudolf and I often used our own salaries to buy watches and other materials for mines. But it all worked out. Rudolf managed to obtain naval depth charges, to get the TNT melted from them, to get dynamite, potassium chlorate, and ammonium nitrate, and to arrange the preparation of hand grenades and various automatic mines. Even regular troops were short of grenades; in return for what we could supply them, we received gasoline and other materials we needed. But we got everything with difficulty. The lack of radio communications made verification of the results of the actions of our groups difficult so that only when a group returned could we ask the command to send planes to attack the rebel trains which it had derailed. Of course, the command rarely managed to do that in time because the enemy had time to avoid the consequences. There were other intelligence-sabotage groups in a better situation, where the advisers were A. K. Sprogis, M. K. Kochegarov, N. A. Prokopyuk. We even helped them with grenades and homemade mines. Things went better after Kh. D. Mamsurov became our senior adviser; his distinguished participation in the defense of Madrid earned him the recognition and respect of the command of the front and of the Republican command.

All our ordeals ended in February 1937, after one of our groups derailed a train carrying Italian Fascist pilots near Cordoba. The obituaries with large crosses, and some with photographs of the vultures who had perished were published in the press. And they recognized us. For that achievement, Domingo Ungria's detachment was turned into a special battalion. All the personnel received flyers' rations and were paid at time and a half. Until then, the men of Domingo Ungria's groups were drawing allowances from many different battalions and had to beg for necessary resources. Afterward, many intelligence officers from other units who had worked with us joined the special battalion. The echo of the partisan struggle at Cordoba and Granada, where our groups operated, found reverberation in the article "Partisans of Spain," which appeared in *Izvestiva* on March 23, 1937.

During the summer of 1937, the special battalion, which had taken volunteers from the international brigades, was turned into a special brigade.

In October 1937, the general staff of the Spanish Republican Army decided to unite all partisan forces, and the XIV Special Partisan Corps was created. The backbone of the corps was made up of personnel trained by us. Domingo Ungria was appointed commander of the corps, deputy commander was Antonio Buitrago, chief of staff was Lyubo Ilich, senior advisers and instructors of the brigades were Ivan Kharish, Vladek Tikhii, and Antonio Rubio. Many of the other pupils of our Jaen school rose to command groups, battalions, and brigades.

Thus, beginning literally with nothing in November 1936, by the summer of 1937, we had trained so many officers and specialists that they were sufficient to bring up to strength the staff of the XIV Partisan Corps. In the course of battle, the XIV Corps became, in essence, a partisan army. By the summer of 1938 it had four divisions of three or four brigades each. They operated behind enemy lines even after the capitulation by Casado.

In spite of the courage of its people and of the soldiers of the international brigades, the Spanish Republic fell in the unequal struggle against the rebels and their allies. The governments of England, France, and the United States of America, which had organized the blockade of Republican Spain under the banner of nonintervention, furthered the victory of fascism in Spain. The Republic fell but troops of the XIV Partisan Corps were in the first ranks of the resistance and partisan forces in the Second World War.

The soldiers of the XIV Partisan Corps who ended up in prison camps in France escaped from them at the beginning of the Second World War and joined in the partisan struggle behind enemy lines in countries occupied by Fascist soldiers, in particular in Yugoslavia, Italy, and Poland.

In France, the XIV Corps was reestablished under the command of Antonio Buitrago. But he was soon mortally wounded in battle, and Jesus Rios became commander of the corps. By the end of 1943, the corps had been turned into a terrible force with *seven* divisions of two to four brigades each. The Spanish partisans, mainly veterans of the XIV Partisan Corps, carried the fight against the Germans with French partisans until the complete liberation of France. More than four thousand Spaniards took part in the battle for the liberation of Paris.

The enormous contribution of the Spanish partisans to the struggle against the German invaders in France, 1940–1945, was briefly but persuasively shown in the book of Miguel Angel *Spanish Partisans in France 1940–1945,* published in 1971 in Havana. For valor and courage in the struggle against the Fascists, many Spanish partisans were decorated by the French government. In Saint-Denis, near Paris, a street bears the name of the commander of the 3d Spanish Partisan Division, Cristino Garcia. Hundreds of graves with inscriptions, dozens of monuments, and memorial plaques remind us about the contribution of Spanish partisans in accelerating the victory over the Fascist invaders in France.

During World War II in the Soviet Union, more than three hundred former soldiers of the Spanish Republican Army fought in the special units commanded by Col. I. G. Starinov. Among them was the former commander of the XIV Partisan Corps, Domingo Ungria.

Behind the lines of the Blue Division, which Franco sent to help Hitler, Fransisco Gullion, Angel Alberque, Pedro Podalier, Benito Ustaros, Joaquin Gomez, and their fighting friends carried out attacks and mined communications.

In the forests of the Leningrad, Kalinin, Smolensk, and Orlov regions and in Belorussia, in the mountains of the Crimea and the Caucasus behind the invaders' lines, the Spaniards operated jointly with Soviet partisans, destroying troops and military equipment of the invaders. They operated successfully under the conditions of the harsh Russian winter. In the unequal battle, Manuel Belda, Francisco Gaspar, Juan Eglesias, Leonardo Garcia, Gusto Rodriguez, Seijo Garcia, Jose Fusimales, and many others perished.

Francisco del Castillo, Luiz Castillo, Jose Vieska, Manuel Alberdi and many others fought the Fascists until complete victory.

In Yugoslavia, Ivan Kharish became Gromovnik—the Crusher—who organized special sabotage partisan units and destroyed the enemy and his military equipment, without entering into battle, using mines he had learned to make in Spain with Rudolf and which he wrote about in his reminiscences *Saboteur,* published in Yugoslavia in 1961.

Many other soldiers of the XIV Partisan Corps operated successfully in Yugoslavia, Italy, Poland, and other countries. After the fall of the Republic, many of them went to Algeria and from there to the countries of Latin America where they used their experience in the struggle against reactionary regimes.

How pleasant it was to learn that most of the soldiers of the XIV Partisan Corps made their contribution to the achievement of victory over fascism in the Second World War.

After the death of Franco, many Spaniards who had been living in the USSR began to leave for their homeland, and some of them later regretted that they had left the Soviet Union.

Thus, Luiz Castillo, former soldier of the Spanish Republican Army and participant in the Great Fatherland War, received a pension and worked on a radio committee. His wife, Zinaida Ivanovna, worked in the pharmacy administration, and their son graduated from an institute and worked as an engineer. They lived in comfortable separate apartments, their medical treatment was free, and each year they received a vacation, a health cure, and other benefits. But in 1978, they left for Spain. For almost two years, they did not have their own place and lived with relatives because apartments there are expensive, there was no steady work, and they had to pay for medical treatment. Only the son found work, as an engineer, and there were five in the family.

In 1979, the wife of Luiz came to visit her brother and said, "Luiz has lost a lot of weight from the difficulties and his sleeplessness. I never thought that he would miss the Soviet Union so much."

In spite of the fact that Franco died, many former soldiers of the Spanish Republican Army who were living in the USSR, decided not to leave the Soviet Union where, as political émigrés, they enjoy all rights and privileges; they have no worry that they will be left without work, or without a pension or without an apartment. Their children receive free high school and higher education. They have everything that all Soviet citizens have guaranteed by the Soviet constitution.[1]

The blood spilled in the common struggle against the forces of Fascism by the Soviet people in Spain and that of the Spanish comrades in the Great Fatherland War, is a pledge of friendship of our peoples and the common struggle for peace. This was brightly shown during the stay in the Soviet Union in 1982 of four groups of former soldiers of the Spanish Republican Army.

Everyone who spoke at the ceremonial gathering of those Spanish veterans spoke of the Soviet Union as a second motherland and the active fighter for peace in all the world.

---

[1]These words were written before the fall of the Soviet Union.

Index

Printed in the United States
by Baker & Taylor Publisher Services